INSIDE THE BAUHAUS

INSIDE THE BAUHAUS

HOWARD DEARSTYNE

Edited by

DAVID SPAETH

Rizzoli   New York

First published in the United States of America in 1986 by
RIZZOLI INTERNATIONAL PUBLICATIONS, INC.
597 Fifth Avenue, New York, NY 10017

Library of Congress Cataloging-in-Publication Data
Dearstyne, Howard.
  Inside the Bauhaus.
  Bibliography: p.
  Includes index.
  1. Bauhaus—History. 2. Art schools—Berlin (Germany)
3. Art, Modern—20th century—Germany. I. Spaeth,
David A. II. Title.
N332.G33B443 1986   707′.11′4318   85–43483
ISBN 0–8478–0699–5
ISBN 0–8478–0702–9 (pbk.)

Art Direction by Charles Davey
Designed by Beth Tondreau
Composition by Rainsford Type, Ridgefield, CT

for my wife
BARBARA TIMMINS DEARSTYNE

contents

editor's acknowledgments

I would like to thank the following individuals for their help in bringing this work to realization: Marjorie Smolka, for allowing me to undertake the work and for her continued support; Carter Manny Jr., director of the Graham Foundation for Advanced Studies in the Fine Arts, as well as the members of the foundation's board of directors for underwriting part of the production of this book; Peter Nisbit, Assistant Curator of the Busch-Reisinger Museum for his help in locating photographs; Cheryl Akins for typing the two revisions of the manuscript and for her unfailing good humor; Mark Cordray for his friendship, his critical support, his generosity of spirit, as well as the use of his apartment during my many trips to New York City; Solveig Williams and Charles Davey for their enthusiasm and the care they brought to this project; my sons, Anthony and Sloan, for their understanding when I was preoccupied with editing and neglected my parental duties; and lastly, Howard and Barbara Dearstyne, for what they taught me and for their friendship.

DAVID A. SPAETH
LEXINGTON, KENTUCKY
JUNE 1985

introduction

This is the story of an idea, an idea full of hope and promise. It is an idea about how people might live. It is also the story of a school, the Bauhaus, whose life span coincided with the Weimar Republic's and whose history mirrors German history between the two world wars.

Through mass-production, the Bauhaus, like the German Werkbund, hoped to change the quality of the designed object and the designed environment for everyone. Quality of life was an important design consideration in the housing schemes developed by Walter Gropius and Hannes Meyer, respectively the first and second directors of the school, and Ludwig Hilberseimer, whose teaching responsibilities at the Bauhaus included the planning curriculum. Frequently predicated on the concept of prefabrication as a way to reduce building costs, their proposals to house Berlin's (and Germany's) working class were also based on a genuine concern for function as well as hygiene; on the importance of solar orientation, cross-ventilation, and easy access to open green space; and a convenient relationship to places of employment. From our vantage point, it is easy to see how naïve this boundless faith in technology was. However, Walter Gropius and his new school offered hope, based on a new order that was life-giving, humane in its application of technology, and full of light, not just light reflected from polished metal surfaces or unadorned planes—seemingly, the Bauhaus hallmark—but the light of reason and objectivity.

Under Gropius and the Bauhaus masters, students were urged to discard their preoccupations and approach each problem as if it were completely new, from zero, studying both functional requirements *and* the technical means necessary to realize a solution—a synthesis of art and craft, of aesthetics and serial production. There was also a subjective, non-rational aspect to the Bauhaus experience which, in the teachings of Johannes Itten, had a quasi-mystical quality.

Howard Dearstyne, the author of this work, was one of a handful of Americans to study at the Bauhaus and the only one to earn a diploma in architecture. He learned of the Bauhaus in the summer of 1928 when he was touring Europe. Like so many other Americans, Dearstyne was drawn to Europe for the educational opportunities travel abroad offered. Seeing Europe's monuments and experiencing its cultural legacy confirmed a passionate interest in architecture which was to last his lifetime.

It was in the summer of 1926 that Dearstyne made his first trip to Europe. That fall he returned to Columbia University to resume his graduate studies in architecture, which he completed in 1928. After graduation he returned to Europe still not satisfied with his education but unclear as to how to proceed. (As an undergraduate he briefly studied journalism and also for a time pursued medicine.) Dearstyne was aware only that a gulf existed between what he had learned in school and what he had seen in Europe.

At this time, architectural educators considered the monuments of the past as the "creative well" to which talented and astute designers would continually return, imitating and adapting past solutions to their own work. Dearstyne viewed history differently, not as a source for so-called creativity but as a source of intellectual inspiration. Unconsciously, he had come to understand that architecture is an expression of its time, its structure, and its technology. In Europe Dearstyne discovered the emergent and as yet unnamed Modern Movement. Its appeal was immediate: the Modern Movement manifested a new way of thinking about how to make architecture.

During the summer of 1928, Dearstyne began to articulate the limitations of his professional education. A visit to the Bauhaus reinforced his misgivings. In retrospect his matriculation at the Bauhaus seems both obvious and inevitable. He was seeking an approach to problem solving (and ultimately to architecture itself) based on something more rational than historic precedent.

The Bauhaus attracted students from all over Europe. Americans were in the minority, and at the onset Dearstyne was essentially an outsider. However, being both egalitarian and gregarious, he sought people out, making friends among students and faculty regardless of social class: an outsider became insider.

Dearstyne's tenure at the Bauhaus coincided with important changes taking place within the school. In 1925 Gropius moved the Bauhaus from Weimar to Dessau, resigning as director in 1928.

He was succeeded by Hannes Meyer, who attempted to change the curriculum and offer a diploma in architecture, one of Gropius's stated, but unrealized, intentions.

Dearstyne witnessed the events surrounding Meyer's departure after two years, Mies van der Rohe's appointment as Meyer's successor, and the closing of the Dessau Bauhaus. He followed the school to Berlin, as a special student, remaining until the political turmoil surrounding Hitler's assumption of power in 1933 forced the closing of the school.

From the richness of this experience coupled with his long-term friendship and professional association with many of the Bauhaus faculty, Dearstyne decided to write his account of the school. What began as a short article in 1958 became, twenty years later, an exhaustive commentary on the Bauhaus and its times.

Dearstyne sent numerous letters home during the summer of 1928 and later, which his mother had the foresight to preserve. When he began work on this manuscript, he used these letters as one of the sources for his work. The letters were very much of the moment—not written with posterity in mind. They are full of descriptions and observations which were of interest or concern to him and which he shared with his family.

His account of life and education at the Bauhaus is drawn chiefly from contemporary sources, from his letters, from journals and letters kept by members of the Bauhaus faculty, from newspaper articles, and from the recollections of others. There is a vitality in his prose, a sense of actual participation. We are part of the forces which shaped the Bauhaus; we are caught up in the internal and external struggles which beset the school. Dearstyne includes historical background of the structure of the curriculum of the Bauhaus as well as discussions of the various workshops and how they functioned prior to his admission to the school.

Dearstyne learned about the Bauhaus from a young woman he met in Düsseldorf and later married, Maria Gödde. When the Bauhaus closed, Dearstyne returned to the United States. Their subsequent divorce was an unpleasant topic about which he seldom spoke. If his narrative is vague about the first Ms. Dearstyne, it is because of the rancor associated with the dissolution of their marriage. After his return to the United States, he worked as an architect in New York City. For a time he was employed in Wallace K. Harrison's office. During World War II, Dearstyne held teaching positions at Black Mountain College, Lawrence College, (now Lawrence University) and the Cranbrook Academy. It was during his year at Lawrence College (1944) that he met Barbara Timmins, who later became his wife and to whose memory this work is dedicated.

After the war, Dearstyne was employed as an architect in the restoration of Colonial Williamsburg and taught at the College of

William and Mary. During his years in Williamsburg (1946–1957), he published the following books: the English translation (with Hilla Rebay) of Wassily Kandinsky's *Point and Line to Plane* (1947); *Colonial Williamsburg—Its Buildings and Gardens* (1949); and *Shadows on Silver* (1954), (the last two in conjunction with A. Lawrence Kocher). In 1957, Ludwig Mies van der Rohe invited Dearstyne to teach architecture at the Illinois Institute of Technology, where Dearstyne remained until his retirement in 1970.

There is no question that Mies's influence on Dearstyne was profound and long-lasting. Obvious affection colors the description of his experiences as one of Mies's Bauhaus students. The same can be said of his attitude toward the Bauhaus, for the experience there changed his life, opening up a new way of thinking about and making architecture, and marked his coming of age. Perhaps this helps to explain the tension which came to exist between him and Gropius. For, while Gropius is rightly given praise for founding the Bauhaus and preserving the idea of the Bauhaus through its difficult early years, it was Mies who worked to preserve both the school and the idea against forces which, to Dearstyne, were far more hostile and threatening than the provincial legislature Gropius faced. In Dearstyne's mind, Mies was the more heroic figure as well as the better architect.

At the time of his death in 1979, Dearstyne was editing the manuscript, and seemed pleased with his results. Three years passed before work resumed when I undertook the task of editing with the support and encouragement of Dearstyne's sister-in-law, Marjorie Smolka, his literary executrix. I had many reservations about this and did not excise one word until I had read the complete manuscript several times. When the actual process began, I started each day by recalling Dearstyne's voice—not just the sound of it but his manner of speaking. As one of his students during my undergraduate years at the Illinois Institute of Technology's Department of Architecture, where he was a professor, and as a frequent guest in his house, I had ample opportunity to hear him speak. It was not hard, then, to bring him to life again, if only in my mind.

In general the deletions I made were done to strengthen the narrative and sharpen the focus of Dearstyne's work. An entire chapter on the history of the *Novembergruppe* was removed: as important as this chapter was, it disrupted the narrative flow. The most important historical facts concerning this group are included in a footnote. I made one addition: Mies van der Rohe's description of the closing of the Berlin Bauhaus. Mies's description was so poignant that it demanded inclusion. It is my hope that Dearstyne would have approved these changes and that he would have understood my deletions. Like any good editor, I hope that I have made another's work better, leaving few "tracks" of my own in the process.

preface

Several considerations have led me to hazard the writing of a book on the still controversial subject of the Bauhaus. I spent five years, from 1928 to 1933, as a student there, first in Dessau and then Berlin; and following the ultimate closing of the Bauhaus in Berlin, I remained a further year in that city, continuing my architectural studies with its third and last director, Ludwig Mies van der Rohe, hopefully awaiting the reopening of the school. So I actually observed the inner workings of that exciting, embattled, and ill-starred academy for more than a third of its all-too-brief existence—a fact that also seemed to justify calling my book, *Inside the Bauhaus*.

In the summer of 1957, my wife and I spent an evening with Mies van der Rohe at the Barclay Hotel in New York, where he was living while the plans for the Seagram Building were being carried out. In the course of some hours of reminiscing, over uncounted martinis, I told Mies that I had in mind to write an article on the Bauhaus. To this he replied, with emphasis, "Write it down, write it down. You might be run over tomorrow by an automobile! And," he added, "say anything you want to." Mies made this article appear more like some obligation to posterity than a mere possibility, so I returned to Williamsburg, Virginia, where we were then living, resolved to write it.

I informed my long-time friend, Ludwig Hilberseimer, that I had seen Mies in New York and that he had recommended that I write an article on the Bauhaus. Hilberseimer replied immediately, urging me to write a book about the Bauhaus rather than an article, and I decided to take his advice. In the meantime, Mies had invited me to teach in the architecture school at the Illinois Institute of

Technology, where he was director. Barbara and I packed our belongings in a hurry and moved to Chicago. I taught in the school for the next thirteen years. This experience and my close association with Mies, Ludwig Hilberseimer, and Walter Peterhans, all dead now, did much to deepen my insight.

It would probably have taken me a dozen years to finish the book had it not been for a wholly unexpected windfall, my receipt of a magnificent fellowship from the Graham Foundation for Advanced Studies in the Fine Arts, which did much to solve the financial problems I encountered in the early stages of writing the book. I am very grateful to Dr. John Entenza, then director of the foundation, for awarding me the grant and to George Danforth, successor to Mies as director of the School of Architecture and Planning of the Illinois Institute of Technology, for having proposed me for the fellowship, without my urging and without my knowledge.

In pursuing a long-drawn-out project such as the composition of this book has been, one needs encouragement and advice. I am most fortunate to have received these in rich measure from my friend Nathaniel Carlos Hudson. Mr. Hudson has reviewed the book, chapter by chapter, and has made recommendations that have been invaluable to me.

I would be most remiss if I failed to express my gratitude to my close friend Erdmann Schmocker for having devoted many full days of his valuable time to doing the tedious work of compiling a bibliography, listing the authorship and ownership of many of the illustrations, and writing captions. Messrs. Schmocker and Hudson also helped me put the many notes in acceptable form.

In the summer of 1972, I made numerous alterations in the manuscript including revision of the captions and notes. These badly needed retyping and Mrs. Eleanor Tolson, wife of my former architecture student Fred Tolson, volunteered to do this for me. The following summer Mrs. Tolson proposed retyping the text of the manuscript and completed a large part of it. It was completed by Curtis L. Adkins of Alexandria.

I am grateful to those persons, publishers, and institutions who and which have permitted me to reproduce photographs, drawings, and text from their personal collections, publications, and archives. Prominent among these are Dr. Walter Gropius and Dr. Charles L. Kuhn, former director of the Busch-Reisinger Museum. I am also deeply indebted to Hans M. Wingler, director of the Bauhaus Archive, for allowing me to reproduce photographs and quotations from his Bauhaus book. I am likewise greatly obliged to Mrs. Oskar Schlemmer for permitting me to reproduce many photographs of her husband's work—dance, painting, sculpture— and to quote numerous passages from his most informative book, *Oskar Schlemmer: Briefe und Tagebücher*. I am also beholden to a number of my Bauhaus student friends, with whom I have remained in contact over the years, for allowing me to reproduce works made by them at the Bauhaus and subsequently. Among them are Pius Pahl, Hermann Blomeier, Wils Ehert, and Eduard Ludwig. To my everlasting sorrow, Ludwig was killed on the Berlin Autobahn on December 12, 1960. A packet of photographs of his work, prepared by him for me, along with a letter to me, typed by his secretary the day of his death and unsigned by him, were generously forwarded to me by a nephew of his. Most of the photographs used in the book were faithfully copied by my Chicago friend, Douglas Baz.

The many passages translated from the German in the book were rendered into English by me, except in those cases in which I expressly credit someone else. Even when translations of certain texts have already existed, I have preferred to rely on my own knowledge of German and French and have made my own original versions of these.

HOWARD DEARSTYNE

A
PERSONAL
JOURNEY

1 the road to the bauhaus

In the summer of 1926 my mother, brother, and I went to Europe. We saw all manner of architectural masterpieces, from St. Paul's to St. Peter's, and many old towns, from Amiens to Istanbul. I returned to the United States with my interest in architecture fully awakened. I graduated in 1927 but did not think of studying architecture at the time. However, during a year-long "detour" into pre medical work, I realized that architecture was my main interest, and I decided to enter Columbia University's School of Architecture.

At the time, the majority of American architects were performing amazing feats of aesthetic dexterity with the sacred relics of half-a-dozen ancestral styles. Greek temple was piled on Greek temple to achieve a skyscraper; steel skeletons were cloaked with the once eminently structural forms of the Gothic; and the restrained and dignified architectural vocabulary of our colonial ancestors put to many perverse uses. Some architects who felt the need for a change of ornamentation turned to the arbiters of fashion in Paris. Having discovered neo-Art Nouveau ornamentation in the Decorative Arts Exposition of 1925, they proceeded to apply its plant-like forms to the stone façades of their buildings. Today these patterns seem flat and utterly dull, and I wonder how anyone could have enthused over them sixty years ago.

europe bound

When I returned to Europe, in the summer of 1928, I had completed three semesters and a summer session of architectural studies, during which time my appetite for architectural history had

From left: Mrs. Ralph Fletcher; Mr. Ralph Fletcher; Henry Dubin

been whetted by three courses given by Hudnut, then a professor at Columbia. This second trip abroad was to prove crucial, for it carried me to the Bauhaus.

There was a mass exodus of Europe-bound tourists that summer. When I came to book my passage, only the Holland-America Line could still offer me a berth, and this was on a ship which stopped at Plymouth and then proceeded to Rotterdam, bypassing France. I boarded the ship in Hoboken, New Jersey, toward the middle of June, having no notion that this summer excursion to Europe was to turn into a six-year sojourn.

During the crossing I became acquainted with Henry Dubin, an architect from Chicago several years my senior. He carried with him a copy of *Vers une architecture* (*Towards a New Architecture*) by Le Corbusier, which he urged me to read. This was my first introduction to the work and thinking of the French pioneer whose influence on world architecture was to be so profound. The book made a great impression on me and helped prepare me for the architectural awakening I was to experience in Holland. Despite this, when I first set foot on Dutch soil, my goal was to seek out the monuments of the past.

Amsterdam was my temporary headquarters. I found the "Venice of the North" a fascinating city, with its concentric, crescent-shaped canals, picturesque squares, twisted streets, stately old houses, and imposing public buildings. However, I quickly became aware of the presence of a surprising number of "modernistic" structures, built in a style that was new and strange to me.

An anonymous German reporter, sent by *Wasmuths Monatshefte* in 1924 to review the architectural scene in Holland, had spoken with scorn of "that chamber of horrors" and had singled out for particular ridicule the buildings of the architect Michel de Klerk, then highly esteemed throughout the Netherlands. Since World War One, that once-so-conservative land had indulged in an orgy of construction. Numerous buildings were of a willfully individualistic and expressionist style: the grand old pioneer of Dutch modernism, Hendrik Petrus Berlage, who had, in his Amsterdam Stock Exchange, erected in 1898, bestowed upon his country one of the first great monuments of the new architecture, lived on into the 1920's only to see his sound and sober precepts inundated in a wave of romanticism.

Unlike the *Wasmuth* commentator, I was far from being incensed at the modern structures I began to see on every hand in Amsterdam. This "chamber of horrors" became an exciting new world for me; in those days, as far as modern architecture went, I was a veritable "innocent abroad."

Herbaceous ornamentation was not the only new star seen in the architectural heavens of the 1920s. Certain daring innovators thought they discerned in color the seeds of an architectural renaissance, and introduced patterns of colored tile into the brickwork of their buildings. Had the Greeks, who could do no wrong in their eyes, not painted the Parthenon in various and vivid hues? Again, today one can see that structures embellished in this style could never have been the basis for architectural renewal.

If any single event served to demonstrate the bankruptcy of American architecture during this decade, it was the 1922 competition for the design of the Chicago Tribune Tower, "the world's most beautiful office building." The great tome containing the projects submitted includes many so grotesque and so remarkably ugly that I took to using the volume as a textbook of architectural ineptitude. Meanwhile, the works of Louis H. Sullivan and Frank Lloyd Wright were ignored.

My own introduction to Wright's work came by accident, and without the benefit of any recommendation from my instructors at Columbia. Browsing one day in the Avery Library, I found the handsome volume of the sumptuous Dutch periodical *Wendingen* devoted to Wright. (This collection of the great architect's early work is surpassed only by the magnificent two-volume portfolio of drawings of his buildings issued by Ernst Wasmuth in Germany in 1910–11.) *Wendingen* opened up a new and hopeful architectural world for me, a world completely ignored by my teachers, who bent all their efforts to rear their protegés in the well-worn ways of orthodoxy. Our preliminary course, for example, consisted of drawing, with scrupulous exactness, the classic orders of architecture.

Architectural design at Columbia and elsewhere concerned itself with the planning of buildings, utilizing the paraphernalia of ancient, medieval or Renaissance architecture. These styles provided an architectural vocabulary of vocabularies which had been tested by time and found good and useful. Why, then, should one try to invent some new form language? The argument seemed to make sense; the results of its application did not. During the time I remained at the school, I saw the gamut run from "purest" Greek via Roman to Romanesque and Gothic, with numerous excursions into Renaissance and baroque. Whatever the style, the plates were elegantly rendered. I remember the awe and envy with which I viewed the masterfully colored double-elephant sheets of the upperclassmen, in which the art of painting frequently took precedence over architecture. A few of us, not without feelings of guilt, made some tentative essays into the *moderne*. Our ardor was generally cooled; classicism carried all before it. Joseph Hudnut's "new deal for architecture" was still a half-dozen years away.

I had come to Europe expecting to see old buildings. Suddenly (and unexpectedly) I encountered seemingly endless new housing developments and countless new commercial structures which had been erected in this ancient city. A number of the new buildings in Amsterdam bore Wright's unmistakable imprint. "The old master has been here!" I thought to myself. But only *Wendingen* and *Wasmuth* had been there. The prophet, so long without honor in his own country, had, through these publications, spoken with authority to the Dutch, winning many converts. So enthusiastic did I become over the new buildings I had stumbled upon in the old seaport that I bought no fewer than five books about contemporary Dutch architecture, studied the illustrations—which had captions in three or four languages, including English—and picked out the structures which seemed most worth seeing.

I also recall examining Walter Gropius's book, *Internationale Architektur*. I had only a smattering of German, the pitiful residue of a college course taken several years before, and failed to grasp the fact that the word *Bauhaus*, which figured on the cover and the title page, was the name of a school, and I had no idea who Gropius was.

Though I had by no means abandoned the past and continued to look up many of the buildings and points of interest starred in my *Baedeker*, I now charted an itinerary which carried me from one twentieth-century architectural highlight to another.

I saw a picture of Rietveld's Schroeder House (built 1923) in Utrecht in Gropius's Bauhaus book and made a note of it. This white-stuccoed building, I thought, resembled houses of Le Corbusier which I had seen in his *Towards a New Architecture*. I didn't realize then how fundamentally different this house was from those of Le Corbusier, who invariably enveloped the neobaroque interiors of his so-called "machines for living" in a serene boxlike sheath, the integrity of which he was at pains to preserve. Rietveld's house, the most noteworthy dwelling executed by any de Stijl ar-

Gerrit Rietveld, Schroeder House, Utrecht

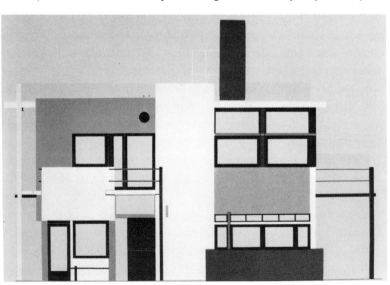

chitect, was not a box punctured by openings, but a space enclosed by a series of overlapping vertical and horizontal planes.

When I saw the Schroeder House, I was much impressed by it. The lightness and "loose-jointed" quality resulting from the nature of its assembly are still attractive today, even though the house shares the mannerism of most de Stijl designs, that is, the unmistakable intent of the architect to make of it a three-dimensional composition of abstract forms.

The other building that I had singled out for investigation in Utrecht, van Heukelom's administration building of the Dutch railways, had been completed in 1921. In the matter of style, a generation separated the two buildings. The vast office structure with its elongated brick piers and mullions and its narrow vertical windows was, to borrow a phrase of Wright's, "an old building built recently."[1]

I have always regretted not having gone to the Hook of Holland to see J.J.P. Oud's charmingly unpretentious row houses—clean-cut architecture and as simple as rolling off a log. To my neophyte's

Row houses, Hook of Holland, by J.J.P. Oud

eye his four-story housing blocks in Rotterdam (Spangen and Tusschendijken, built in 1919 and 1920 respectively) looked forbidding in their stark severity, unmitigated by ornamentation or any eye-catching, gratuitous elements such as those with which de Klerk and his colleagues had sought to lend interest to their comparable housing blocks in Amsterdam. The fine proportions and crisp detailing of the façades of Oud's brick structures, even if I had been fully aware of them, did not at that time compensate in my eyes for the lack of more striking or sensational features. What did interest me, however, were the enclosed garden courts, the first of their kind that I had ever seen. They were completely insulated from the surrounding streets and were long enough and wide enough to allow the sun to fall upon the central grass plots and the individual gardens which bordered the buildings at either side.

Now, looking at photographs of Oud's apartment blocks, I have no difficulty recognizing their distinction or determining where this lies: the exteriors possess a clarity of structure and simplicity of form which make them timeless. These qualities are as elusive as they are essential. I had to train my eye to detect them.

I also visited "Oud-Mathenesse" in Rotterdam, a development of more than three hundred story-and-a-half, pitched-roofed row-houses erected by Oud on a triangular plot of ground, with a triangular garden at the center flanked by shops. Four concentric lines of white stuccoed houses, served by internal, intermediate, and peripheral streets, surrounded this open core on the triangle's three sides. Oud's emphasis on the center, with its park and stores, stemmed, no doubt, from the idea which underlay the courts of his apartment blocks. "Since the present city is an unlovely place," he may well have thought, "we will create a community within the city with its own sheltered and peaceful village green." In his Rotterdam housing blocks and his settlement of small houses, Oud may be said to have borrowed from medieval practice, setting up fortress-like enclosures to shield the occupants from the city and enable them to defend their bodily health and peace of mind.

Significantly, my recollection of many of the modern structures I saw in Holland is clear and distinct, whereas that of most of the old buildings is dim. Even so, of all the buildings I saw in Holland, time has reduced almost to the vanishing point the number of those modern structures which still today have intrinsic value for me. I was impressed by the Van Nelle Factory, in Rotterdam, by Brinkman and van der Vlugt, and I continue to admire it. At the time I saw it, the main block was under construction; the curved three-story extension was added later and this, I have always thought, impaired the clean-cut effect of the main structure. The latter presented a street façade composed of horizontal bands of glass uninterrupted by columns and alternating with narrower stuccoed

Van Nelle factory, Rotterdam

spandrels. Monotony was avoided in the long façade by breaking it at intervals with projecting vertical towers containing the elevators and staircases. The total effect was one of lightness, airiness, and grace. It came closer to being an all-glass building than anything I had ever seen. Indeed, it may be said to have anticipated our "glass skin" architecture of today. Present here was a sense of form, one which required for its sufficiency no "additives." There was no feeling about the Van Nelle Factory of a striving after "significant" form such as we find in Behrens's factory buildings in Berlin, as important as these buildings were in their day and as fine as they still appear to us.

I was unaware, when I saw the Van Nelle Factory, that the central idea underlying its structure and form, that is, the setting of the reinforced concrete supporting columns back from the face of the building, which permitted the use of continuous bands of glass, proceeded directly out of Mies's Concrete Office Building project of 1922–23. It also served as the inspiration for Erich Mendelsohn's famous Columbushaus on Potsdamer Platz in Berlin. Neither of these executed buildings was as effective as the project from which they were derived; yet of the two, the Van Nelle Factory, to my mind, was by far the greater achievement.

architecture of the future

From Holland I journeyed through Germany to Vienna, where I knew a Columbia classmate, Russell Shiman. Though our occupations were rather different, we spent most of our evenings together. He spoke frequently of his experiences as a student in London and Vienna, and I was an attentive listener. Repeatedly he enlarged upon the advantages of study in Europe over study in the United States. "Why," he asked, "should I return to Columbia to complete my course in architecture when I could study the subject better in Europe—at better schools and with great monuments of architecture all around me?" The question soon became not whether I should study in Europe but where I should do it.

I wrote to the *Technische Hochschule* in Charlottenburg, Berlin, but, receiving no answer after ten days or so, I parted from Shiman and went there. I was told that to be admitted, I would first have to pass a proficiency examination in German. But by that time I was resolved to stay in Germany in spite of disappointments and obstacles. Upon the invitation of a young lady, Maria Gödde, whom I had met in Düsseldorf and with whom I had remained in correspondence, I went to stay at her house in Bernburg-on-the-Saale. It was she who dissuaded me from studying at the Technische Hochschule in Berlin and introduced me to the Bauhaus in Dessau.[2]

Russel Shiman (right) and author on the Lido, Venice

Bauhaus faculty, Dessau, 1926. From left to right: Joseph Albers, Hinnerk Scheper, Georg Muche, Laszlo Moholy-Nagy, Herbert Bayer, Joost Schmidt, Walter Gropius, Marcel Breuer, Wassily Kandinsky, Paul Klee, Lyonel Feininger, Gunta Stölzl, and Oskar Schlemmer

Maria Gödde took me one day to Dessau to see the Bauhaus. This was early in October 1928. Fräulein Gödde was acquainted with Frau Sachsenberg, the secretary of the school, so we were cordially received and shown around Gropius's impressive new building. Our guide was a student who spoke good English. The first instructor I met that day was Josef Albers, who was also to be my first teacher. He proved very persuasive, pointing out the advantages of studying at the Bauhaus over studying at any German *Technische Hochschule*. Then and there I decided to enroll as a student.

I visited the Bauhaus several times before beginning my new and exciting work. After one of these visits I wrote a letter to my mother, in which I described the architectural aims and philosophy of the Bauhaus. I was happy to discover, many years later, that my mother saved this letter, along with the hundreds of other messages, that I had sent home during my six years' sojourn in Germany. I was fairly garrulous in those days, describing in detail persons and events which could hardly have interested my mother particularly but which were of moment to me.

In a few days I will go to Dessau where around the 1st of November I'll start to study in the Bauhaus. The Bauhaus, they say, is the only place, not only in Germany, but also in Europe, where they teach the modern architecture I'm interested in . . . This modern style, I believe, is bound to have a great future. It is as simple as possible, without decoration, frills or unnecessary elements. It is the architecture of the modern age . . . The nearest approach we have made to this new architecture is our simple white steamship staterooms. We have one or two architects who have approached this architecture in the United States but they have not gotten very far with it. It is not yet widely accepted here in Europe (since the majority of people are always slow to grasp the importance of new things; can only slowly make radical changes in their ideas) and it is almost unknown in America.

. . . tho I do not accept all of their ideas (they go too far, like all enthusiasts), I think it is the architecture of the future and will gradually make headway . . . And the atmosphere at the Bauhaus is different and more free. They get down to the essentials of architecture and art, I feel . . . I don't know whether I'll stay 1 semester or 2 or more. But at least I'll stay long enough to become acquainted with the spirit of the architecture.

It is interesting, too—one must learn a trade here—rug-making or ironworking or furniture-building. This will be (or would be if I stay long enough) very interesting for me also. Later, when the students have gotten along in modern design, they actually start to build. That is, they coöperate in the design of buildings that will actually be built. So one can get a start and a name. But I don't know too much about all this yet so I don't know how long I'll stay. At any rate, I promise to spend next summer at home. . . . [3]

Walter Gropius and Adolf Meyer, administration building for the Werkbund Exhibition, Cologne, 1914

I found a place to stay with a Fraülein Menzer in the Bismarck-strasse in the old part of Dessau. I had to walk three-quarters of a mile or so each day from my lodgings to the Bauhaus, which was located in the open fields of a little-developed area separated from the city proper by the railroad tracks.

Menzer rented me her big, overfurnished front room and a small bedroom and bath, while she and her elder sister, a gentle old lady with little or no voice in the management of the household affairs, withdrew to some region of the apartment which I never saw. The younger Menzer was a close-fisted woman who left no stone unturned to earn one more Reichsmark, and she doubtless saw in her roomer a golden financial opportunity, for all Americans were supposed to be rolling in wealth. She was of a prying disposition and this annoyed me at first to such an extent that I instructed my mother to continue sending her letters to the Dessau general delivery because, I wrote, "I think my landlady is kina snoopy."[4] However, she made me quite comfortable.

I lived close enough to the Bauhaus to permit me to return home for a couple of hours in the afternoon when I felt the need for peace and quiet and wanted to be alone. I could also bring a friend home for coffee and cakes or a *Butterbrot* whenever I wished to. One of the friends who visited me on occasion was Edward Fischer, the only other American at the Bauhaus during my first year there. We

Lyonel Feininger, *Domchor, halle*

Bauhaus, Dessau. View from soccer field. On the right is Preller House (dormitory); center is the canteen (cafeteria) and auditorium; left is the workshop wing

Walter Gropius, workshop wing of the Bauhaus in Dessau shortly after completion, 1925–26

were the first Americans ever to attend the Bauhaus. Fischer had taken a leave of absence from his job at the Berlin branch of the J. Walter Thompson advertising agency to enable him to study for a while at the Bauhaus. We sometimes worked together in my room on problems for Albers's *Vorkurs* (beginning class in design). Fischer eventually became so intrigued with Oskar Schlemmer's abstract theater that he spent most of his time working on this.

When I enrolled at the Bauhaus, I thought it would be for a semester or two at the most. I still intended to return to Columbia after the novelty of living and studying in Europe had worn off. But I failed to reckon with the Bauhaus and its influence. It became impossible for me to leave after two semesters. I began to thrive on life in Germany and the work at the Bauhaus; it became almost inevitable that I would remain in Europe much longer than I had originally intended. I have never regretted this turn of events.

2 henry van de velde and his prototype bauhaus in weimar

On the face of it, it was not unreasonable for a school which was to gain such renown in the arts to have been established in Weimar. This small town, capital of the grand duchy of Saxe-Weimar-Eisenach, had won the titles of "poets' city" and "the German Athens." Goethe had lived there, from 1775 until his death in 1832, as had Schiller, Wieland, Herder, and Nietzsche. In addition, Weimar could claim distinction as a musical center, as it had been the frequent residence of Franz Liszt, who had conducted its orchestra.

When Gropius took up residence in Weimar in 1919, he already had a well-conceived program worked out for the new school he was to head. For three years, while serving as a lieutenant in the German army, he had corresponded with the Grand Duke of Saxe-Weimar-Eisenach about his possible assumption of the directorship of the Weimar Academy of Art (*Hochschule für bildende Kunst*). Gropius had proposed the union of the Academy with the Weimar Arts and Crafts School (*Kunstgewerbeschule*), which had been closed since 1915. When, at the end of the war, he finally reached an agreement with the republican government of Saxe-Weimar-Eisenach, which had succeeded the deposed grand duke, it was with the understanding that the two institutions should be merged to form a new school. Indeed, in 1915 Fritz Mackensen, the director of the Art Academy, recognizing the need to broaden the curriculum of his school, had corresponded with Gropius about the possible establishment of an architecture class in the academy with Gropius to teach it. Two years later, Mackensen and his colleagues Theodor Hagen, Walther Klemm, and Richard Engelmann had proposed a program which included the introduction of craft training

Ernst Ludwig Kirchner, *Henry van de Velde*.
Woodcut

into the Academy. These men, with whom Gropius would have to deal, seemed well disposed towards two main features of his own program, architecture and handicraft.

It was a different story with the Arts and Crafts School, which already had a distinguished reputation. The school had been started by Henry van de Velde eight years earlier, in Weimar, and he had remained its guiding spirit. Van de Velde had been invited to Weimar in 1902 for the stated purpose of acting as artistic advisor to the industry and handicrafts of the grand duchy and to establish, for the benefit of these domestic enterprises, an experimental laboratory in which new models would be designed and new forms of technology tried out. In this research institute, which was given the name Arts and Crafts (*Kunstgewerbliches*) Seminar van de Velde employed a radical pedagogic system, based upon study and analysis of the project at hand rather than the application to it of a preconceived formula. Of this system, Hans Curjel says, "A direct line leads from this to Gropius's Bauhaus establishment of 1919, the pedagogic principles of which have become fundamental in the present-day education of creators of form."[1]

Out of the Arts and Crafts Seminar grew the Weimar Arts and Crafts School established in 1906. To accommodate this school, van de Velde erected a new building which later came to house the Bauhaus workshops. Opposite this he built a more impressive edifice to serve the Weimar Art Academy. In the *Kunstgewerbeschule*, van de Velde introduced his new method of instruction. Karl Ernst Osthaus, in his biography of van de Velde, explained it as follows:

A project from which van de Velde expected great things was now actually carried out. This was the school which had already been contemplated, in connection with the total art policy of the grand duchy, at the time of his appointment. Its purpose was to be the education of the younger generation of artists. In contrast to the other arts and crafts schools, van de Velde here stressed, above all else, the workshop system. He could easily do without a life class since the "Art School" (the Academy) already supplied this need. And he also steered the drawing courses wholly toward the development of the new style. He had his students derive motifs from flowers and butterflies and then, bearing in mind the quality and quantity of color, develop them into patterns. This was done directly on graph paper, in order to awaken a feeling of rapport. Another requirement was that every student should learn modeling. It was only in this way that he could gain command of the third dimension and make himself understood by the craftsman. After these preparatory courses, the student, whenever possible, was transferred to one of the workshops. A foundry, a metalworking and chasing shop, a workshop for rug-making and weaving, a batik workshop, a book bindery, and a pottery

Henry van de Velde, samovar, 1902

shop were set up, as well as shops for enamelwork and jewelry. In these, special emphasis was placed on the speed of the work in order to teach the student the value of time. The whole system naturally depended upon the possibility of selling the products of the workshops and upon the acceptance of orders by the school administration. This policy, which, inexplicably, still meets with opposition in many quarters, was carried out in Weimar from the start. . . . [2]

It should not be concluded from this that van de Velde expected handwork to continue as the prevailing method of manufacture. At many points in his provocative writings he praises the works of the engineer and extols the beauty of machine-made objects as in this passage, from an article entitled "The Role of Engineers in Modern Architecture," written in 1901:

> There is a class of people from whom we can no longer withhold the title of artist. Their work is founded, on the one hand, upon the employment of materials whose use was hitherto unknown and, on the other, upon an audacity so extraordinary as even to surpass that of the cathedral builders. These artists, the creators of the new architecture, are the engineers. [3]

Implicit in van de Velde's praise of machine-made products is an acceptance of the principle of mass production. He made it quite clear, as early as 1897, that he designed his own furniture for mass production:

> . . . to avoid in furniture everything incapable of realization through *major industry*. My ideal would be a thousandfold multiplication of my creations, under the strictest supervision, to be sure, because I know from experience how quickly a model can be debased in the course of mass production and can become, through all kinds of dishonest or unintelligent manipulations, just as inferior as the thing which it is intended to oppose. I can hope for a decisive influence only from the moment when increased machine productivity allows me an effectiveness commensurate with the maxim which has directed my social creed: viz., that a person is worth more, the more numerous are those to whom his life work brings benefit or improvement. [4] . . .

Writing in 1901, van de Velde almost completely formulated the fundamental principle of the philosophy of design of the 1960s:

> What I recognize to be . . . the crux of all the artistic endeavors of our time is a yearning for a new harmony and a new aesthetic clarity. I adhere to this by proclaiming in the arts and crafts the sole principle which, in my opinion, is valid—that of construction. And I extend this structural principle just as far as I possibly can—to architecture as

well as to household utensils, to clothing, and to jewelry. I strive to eliminate from the decorative arts everything which degrades them by making them meaningless; and I wish to replace the old symbolic elements, in whose efficacy we no longer believe, with a beauty which is new and equally imperishable.[5]

Henry van de Velde, Bloemenwerf house in Uccle, Belgium, 1895

With the outbreak of the war, being an enemy alien (he had never relinquished his Belgian citizenship), van de Velde was relieved of all his duties in Weimar and placed under virtual house arrest. After suffering many indignities at the hands of reactionary artists and government officials (not the least of these the grand duke), whom the international conflict provided with a convenient pretext for venting their stored-up antagonism to him and his ideas, in 1917 he was finally permitted to take refuge in Switzerland.

It was early (December 1914) in the long, disheartening period of van de Velde's enforced inactivity in Weimar that Gropius wrote him from Alsace-Lorraine the following letter of commiseration:

I thank you heartily for your friendly communication. This gives me reason to hope that the letter I sent to Constance may have reached you. In this I wanted to tell you how much I condemn the brutal, boundlessly foolish behavior of my countrymen toward you. I am ashamed for them, and their lack of tact and judgment pains me exceedingly. We have much for which to make amends to you, my dear professor, and when the ears of the world again become receptive to sounds more delicate than the thunder of cannon, then surely some will arise who will settle with those fools according to their desserts [*sic*] and before the eyes of everyone express thanks to you for all that you have bestowed upon our country. . . . [6]

In July 1915, about six months after Gropius had sent his sympathetic letter to van de Velde, the latter wrote back from Weimar, informing him of the deplorable status of his Arts and Crafts School. This was, he says, "sad and lamentable enough to make one weep." The grand duke had decided to close the school on the approaching first of October, and the ministry of the interior was casting about for something to replace it. It had hit upon nothing better than the revival of the old consultation bureau, the business of which was to furnish advice to industrialists and craftsmen, and this project did not appeal to van de Velde. He had, nevertheless, suggested to the ministry three architects as possible directors of whatever organization finally emerged from the confused situation. These three persons were Gropius, August Endell,[7] and Hermann Obrist.[8] He goes on to say this:

Henry van de Velde in later life

I assure you that I have given all three of you—you, Endell, and Obrist—the same recommendation and that I have always stressed the fact that you were all equal in my eyes.

Whatever else comes out of this, my dear Mr. Gropius, can be a matter of indifference to us, except that you could still be of service to Endell. This is no longer the kind of job for you and other tasks await fulfillment through your talents, your artistry, and your determination to seize upon great projects of this sort.

Take heart! You are, after all, going through the school of courage and also the school of perseverance and patience. I envy you, and it helps me to endure everything (for the violent strangling of my school is a deep sorrow to me) when I think of all the friends who are fighting and bearing up in the armies of the various nations at the front. . . . [9]

This exchange of letters attests to the esteem in which the two men held each other. The older (van de Velde was over fifty and Gropius's senior by some twenty years) was rich in experience and prestige, so it was proper that he should offer advice to the younger, who stood on the threshold of his career. Gropius had, to be sure, already made an impressive start with his Fagus Factory in Alfeld in 1911 and his two exhibition buildings in Cologne in 1914, and his future looked very promising. But far from relinquishing his effort to land the job at Weimar, he continued negotiations throughout the war until he was at length successful.

To his new school Gropius gave the name *Bauhaus*. It was well chosen not only for its brevity but also because the word *Bau* in German embraces the act of constructing a building, its physical structure, the building itself, and, by extension, the interior decorations, including furniture and other utilitarian objects.

3

the launching of the bauhaus in weimar

the bauhaus program

Gropius had the program of his new school well in mind when he took up residence in Weimar. He lost no time, after he became director on April 1, 1919, in issuing the four-page brochure carrying his first Bauhaus proclamation and the program of the school; it is dated April 1919. On its cover is a woodcut by Lyonel Feininger, which must have been executed in Berlin as he did not reach Weimar until May 18. The proclamation is a state document only a little less famous than other documents of the time and quoted here in its entirety:[1]

The final goal of all artistic activity is architecture. Its embellishment was once the noblest task of the plastic arts, which were inseparable parts of the great art of building. These stand today in self-sufficient isolation, from which they can be released only through the conscious, coöperative efforts of all working men. Architects, painters, and sculptors must once more acquaint themselves with and come to understand that many-membered entity, the building, as a whole and in its parts, for then their works will, of themselves, again become infused with the architectonic spirit which, as salon art, they have lost.

The old art schools were unable to achieve this unity and, after all, how could they, since art cannot be taught? They must be absorbed once more by the workshop. This world of designers and decorators who only draw and paint must finally become one of builders again. If the young person, who feels within him the urge to create, again, as in former times, begins his career by learning a handicraft, the unproductive "artist" will, in the future, no longer remain condemned to the creation of mediocre art, because he will also be skilled in handicrafts, in which he will be able to produce things of excellence.

Architects, sculptors, painters, we must all return to handwork! For there is no such thing as a "profession of art." There is no difference in kind between the artist and the craftsman. *The artist is an enhancement of the craftsman.* The grace of heaven, in rare moments of inspiration, which lie beyond the control of his will, causes art to blossom unconsciously from the work of his hand. *But a foundation in handwork is indispensable for every artist.* Therein lies the wellspring of creativity.

Let us, therefore, establish a new *guild of craftsmen*, free of that class-dividing arrogance which seeks to erect a haughty barrier between craftsmen and artists! Let us desire, conceive, and create together the new building of the future, which will embrace everything—architecture, sculpture, and painting—in one entity, and which will mount toward heaven from the hands of a million craftsmen as the crystal symbol of a new and coming faith.[2]

The central idea of this proclamation is the revival of the medieval conception of the arts in which they were all united under the aegis of architecture (for example, the great cathedral). Since, at that time, the arts were sound and vital, architects, sculptors, and painters should again be trained to work, as they did then, with their hands. All workers must unite to create the great structure of the future, which will herald the advent of a new belief. Gropius had previously referred to this "crystal symbol of a new and coming faith" as the "Cathedral of Socialism,"[3] and, director as he was at the time of the Arbeitsrat für Kunst (Workers Council for Art), he might justifiably have been accused of viewing socialism as the new religion. It is likely that he subsequently rued coining the term "Cathedral of Socialism," as it was used against him for years afterward, in jest and in earnest, by his bourgeois deprecators.

As visionary as this call for unity of the arts on the basis of handwork was, it could certainly be interpreted as outdated and retrogressive. Instead of addressing itself to the future, it went straight back to John Ruskin and William Morris. The best that one can say for the document is that, like the preachments of Ruskin and Morris, it pleaded for a return to honest workmanship; but it betrayed no awareness of the fact that the face of the world—the character of society and the tools of creation—had changed since the Middle Ages. The proclamation was a romantic and unrealistic paean to the past.

Lyonel Feininger, cover of Gropius's manifesto, 1919.

Something more than half a page of the brochure is given over to a recapitulation, in somewhat different terminology, of the ideas in the proclamation. Toward the end of this Gropius states: "The school is the servant of the workshop and will one day be absorbed by it. Therefore, not teachers and students at the Bauhaus but masters, journeymen, and apprentices." It is evident that one of Gropius's major models for his pedagogical method was the medieval guild and the guild's relationship between masters, journeymen and apprentices in his own school. The people of Weimar, however, couldn't break themselves of the habit of referring to a teacher at a school of collegiate rank, such as the Bauhaus, as "professor" and to the students as "students." The antiquated terminology of the proclamation was dropped when the Bauhaus moved to Dessau.

The actual "Program of the State Bauhaus in Weimar" occupies two pages of the brochure, with a list of projected plans and principles:

The character of the teaching derives from the nature of the workshop:

Organic creation developed out of skill in handwork. Avoidance of all inflexibility; advancement of the creative; individual freedom, but hard study. Masters' and journeymen's examinations, in conformity with guild usage, before the Council of Masters or outside masters. Securing of commissions, for the students also. Coöperative planning of extensive Utopian building projects—buildings for the people and for worship—with a far-reaching goal. Coöperation of all masters and students—architects, painters, sculptors—in these designs with the aim of a gradual harmonizing of all members and parts of the building.

Constant contact with the leaders of the crafts and of industry in the province [of Thuringia]. Contact with public life and with the people by means of exhibitions and other events. New attempts in the exhibition field to solve the problems of displaying pictures and sculptures within the framework of architecture.

Promotion of friendly intercourse between masters and students outside of the work; to this end, theater, lectures, poetry, music, costume festivals. Building up of a gay ceremonial at these get-togethers.[4]

Oskar Schlemmer, *The Bauhaus Staircase*, 1932.

There is nothing startling or revolutionary about the points of this program. Running through these and the statements which immediately precede them is the same strong emphasis on handwork found in the proclamation. Gropius does address the need to keep in touch with the local crafts and industry. However, the mere mention of industry in a program so heavily weighted on the side of handwork for the sake of handwork hardly justifies his claim that the Bauhaus started its career as a series of laboratories devoted to the development of models for mass production.

The final page of Gropius's initial Bauhaus announcement goes into the details of the curriculum. It was to encompass all the practical and scientific aspects of the plastic arts—architecture, painting, and sculpture—together with all of their handicraft branches. The students were to be trained in handwork, draftsmanship, and theory.

The handicraft training was to comprise most of the three-dimensional arts and crafts customarily taught in a design school of that day (or the present). Practical training in draftsmanship was to cover the various kinds of freehand and technical drawing and painting techniques required by an architect or a pictorial artist, as well as architectural design and product design. Theoretical discipline ranged all the way from art history to bookkeeping. In addition to regular classroom work, special lectures would be held in all the fields of art and science.

The educational program was to consist, in sequence, of (1) the course for apprentices, (2) the course for journeymen, and (3) the course for young masters. Males or females, regardless of age, judged by the Council of Masters to have the necessary educational background, would be admitted to the Bauhaus. The tuition was to be 180 marks per year, with double this amount for foreigners.* As the earnings of the Bauhaus increased, this tuition was to gradually disappear altogether.

As far as one could gather from the program, this was the same outline of courses offered by any respectable school of art and architecture anywhere. The crucial question concerning any school, however, is not *what* courses are taught, but *how* they are taught. When Gropius compiled his program, the only insurance he had that his school would turn out to be more than just another humdrum institution was his own insight and determination. The fact that the Bauhaus did become an extraordinary educational venture was due in large part to his felicitous choice of collaborators. No art school of modern times has been able to boast of anything like

*Early in 1919, annual cost for tuition to the Bauhaus was (approximately) $14.50. The value of the German mark fell as the year progressed. Calculated in December, the approximate annual tuition cost would have been $4.50. By way of comparison, the annual tuition cost in 1919 for the University of Florida was $20.00.

the galaxy of brilliant teachers Gropius persuaded to join him in this undertaking. According to Mies van der Rohe, it was Alma Mahler, Gropius's wife, who advised him to engage celebrities to *x* teach at the Bauhaus, maintaining that this was the only way to make a success of the school.[5] Gropius did so, and he managed to hold these people together long enough to put the Bauhaus on the highroad to fame.

His first appointees were Feininger, Johannes Itten, and Gerhard Marcks, who came in 1919; Adolf Meyer came shortly after. They were followed by Georg Muche in 1920; Paul Klee in January 1921; Oskar Schlemmer and Lothar Schreyer in January and June, respectively, of the same year; Wassily Kandinsky in June 1922; and, early in 1923, László Moholy-Nagy. Of these, only Meyer was an architect. Marcks was a sculptor; and the rest were painters—painters, to be sure, but painters who frequently made excursions into one or more of the other arts. One of the weaknesses of the school was, thus, in the composition of the staff, and it must be considered peculiar that Gropius invited nine artists and only one architect to assist him in the implementation of a program directed toward *building* as its culminating objective, even if the script did read, "the union of the arts in architecture."

The teaching program which accompanied Gropius's first proclamation was primarily what each individual master, and the masters collectively, made of it. It is desirable, nevertheless, to trace its main outlines as Gropius conceived them. Handwork was to be the cornerstone, and the final, though remote, objective, was to be the great "total work of art," the culminating, coöperative achievement of countless artists and artisans.

Oskar Schlemmer, ca. 1920

Lyonel Feininger, photographed by his son, Andreas Feininger

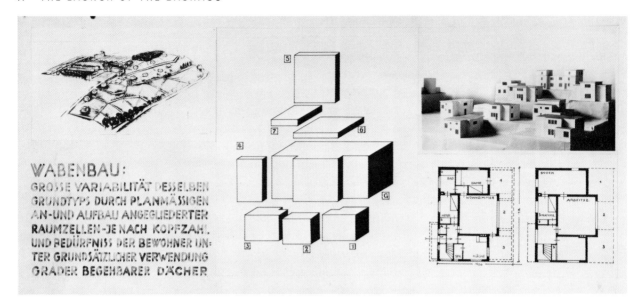

WABENBAU:
GROSSE VARIABILITÄT DESSELBEN
GRUNDTYPS DURCH PLANMÄSSIGEN
AN-UND AUFBAU ANGEGLIEDERTER
RAUMZELLEN-JE NACH KOPFZAHL
UND BEDÜRFNISS DER BEWOHNER UN-
TER GRUNDSÄTZLICHER VERWENDUNG
GRADER BEGEHBARER DÄCHER

Walter Gropius, Bauhaus housing settlement,
Weimar, 1922

Craft instruction at the school embraced work in stone, wood, metal, clay, glass, paint, and fabrics. Shops for these various branches of handwork were promptly established in name, but it was some time before the work really got underway in many of them. In the course of a speech to the state legislature in July 1920, Gropius explained what gave the workshops their slow start:

We had to wait a year, we had no money with which to equip the workshops, to obtain raw materials and tools. With this same money today, as you yourselves know, we can buy, at most, a fourth or fifth of what it would have been possible to get with it a year ago. . . . You can see how tremendously difficult it is today to set up workshops. I also have to voice an objection to the false reports which are being published in a certain newspaper about the number of fully equipped workshops which I took over here. I pass nothing off as my own work which is not actually that. With the exception of the book bindery, the private business of Mr. Dorfner, which has remained essentially as it was, the workshops have been rebuilt under my direction. The textile department has been changed completely and, except for a few looms, it is not private property but was taken over by the Bauhaus and newly organized. All the work which you saw there (on your recent tour) falls to the credit of the Bauhaus and not to that of the previous school. Everything looked quite different then. The metal workshop didn't even exist when I came here. All of van de Velde's workshops had been dismantled, every piece of equipment had been sold, and I was confronted by completely empty rooms; and these rooms were to be filled again out of nothing. In this metal workshop, which you saw, every single article was newly procured and in part very recently, because we received our first money only eight weeks ago. Everyone knows that a project cannot be set up in actuality in the short time it takes to put it on paper or into words.[6]

Two masters were placed in charge of each of the workshops, a "form master" and a "technical master." Gropius explained the necessity for this division of labor:

> The best way to train such artists remains individual instruction by masters, individual instruction by masters as we see it in the Middle Ages when no institutions for art education, no academies whatever, existed, but when there were creative masters who combined in one person both formal and technical ability. This instruction by masters still remains the goal to be striven for. But if we look around us today, we are no longer able to find such masters. With but a few exceptions, we don't have this personal study under masters any more. Craftsmanship has sunk very low. We no longer have any universally creative persons who are able to guide young learners not only in technical matters but also, at the same time, in a formal way. But thinking this through logically, one realizes that we must seek a way that will gradually lead us again to this objective which we hope later, after generations, to attain. The Bauhaus plan is just such a way. It is therefore a fundamental principle of the state Bauhaus that the young person who is learning be influenced simultaneously from two sides: first, from the craftsmanship side, by technically outstanding masters of handwork; and second, from a formal standpoint, by artistic personalities. Thus it will already be possible for the coming generation to unite both capacities in one and the same person. For this reason I have set up the basic requirement, in agreement with other experts, that every architect, sculptor, painter, etc. must learn a craft as a matter of principle.[7]

the beginning of the school

The story of the Bauhaus may be said to have begun with Gropius's trip on his thirty-sixth birthday, May 18, 1919, from Berlin to Weimar. He was accompanied by Feininger, the first of his chosen teachers to set foot in Weimar and the first American at the Bauhaus. (Although Feininger had lived in Germany since he was sixteen years old, he was born in New York City in 1871; he had managed for over thirty years to retain his United States citizenship.)

The first report which Feininger sent to his wife, Julia, in Berlin, on the day after his arrival in Weimar, was full of hope and optimism:

> . . . how shall I begin? Is it possible to experience so much in twelve short hours? . . . the most wonderful of all is my new studio! . . . a room in the top story, about 45' x 45' x 18' and at the skylight a curtain like the giant mainsail of a full-rigged ship, adjustable in every direction—and the view! over the gardens, over the roofs of the whole town out to the mountains—here I shall be able to work . . . I am very

happy indeed! Dear good Gropius, he has appointed this studio to me rightaway. I have been all over the school with him, and I have seen the printing-shop [Feininger's special domain later], marvellous—here we shall be like in a painter's heaven . . .[8]

Feininger does not voice his disillusionment when, two days later, he tells his wife of the gathering storm clouds, those clouds which were to hover almost continually over the Bauhaus, whatever its site, during its existence:

. . . had tea with Gropius and the museum director . . . very important talk about the already beginning intrigues of our opponents . . . how best to counteract, and to deal with them in this wasp's nest . . . the students I have so far seen, look very self-conscious. Almost all have been in the war for many years. It is a new type of youth. I believe them to be after something new in the field of art, and they are by no means so timid and harmless as the old professors here imagine them to be . . .[9]

Meanwhile, Gropius's proclamation and his original program had been widely distributed and had called forth a quick, enthusiastic response. Keyed to the needs of the generation of young people who fought in the war, or, who at least suffered from it, it attracted eager and hopeful students to the Bauhaus from all over Germany, from Austria, and elsewhere. Many who were enrolled in other schools wished that they were at the Bauhaus instead, as Feininger, in a letter of June 30, 1919, commented:

. . . you won't believe it, how from Munich, for instance, they look upon "free" little Weimar with jealousy and longing . . . And it really will develop into something very wonderful: the Bauhaus.[10]

Gropius had the power to inspire the youth of that day through both his written and spoken word. Reactions to his program and his inaugural address were published in *Der Austausch*, an excellent student "newspaper" carrying original essays, poetry, woodcuts, and reviews of books and exhibitions.[11] The first issue of the paper appeared in May 1919 and featured on its front page this eloquent plea for solidarity by E. Schrammen, one of the student leaders:

The old, easygoing art school, the proud exalted college of the plastic arts—and now the state Bauhaus! The Bauhaus which is coming into being under its new director, Walter Gropius, with a plan of study looking backward to the times and countries of the highest culture and pointing forward to new, high goals, is both rigorously down-to-earth and far-ranging in fantasy! The Bauhaus, itself, [is] in its conception a "Utopian structure," such as its leader advances as a new requirement of our time.

"Easel photograph" of van de Velde's Art and Craft School. *Lower right* atelier house for students

Long, crippling years of war and then, in the direst need, a breath again and hope of freedom through the great upheaval. And now, in spite of all material restrictions, the reawakening of the will to creative life, of the joy in work which brings fulfillment, in activity worthy of human beings; constructive work after being compelled to devastate and destroy unworthily; friendship, helpful love after embittering hatred and remorseless persecution.

Arise, human beings, fellow human beings, join in the reconstruction of our common life, in the creation of new and nobler ways of living, in a spirit of mutual trust, reciprocal help: work community, community work![12]

Schrammen's piece, of which I have quoted the more interesting half, is followed by other comments on the program and the speech. A student who describes him- or herself only as Auerbach (probably Johannes Auerbach) says, addressing Gropius:

The fact that your views, aims, and efforts represent the fulfillment of the wishes of many and that you by no means have to fight alone against one hundred and fifty who think differently, has perhaps already become apparent through our behavior and will be emphasized in this paper. If the hopes which we repose in the realization of your plans should be fulfilled, then the school which provides a one-sided and therefore restrictive education and which nourishes the desire for freedom, would be transformed into a showplace of many-sided, stimulating, and creative life . . . Your remarks about our relationship to craftsmen, furthermore, seem to me to be of great importance. It is surely high time that we tore down the barriers between us and the class to whom the future, admittedly, belongs. It will otherwise be our fate to miss the path of true vitality and culture, just as those who, when the political and cultural power passed from the aristocracy to the bourgeoisie, sought to deny the progress of world history and became mired in old forms.[13]

It is interesting to learn from this that there were as many as one hundred and fifty students at the Bauhaus a month or so after it opened. It is also worthy of note that the student, reflecting Gro-

E. Schrammen, woodcut from July 1919 issue of *Der Austausch*

pius's viewpoint, believes the handworker to be the man of destiny.

The next student, Käthe Brachmann, spoke with a full heart:

> This vibrates and resounds within me: I may take part. It must vibrate and resound in the same way, these days, within all those who hear their names named among the ranks of the Bauhaus students. And I cannot rest until I have expressed my gratitude. . . . [14]

Brachmann devotes the remainder of her composition to a justification of her being at the Bauhaus rather than following a woman's natural calling, motherhood:

> So we women, too, came to this school because we, every one of us, found work to do here, which we durst not neglect! May no one begrudge us this work! Thanks to those who already accord it to us. [15]

It will not surprise us today that she found it necessary to defend a woman's right to a higher education, even though the watchword of the school was emancipation of the spirit.

Heinrich Linzen, the next to bear witness to the virtues of Gropius's program, had reservations when it came to the director's campaign against "l'art pour l'art":

> The joyful approval with which the new program has been received by the young artists proves right from the start how justified it is. Most of them hope that it will release them from "purposeless" art and a spiritual standstill.
>
> Honesty is the greatest thing in art, so that the new program will rescue many from artistic falsehood. But let us not forget to accord respect and recognition to those who pursue old, exalted aims which will always be vital, and for whom art, also in the form of the "salon painting," is the highest revelation of life. [16]

It is remarkable that Linzen had the temerity to challenge one of Gropius's fighting issues, the abolition of easel painting and the other self-sufficient arts. It is possible that he had been "corrupted" by attending the old Academy of Fine Arts, which had surely been dedicated to "art for art's sake." Whether he realized it or not, he was calling into question the ultimate objective of Gropius's program, the unification of the arts in architecture; for there could be no place in such a plan for the self-contained works of art which he, Linzen, still revered. The painting and sculpture which were to be incorporated in Gropius's ideal structure would be subordinated to it and therefore modified by it, just as Gothic sculpture was rigorously stylized to integrate it with the architectural whole. In Gropius's view, art achieved legitimacy by playing an ancillary role in a composite work but forfeited this when it led an independent existence.

These passages from *Der Austausch* are infused with idealism, with eagerness, and with hope for a better future. Those who would like to believe that they reflect the prevailing state of mind at the school will take comfort in the words of Schreyer, one of the Bauhaus masters, when he says:

The few short years of the Bauhaus in Weimar were fired through and through with dedication to the idea. Masters, journeymen, and apprentices strove to outdo each other. We believed literally that we were privileged to participate in the building of a new world, conscious of an actual historical turning point in which, as in an hour of destiny, creative energies were welling forth directly out of the depths of life into the light.[17]

Walter Gropius

Schreyer wrote this thirty years after the Bauhaus in Weimar had ceased to exist. The passage of time can lend perspective, clarity of view. Closeness to the situation or the events can obscure the vision and distort the interpretation of them. So it may be that when Schreyer implies that the Bauhaus was one big happy family, working together in harmony, he is giving us a valid appraisal of the state of affairs; whereas two of the students, writing in the July 1919 issue of *Der Austausch*, in the midst of the events, may be presenting us with an inaccurate one. These two students, who in the May number had spoken so feelingly of such things as mutual trust, reciprocal help, and coöperative effort, turned this forum for the trading of noble ideas into an arena for the swapping of verbal brickbats. Thus the *quondam* apologist for coeducation, Brachmann, no longer shy and suppliant, in an article entitled "Bauhaus Spirit," says:

Dear comrades—It is almost ironic to address you in this manner for comradeship is in a damn bad way with us—tell us sometime what you think about this:

There goes our first student president, having just resigned his office, running his legs, already short, still shorter. There he is making his round skull still rounder with thinking and using his "loose snout" to deliver well-composed speeches for the good of the community. And how does the community react? It continues to stick, well-satisfied, to the old clique business.

Do you think it was any honor to us that Schrammen, Linzen and Teichgraber, happily relieved after going through the formality of resigning, shook hands with each other?

Dear Bauhaus students, here we are in the most beautiful building that one can imagine but, so far, we are not worthy of it.[18]

Side by side with Brachmann's piece on the last page of the July issue of *Der Austausch* is a vitriolic diatribe by Schrammen in which he castigates his fellow students who are running the magazine:

> Believe it or not, honored Bauhaus students, the third number of *Der Austausch*!
>
> Look it over, the third, this splendid specimen!
>
> The same, brave, tame, little paper as the first two famous numbers.
>
> But remember, honored *Austausch*—you dishrag—(and you also bear this in mind, all of you fine parents and noble relatives of this spotty bastard), the foremost and the strongest spirits have long since denied you every right to existence!
>
> Shrink into yourself in shame, buy yourself out, creep away to some still, remote place, pitiful candidate for death—and reduce yourself to ashes, burn yourself up! . . . [19]

The remaining two-thirds of Schrammen's blast is as ill-tempered as the part quoted. No invective was too strong for him to hurl at this very creditable student paper. His article and that of Brachmann's reveal that the united front heralded in a number of Bauhaus declarations of solidarity was already crumbling (which proves once again the instability of human resolutions).

the 1919 exhibition

If some of the students were so early in a frame of mind to wrangle with each other, it is not surprising that they readily found a reason to turn against Gropius, whom they had so recently acclaimed and honored. In June 1919 an internal exhibition was held to enable the masters to evaluate the student's work. Coming little more than a month after his arrival in Weimar, Feininger wrote:

> . . . at 4 p.m. meeting of the "masters" for the purpose of examining the show of students' works and to decide upon federal stipends, awards, etc. For the first time I saw an assemblage of their works. In the beginning I had great difficulty in adjusting myself. Some works simply dumbfounded me . . . and again there was a confused mass of industrious studies without any signs of talent . . . but after a while I was able to discern more clearly. Gropius had told me privately that he intended to deal harshly and go against certain elements uncom-

promisingly—and so he did. I have to admit that he was perfectly right. He has a very precise judgment, of tradition; he is apt to overthrow. This seems hard, but it is stimulating and clears the road . . . and that is what we are here for: to fight sterility in the arts.[20]

Feininger had certainly seen bad art before but possibly never so much of it together in one place. This gives us a clue to what had been going on at the old Academy of Art, since many of the students whose works were up for judgment were holdovers from that school. It is evident that Feininger, whose tendency was to be kinder to the students, bent over backward to justify Gropius's strict appraisal of the student works.

It was up to Gropius, as director, to report the decisions of the jury. He did this in a carefully prepared statement, and at the same time he told the students bluntly enough what he thought of their work and outlined what they would have to do to improve it. Since the talk is an eloquent presentation of Gropius's ideas and feelings of that day, I will quote a substantial part of it:

The exhibition made the Council of Masters rack their brains. We couldn't reach a decision on the first day about the awarding of the prizes and so, after much deliberation, we met again. Confronted by your works, I myself felt a crushing responsibility, and I have been disturbed about them for days. For we are living in a terribly chaotic time and this small exhibition is a faithful reflection of it. I also spent the whole of Sunday in the exhibition rooms because I wanted to arrive at an understanding and estimate of each one of you, in order to get a true cross section of the Bauhaus. Ladies and gentlemen, there is talent there but also tremendous disintegration.

Ladies and gentlemen, first, external considerations: many fine frames, splendid getups, finished paintings, but for whom, after all? I asked you especially to turn in design sketches and ideas. Not *one* painter or sculptor brought in composition ideas, which should really form the core of an institution such as this.[21]

Here Gropius speaks at some length about the works of De-termann, Röhl, Herrmann, Breustedt, and Käthe Brasch.[22] He continues:

I will mention other names afterwards. I am certain that a year from now everything will have changed tremendously. The chief thing for all of us remains, after all, spiritual experience and what each indi-vidual makes of it. We are in the midst of a momentous catastrophe of world history, of a transformation of all aspects of life and of the entire inner human being. This is perhaps fortunate for the artistic person, if he is strong enough to bear the consequences, because what we need is the courage to have inner experience. For then, suddenly, a new way will lie open to the artist.

Our impoverished nation has scarcely any more resources to devote to cultural things and cannot provide for those who only want to dabble in art. Ladies and gentlemen, I am compelled to say this with so much emphasis because my conscience demands it of me. For I foresee that many of you, unfortunately, will be forced, not too long hence, to turn to some paying employment; and the only one who will stick to art will be he who is willing to starve for it. We must forget the prewar time, which was totally different. The sooner we adjust ourselves to the new, changed world, to its new, albeit harsh, beauties, the sooner will each individual be able to find his own personal happiness. The distress of Germany will spiritualize and deepen us. With the falling away of material opportunities, the spiritual possibilities have now risen enormously.[23]

Here the photocopy of the typescript ends. It appears, in any case, that Gropius is about to wind up his remarks and proceed to the awarding of the prizes. The awards had some unexpected consequences, as Feininger related in a letter of June 27 to his wife:

. . . these days the Bauhaus resembles a mad-house—there is flaring or brooding rebellion all around. Reason: the prize awarding . . . some even intend to apply to the government to demand nothing less than Gropius's dismissal right away! So yesterday evening Gropius called in the rebels for a heart-to-heart talk and he listened to everybody's complaints. That eased their minds and helped to clear the situation. . . . What the students resented most was that Gropius had declared he would always intercede for the most extreme in art, as a manifestation of the times we live in.[24]

So Gropius succeeded in restoring calm. Returning to his speech, one cannot deny the moving quality of his words, the sincerity of his plea for spirituality in a country racked by war. One must also grant that he sized up the situation accurately when he said that things could not continue along the old track.

Gropius had an almost hieratic sense of his mission to reform art and, along with art, the world. He knew he couldn't do this with halfhearted converts to the great cause or with disciples who lacked the gifts to further it. So he set high standards for admission. A major purpose of the student exhibition was to enable him and the other masters to size up the students and decide which ones were to be permitted to continue at the Bauhaus. Gropius was inclined to weed them out a little too drastically to suit Feininger who, in a letter written a week or so after the exhibition opened, took a more sympathetic view of the less brilliant students, those who had to struggle to attain their goals:

. . . again a ''master''-meeting to determine which of the students are to be admitted. That always gives me lots to ponder about. In my mind's eye I see so vividly all our youngsters, over whose fates we hold decision . . . it is a strange thing, the most gifted of our students simply goes ahead unheeding, in a playful way . . . this one remains unmolested, while others, whose talents are less gaily on the surface, who have to take pains to overcome the antiquated methods of the previous system, should have no chance. I very decidedly take sides with those who have to work hard but want to achieve something. Art development is a thing of slow growth, it requires time and plenty of it, it cannot be forced. I always manage to save one or two, they then get a break . . . and Gropius is open to arguments and ready for a discussion.[25]

This excerpt, and the one below, tell us as much about Feininger as about Gropius and the Bauhaus.

. . . there will be a young man coming to see me who wants to study with me, the same I wrote about yesterday, who gazed at me as though expecting all salvation for him to come from me. But what more can the best of teachers in Art impart than guidance, develop inherent faculties and give confirmation . . . all else has to be attained by continual self-education . . . I should like best to have pupils of strong initiative and who are not afraid of it. They ought to learn to obey less my precepts than the compulsion of Art.[26]

I can scarcely do better by Feininger than to let him speak for himself, a man rich in human understanding and compassion.

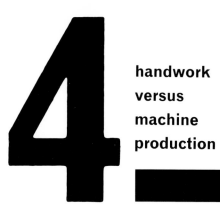

4 handwork versus machine production

Gropius's workshop program was not new. His predecessor, van de Velde, had also "stressed above all else the workshop system" in the Arts and Crafts School. However, the well-known art critic Max Osborn wrote in the *Vossiche Zeitung* (this was a famous liberal newspaper dubbed "Aunt Voss" by its many devoted readers.):

> "He [Gropius] is the first finally to have taken serious steps to meet the demand which has for years been made by all the experts, that art instruction be placed, once more, upon a handwork basis."[1]

The program was not universally accepted, especially by those students intent upon creating *objets d'art*. Because many of the students had been taken over from the old Weimar Academy of Art there was, from the beginning, a large number of would-be artists at the school. Most of the works displayed in the exhibition of June 1919 were paintings and sculpture, and at the time Gropius found it necessary to chide the students for ignoring his program.[2] This dedication to art for art's sake on the part of many of the students was destined to persist at the Bauhaus. Schlemmer, having concluded a contract to teach at the Bauhaus, wrote to his painter friend Otto Meyer-Amden:

> There is danger that the Bauhaus will turn out to be not very different from a modern art academy for the thing which should distinguish

it fundamentally from such schools—handwork and the workshops—
is only incidental. . . . furthermore, the students are said to have little
interest in genuine handwork, their chief ambition being to become
modern painters. The fine thing is that Gropius wants to allow himself
and the Bauhaus time and will exhibit nothing publicly for five years.[3]

It was inevitable that friction should develop between the de-
votees of art and the champions of handwork. From the outset,
Gropius had inveighed against art that was self-sufficient and artists who refused to coöperate in his grand plan—although he packed
his teaching staff with artists. The students may well have wondered why, if Feininger, Klee, Kandinsky, and the others persisted
in creating works which were ends in themselves, they should not
be permitted to do so as well. If the Bauhaus became separated
into two camps, that of the "useful" crafts and that of the "useless"
arts, Gropius, himself, was in part to blame for it.

Muche, contemplating this forty years later, viewed it as a constructive domestic situation:

The hovering equilibrium between the search after architectonic and
purposeful form, on the one hand, and the imaginative method of
creation of the painters and sculptors, on the other, provided the
Bauhaus with an exciting middle ground. If Gropius had not possessed a persuasive power sufficient to hold these tensions in balance, it is possible that the formulas of abstract painting would have
crept into the products of the workshops and a new style of craftsmanship would have developed. As things stood, however, the beauty
of industrial form became the clear and useful goal.[4]

Schlemmer, however, noted the harm this was causing:

I was astonished at the bad feeling that the students with whom I
have so far become acquainted have toward Gropius. They say he is
no longer what he was in the beginning when, as "Father Gropius,"
he lived—and suffered—in true companionship with the students.
They declare that he is greatly changed, a fact which is even visible
in his eyes, in a line about the mouth; and in the recently published
Bauhaus statutes, next to nothing remains of the once-beautiful program . . .

The amount of positive work done by the students, whether art work
or handwork, is small, almost shockingly small. It is quite just to say
that the Bauhaus is a beautiful façade, a conception, an idea in Germany, supported on the names of some artists and on a program. . . .[5]

Gerhard Marcks, *Maisa*

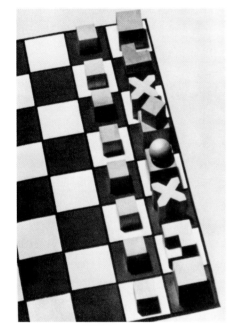

Josef Hartwig, chess set, 1923

Though Schlemmer's contract had gone into effect on January 1, 1921, he was still commuting between Cannstatt (near Stuttgart) and Weimar a month after this. He wrote a long letter to Meyer-Amden relating the goings-on at the Bauhaus. After reporting that about twenty students, agitated by an itinerant crackpot "Apostle of the Truth," who had spoken in Weimar, had picked up and left, "on foot, without concern or money," for Spain and Italy, he says:

. . . the circumstances that the Bauhaus program, itself, called together an insolent band of young people (they are a mad assemblage of today's youth), has caused the Bauhaus to "build" in a quite different direction than it is expected to, viz., the human being. Gropius appears to be very much aware of this and he recognizes therein the failing of the academies, which neglect to mold the individual. It is his wish, he says, that an artist also have character, this first and other things later. Nevertheless, he seems at times to be concerned about the consequences; no work is being done, but there is, instead, a very great deal of talking. So he wishes he could have, temporarily, a wall about the Bauhaus and cloistered seclusion.[6]

And in a letter written on March 2, 1921, to an unidentified correspondent, he continues to dwell on conditions at the Bauhaus:

The departure of students goes on (Italy, in league with the springtime). Few applications this year. . . .

In his book *The New Architecture and the Bauhaus*, published many years later, Gropius attempted to persuade his readers that the Bauhaus concentrated on the making of industrial prototypes from the very beginning:

In carrying out this scheme I tried to solve the ticklish problem of combining imaginative design and technical proficiency. That meant finding a new and hitherto nonexistent type of collaborator who could be molded into being equally proficient in both. As a safeguard against any recrudescence of the old dilettante handicraft spirit, I made every pupil (including the architectural students) bind himself to complete his full legal term of apprenticeship in a formal letter of engagement registered with the local trades council. I insisted on manual instruction, not as an end in itself, or with any idea of turning it to incidental account by actually producing handicrafts, but as providing a good all-round training for hand and eye, and being a practical first step in mastering industrial processes.

The Bauhaus workshops were really laboratories for working out practical new designs for present-day articles and improving models for mass production. To create type-forms that would meet all technical, aesthetic, and commercial demands required a picked staff. It needed a body of men of wide general culture as thoroughly versed in the practical and mechanical sides of design as in its theoretical and formal laws. Although most parts of these prototypes had naturally to be made by hand, their makers were bound to be intimately acquainted with factory methods of production and assembly, which differ radically from the practices of handicraft. . . . In the future the field of the handicrafts will be found to lie mainly in the preparatory stages of evolving experimental new type-forms for mass production.

There will, of course, always be talented craftsmen who can turn out individual designs and find a market for them.[7]

D. Levine, "Father Gropius who lived and suffered with the students."

These comments surprised me greatly. And I was even more surprised at a statement made by Gropius in a letter in the June 1963 number of *The Journal of Architectural Education*. Gropius, replying to certain remarks I had made in the October 1962 number of the same magazine concerning van de Velde's influence on the Bauhaus, wrote: "Accordingly, handicraft in the workshops was, right from the start, not an end in itself, but laboratory experiment preparatory to industrial production."[8] I do not believe that this tallies with the facts as they emerged from an investigation of the documentary material bearing on the matter.

In the same number of *The Journal of Architectural Education* in which Gropius's reply was printed, I questioned the correctness of this assertion, quoting, to prove my point, from statements made by Gropius in 1919 and from a letter written by Schlemmer in 1922.[9] Gropius saw fit to reply again:

> In his answer to my statement on the Bauhaus in your last issue, Mr. Dearstyne has come to a wrong conclusion. Since he alleges that I am trying to "rewrite history," I feel obliged, for history's sake, to offer evidence from my own original files for the correctness of my statement. Mr. Dearstyne, not knowing sufficiently the background to the initial Bauhaus program, errs when he states that the original Bauhaus was set to educate craftsmen only, and that I was only later "persuaded by Doesburg of the error of the Bauhaus way." The craft training in the Bauhaus was indeed, right from the beginning, not an end in itself, but a means to an end. Everyone who cares to look at my own production in architecture (prefabrication and industrial buildings and products) and into my writings *before* I started the Bauhaus and before I met van Doesburg cannot be in doubt that my thinking was all along aiming at industry, and not at craft work as an end in itself: Here is the chronological evidence from my early articles . . . [10]

He then presented excerpts from articles of his of 1911, 1913, 1916, and 1919, in each of which industry and machine production were either mentioned briefly or discussed at some length and from a lecture of October 1919 he quoted himself as having said:

> It has been doubted whether the installation of state workshops would not cause competition detrimental to private enterprises. However, danger of competition can never arise, for the aim of such workshops points to the opposite direction. Their intent is to help all crafts and industries, not to hinder them. They are meant to establish a suitable professional training ground for the rising generation of craftsmen and industrial workers. . . . They want first of all to create models, the particular quality in workmanship and form of which should bring commissions into the country for the benefit of all crafts and industries which have been stimulated by the activities of these workshops.

He proceeded to point out that in referring, in my letter, to his first Bauhaus program, I had failed to mention the fact that this contained the phrase "constant interrelation with leaders of the crafts and with the industries of the country." Gropius then quoted as follows from a talk given by him in the spring of 1919 to representatives of the local crafts and industries in Weimar:

We can reach our aim only when arts, crafts, and industries inter-
penetrate each other. Today they are widely separated from each
other, so to speak, by walls. The crafts and also the industries need
a fresh influx of artistic creativity in order to enliven the forms which
have gone stale and to reshape them. But the artist still lacks the
craft training which alone will safely enable him to shape materials
into masterly form.

He then summarized his reasons for introducing the craft program
into the Bauhaus:

My basic trend of thinking as to the role of the crafts as a means to
an end only, and to the role of industry as the future basis of production, has never changed since the beginning of my professional
activities. . . . The emphasis on crafts during the first three Bauhaus
years has, therefore, not been an error, as Mr. Dearstyne sees it,
but it was the first logical and necessary step. The students knew
very well from innumerable discussions with me—which unfortunately were not written down—that learning a craft was for training's
sake, but not an end in itself.

Though he was critical of me for having omitted the line "Constant interrelation with the leaders of the crafts and with the industries of the province" (meaning, in this case, Thuringia), in
quoting from his first Bauhaus program, he didn't explain why the
program, except for this phrase and the proclamation which pre-
ceded it, stressed handwork—handwork directed, not toward industrial production but, like that of the Middle Ages, toward the
creation of some architectural monument of cathedral-like proportions, some great consortium of all the crafts.

The question at issue, of course, is not what Gropius said or
thought, but what he did. The purpose of Gropius's emphasis on
handicraft instruction at the Bauhaus from 1919 to 1922 was two-
fold: craftsmen would be trained both to collaborate on that ne-
bulous project, the all-embracing structure, and, by pursuing
handwork as a vocation, infuse new vitality into the moribund crafts.
This second objective clearly fell into the category of handwork for
the sake of handwork, regardless of how strenuously he objected
to this interpretation.

The evidence which established this beyond a doubt is contained
in the lengthy address delivered by him in defense of the Bauhaus,
to the provincial legislature on July 9, 1920:

The impossibility of doing quality work, which characterizes our economic life today, stems from the draining off of creative talents from
handwork into the so-called fine arts. The crafts have become des-
titute and art is very mediocre. The normal aim of creative talents
today is the practice of painting, the graphic arts, or sculpture. . . .

Georg Muche, *The Table*

L. Hirschfeld-Mack, composition in tempera

Furthermore we can already observe a strong return current. Many design draftsmen from the factories, many humble persons in the arts and crafts schools and the academies are streaming back and are taking steps to find work. It is one of the main ideas of the Bauhaus to win all of these abilities over to handwork in order that they may enrich the crafts. . . . The young artists, however, of whom I previously spoke, have an entirely different attitude. They want to go into creative work, and the important thing for us is to see to it that these artists, who possess the capacity for regular constructive work, find employment in the crafts and be won over to handwork. This refutes the false assertion that an institution such as the one we have here robs the crafts of talents. . . . On the contrary, we even supply the crafts with additional talents, for the people who want to study with us have never before had a connection with handwork. They were purely draftsmen, graphic artists, painters, etc. . . .

The best way to train such artists continues to be individual instruction by masters—voluntary study under masters, as we see this in the Middle Ages, when no institutions for art instruction, no academies whatever existed, but when there were creative and technical skills. This instruction by masters remains the objective to be sought after. . . . For this reason I established the basic requirement . . . that every architect, sculptor, painter, etc., as a matter of principle, should learn a craft.[11]

The portion of Gropius's address reproduced (in careful translation) constitutes the core of his "idea of the Bauhaus." It is difficult to see how, in the light of this, he could later maintain that the craft training at the school was conceived as preparation for design in industry. The major emphasis is on the sad plight of craftsmanship and the need to inject new life into it by furnishing it with fresh talent. But far from sending trained men into industry, Gropius seems to rejoice that designers already in industry were flocking back to handwork.

This speech to the legislature was undoubtedly a major effort on his part since, even at that early date, it could have affected the decision of the legislature to allow the Bauhaus to continue. We can assume that he prepared it with the utmost care in order to present the Bauhaus case as accurately, and in as favorable a light, as possible. If this was the way he himself interpreted the work, it is no wonder that he convinced many of the Bauhaus students and teachers and the world in general that his objective in introducing the craft program was to pursue handwork for the sake of handwork.

That Gropius should have tinkered around with the established facts can signify only that he was very sensitive on the point as to whether or not handicraft for its own sake or handicraft aimed at machine production prevailed at the Bauhaus in its early days. Two things seem certain: one, that the Bauhaus, until 1922, stood for handicraft production without any strings attached; and two, that in that year there was a complete about-face, calling for the making of industrial prototypes.*

Theo van Doesburg, in Weimar

**theo van doesburg
alters the course
of the bauhaus**

Between 1922 and 1923, a profound change in orientation took place at the Bauhaus. Gropius, no doubt, would have denied that any such basic change took place and would have maintained that what appeared to others as a basic change was merely the pre-conceived logical unfolding of his program. Schlemmer, in a letter written from Weimar at the end of March 1922 to his friend Meyer Amden gives us an intimation of what this change was to be and who was to bring it about:

*Although Dearstyne was not present at the inauguration of the Bauhaus (1919) nor when the focus of the curriculum was redirected (1922), he cites sources who were present to support his contention that a significant change in the curriculum took place. In his desire to preserve the larger view of the importance of the Bauhaus and its historical contributions, Gropius did not wish to acknowledge that any change or redirection took place. Gropius's interest was in the purity of the idea, Dearstyne's in historical accuracy about which he feels strongly.

Theo van Doesburg, *Space-Time Construction No. 3*, 1923

One of those here who goes especially eagerly to the attack is van Doesburg, the Dutchman, who is so intensely interested in architecture that painting, except it be the reflection of this, does not exist for him. He is a very eloquent champion of his ideas, so that he draws the Bauhaus students under his spell, especially those who are interested, before everything else, in architecture, and who seek that architectural center which, in their opinion, the Bauhaus owes to them. The circumstances make it almost easy for him, in the light of his views, to reject the Bauhaus and its masters. I was formerly closest to being in his good graces, although I "still" make use of "soft" forms. He rejects handwork (the focal point of the Bauhaus) in favor of the modern means, the machine. He believes that through the exclusive, consistent use of the horizontal and vertical in architecture and art he will be able to create the style which denies individual expression in the interest of collectivism.[12]

In a letter written by Feininger to his wife, Julia, on September 7, 1922, he confirms Schlemmer's account of the chaos existing in the Bauhaus at the time and of the influence exercised by van Doesburg on the students:

. . . yesterday while we had supper together, I had a talk with Kandinsky about van Doesburg. Kandinsky thinks that Doesburg will leave soon, in the fall, for Berlin, since Weimar offers him too little scope for his activities. Do tell me, how many students are there at the Bauhaus who really know what they want to do or who are strong enough to accomplish something by their own patient work? For most of them the unsentimental but also completely ungifted Doesburg is a kind of support in the midst of all the excited and conflicting individual viewpoints—something definite, clear, to which they can really cling. . . . Why this voluntary submission to the tyranny of van Doesburg and the complete resistance to all the measures and even the mere requests put forth by the Bauhaus? I believe that nothing can be done about it. Either the point of view of the Bauhaus is strong enough to overcome the opposition from within and without or the whole thing will collapse, because there are today actually too few persons who are able to come to its support in a single-minded and clear-sighted manner. We move from suspicion to suspicion, from danger to danger. . . . That is because the Bauhaus imposes an obligation, whereas van Doesburg imposes none. In his case one is free to come and go; it is a completely voluntary submission, from which one can release himself at will, as they all say. Naturally, it is crass sabotage against everything the Bauhaus is aiming at. But almost all of them must first go through something like this before they find their balance. If Doesburg were a teacher here at the Bauhaus he would not be injurious to the whole idea; he would be more likely to be useful since he represents an antidote to the much-exaggerated romanticism which haunts us. But, presumably, he would not be able to contain himself within his bounds and, like Itten in his day, would soon want to command the whole thing.[13]

Van Doesburg's advocacy of the machine stood in contrast to the attitude toward it which prevailed at the Bauhaus. I discussed van Doesburg numerous times with Ludwig Hilberseimer, who knew him and his wife, Nelly, well. He believed van Doesburg to have been very gifted, very energetic, and entirely trustworthy. Conversing at dinner in Chicago in 1958 with Hilberseimer and Hans Richter, I also asked Richter about van Doesburg. He related that he had once lived with him for three months in Berlin at which time, incidentally, he had introduced him to Mies van der Rohe, then a young architect. Richter said that van Doesburg was a man of tremendous energy who liked to argue and who presented his viewpoints forcefully. He was open-minded, however, according to Richter, so that when someone advanced a convincing argument, even though it ran counter to his own thinking, he welcomed the opportunity for debate. Richter was of the opinion that van Doesburg's influence on the Weimar students had been great. Some of the Bauhaus instructors were for him, and some were against him. Gropius opposed him, Richter believed, because he feared that van Doesburg would rob him of some of his authority.

Once, in the summer of 1956, when I asked Gropius about van Doesburg's influence on the Bauhaus, he brushed it off as unimportant.* In a letter in the July 1963 number of *The Architectural Review*, he called van Doesburg "an arrogant and narrow man." And commenting on him in his previously mentioned letter in the September 1963 number of *The Journal of Architectural Education*, he says:

> Theo van Doesburg wanted to teach in the Bauhaus in 1922. I refused, however, to appoint him since I considered him to be too aggressive and too rigidly theoretical: he would have wrought havoc in the Bauhaus through his fanatic attitude which ran counter to my own broader, approach. I was determined to avoid narrow one-sidedness and oversimplification until a new totality and unity would grow organically and naturally out of the initial chaos of the Bauhaus melting pot. We were all interested in van Doesburg's philosophy, but his influence was temporary and has been exaggerated.[14]

Gropius's contention that van Doesburg would have wrought havoc as a teacher at the Bauhaus receives some support from Feininger's closing remark that van Doesburg, in such a situation, would probably have tried to seize control of the works. Werner Graeff, who served under van Doesburg on his magazine, *De Stijl*, says in this connection:

> I can imagine that Gropius might earlier have appointed Doesburg to his Bauhaus teaching staff, for everything of a constructivist nature lay much closer to Gropius's own work than expressionism. Yet Doesburg would surely have fought half of the other teachers to the knife. If Doesburg had entered the Bauhaus, its internal tranquility would have vanished.[15]

Wingler offers an explanation for this switch from formalistic craftsmanship to a preoccupation with machine methods of production:

> A faithful helper for Gropius arose in Moholy-Nagy, who was appointed in 1923. In the preceding years, in the midst of the contest between Gropius and Itten, another propagator of constructivism

---

*During the preparation of his manuscript, Dearstyne maintained a limited correspondence with Gropius. He also had direct access to the Bauhaus files and related materials which Gropius had given to the Busch-Reisinger Museum. The friction between Dearstyne and Gropius stems, in part, from the fact that when László Moholy-Nagy established a school in Chicago, he called it "the New Bauhaus," Gropius having given the permission to use the name. However, Dearstyne was of the opinion that the name was not Gropius's to proffer. Under Mies's directorship when the Bauhaus moved from Dessau to Berlin, it became a private academy, all rights to the Bauhaus name passing to Mies, who elected not to press his claim when the New Bauhaus opened.

Werner Graeff

Werner Graeff, untitled painting

who, in addition to this, resembled Moholy-Nagy in his mental elasticity and activity, had aggravated the growing internal crisis of the Bauhaus, to wit, Theo van Doesburg. He had established himself at that time in close proximity to the Bauhaus in Weimar and had gathered about him many of the younger people who viewed the prevailing intellectual tendency, which extended from Sturm expressionism as far as the tenets of the Blue Rider, as organized, doctrinaire, and stale. As builder of the Sommerfeld House, even Gropius, after all, had paid his tribute to expressionism. In this situation the dangerous intrusion of the adherents of van Doesburg acted as a catalyst. Except for a special case, the constructivist chairs of Rietveld, which inspired Breuer's first chairs, the influence of de Stijl contributed nothing really new to the Bauhaus. It helped, rather, finally to bring into operation the partly overlaid and displaced ideas of Gropius, as these had been embodied in the Fagus Works, and, if you will, to bring the Bauhaus community to its senses.[16]

So van Doesburg shifted the basic orientation of the Bauhaus, bringing Gropius back to his true course, which the latter denied he ever left. This was no small accomplishment. The influence of De Stijl, furthermore, permeated the entire work of the Bauhaus, as is evident from even a casual examination of it.

Graeff, painter, designer, and author, who studied at the Bauhaus in 1921 and 1922, also wrote about van Doesburg's Weimar activities and the matter of craftsmanship:

. . . I came to the Bauhaus at the age of twenty.

Here I found exactly what I had sought—"masters," but this time real masters, great personalities—plenty of them. Never before or after the Bauhaus period in Weimar and Dessau, indeed, has there been such an assemblage of outstanding artistic personalities on one and the same faculty as there was there. In fact, the unusually vital atmosphere of this art school drew other artists to the city. Among these, Theo van Doesburg, the Dutch painter, friend of and tireless propagandist for Mondrian, and publisher of *De Stijl* became of importance to me. He himself was never a teacher at the Bauhaus and yet, through lectures, writings, discussions, and his own "form instruction," he exercised, from the outside, a noticeable influence on many of the students and even on a number of the teachers [also especially on Gropius's most important collaborator, Adolf Meyer].

The change in orientation of the Bauhaus was a change in the founder, a recovery by him of his senses. Gropius lost certain illusions. Whereas he wished, fundamentally, to reform handwork and raise it to a more dignified, higher level, he had to stand by and see his Bauhaus attacked and vilified, not alone by the average citizen, but even in craft circles themselves. Whereas he envisioned the collaboration of all the craft disciplines and arts in building, and though his Sommerfeld House (1921) fulfilled indeed, this program, it remained, as a whole, completely unconvincing, since it fell far behind his famous prewar buildings, the Fagus Works in Alfeld (1911) and the buildings of the Cologne Werkbund Exposition of 1914. In 1922 Gropius found his old, straight road again. . . . [17]

"art and technology; a new unity"

For the first time, in a lengthy statement of policy written by him on February 3, 1922, for circulation among the Bauhaus masters, Gropius soft-pedals handwork and embraces the machine:

It was also necessary to revive sound handwork in order, by means of it, to give young people an understanding of the entire process of genuine creative activity. But a rejection of the machine and industry is by no means involved in this. A basic contrast lies only in the division of work in the one case and the unity of work in the other.

. . . If a factory with all of its machines were placed at the disposal of a creatively endowed person, he would be able to develop new forms, different from those produced by handwork. . . .

Walter Gropius and Adolf Meyer, Sommerfeld
House in Dahlem, Berlin, 1921

Joseph Albers (and the Bauhaus stained glass
workshop), stained glass window in the staircase
of the Sommerfield House, Berlin, 1922

The Bauhaus could become an island of introverts, if it were to lose contact with the work and working methods of the rest of the world. It has the responsibility of educating people who are able to discern the fundamental character of the world *in which they live* and who have the power, through the combination of their knowledge and their imagination, to create forms which express their world. It is, therefore, a matter of joining the creative activity of the individual and the broad productive work of the world. . . . [18]

With this document, Gropius takes over the ideas of van Doesburg and reorients his school toward collaboration with industry. He even takes a cue from van de Velde in his unstinted praise of the engineer. The function of the workshops henceforth is to prepare models for industrial reproduction. This renewed orientation toward industry, attained after nearly three years of floundering around in a futile attempt to revive handwork, remained the course of the Bauhaus for the rest of its time.

Having accepted the machine in 1922 as the new lodestar of the masters in the Bauhaus shops to communicate artistic finesse to the work amounting to a fusion of art and craftsmanship and, after Bauhaus, Gropius proceeded to link this up with art. He stated his thesis in a lecture entitled "Art and Technology, A New Unity," which he gave as part of the program of the "Bauhaus Week," the central event of the exhibition held in the summer of 1923. The theme, which became the *leitmotif* of the show, was that artists should work hand in hand with technologists toward the improvement of industrial products. Gropius had always expected his form the new look was ushered in, to a combination of art and technology. "Art and Technology, a New Unity" was merely a formalization of a previously held point of view.

It was to be expected that anyone inclined to the nonrational nature of art would reject Gropius's high-sounding new proposition, and the Bauhaus masters did just this. Even Feininger, Gropius's great admirer and a man not given to controversy, could not swallow the dubious potion:

I oppose, with all the strength of my conviction, the slogan, "Art and Technology, the New Unity." This misunderstanding of art is merely a symptom of our times. And the demand for its amalgamation with technology is senseless in every respect. A real technologist, rightly enough, will not tolerate any admixture of art and, on the other hand, even the greatest technological accomplishment can never supplant the godlike spark of art. [19]

5

the struggle over the bauhaus in weimar

The Bauhaus was officially launched on April 1, 1919: the opposition to it could be said to have started the day after its founding or even, perhaps, a few days before. Gropius had scarcely set foot in Weimar before the conspiracy to throw him out began. The alacrity with which his opponents joined forces for the assault is strikingly brought out in the letters written by Feininger, when he was in Weimar[1] to his wife, Julia, in Berlin. Feininger's initial enthusiasm was quickly dampened by the enmity shown to the fledgling school by various elements in the town.

The opposition to the Bauhaus continued with ever-increasing momentum until, at the end of 1924, it achieved its goal, the closing of the institution. Apart from religion and race, however, there is no more hate-engendering, no more bitterly contested, no more hopelessly insoluble an issue than art. And, as often happens, the people who cannot understand the new ideas mistrust them and seek, by devious means, to eliminate those who advocate them. This, by and large, was the strategy of the would-be spiritual leaders of the revolt against the Bauhaus.[2]

The opponents of the Bauhaus made one frontal attack on Gropius: they lumped together everything produced at the school and labeled it "expressionistic." Their intention was to stigmatize the work as inferior, subversive, and anti-German; and following from this, they demanded the severing of the Academy of Art from the Bauhaus and its reestablishment, on its former basis, as an independent art school.[3] In actuality, rather than being a Gallic importation, as the ill-informed Weimar art connoisseurs claimed, the expressionism of the 1920s was far more closely allied with the greatest and most authentic works of German painting (for example, Grünewald's *Isenheim Alterpiece*) than were the realism and impressionism of the landscape school of Weimar which they so much revered at this time.

Seeing the hostility mounting between the Bauhaus masters and the academy professors, Gropius put up little resistance to the secession of the latter from his consolidated institution, that uneasy union of two incompatible schools. So the academy was reconstituted in 1921 and given quarters in the right wing of the main Bauhaus building, seat of the old Academy. The wall-to-wall juxtaposition of the two schools, understandably ensured the continuation of the friction between the adherents of Gropius and the old guard.

In view of the growing opposition, Gropius was quick to seek support from distinguished people outside Weimar. When the situation there became widely known, endorsements of the Bauhaus program, by prominent art and architectural organizations, art educators and museum directors, flowed in from all over the Reich. The opponents of the school then slyly pretended to have no quarrel with the program itself but rather with the way it was being carried out. These champions of Gropius, they said, had no knowledge of the disastrous conditions at the Bauhaus; consequently, their expressions of approval carried no weight and could be ignored.

There is no doubt that Gropius's foes resented this attempted intervention of outsiders, regardless of their reputed eminence, in the affairs of Saxe-Weimar-Eisenach and increased their efforts to destroy the Bauhaus in consequence of it. Indeed, Gropius's judgment in trying to pit the outside world against Weimar is highly questionable. Disputes of this kind, if they are to be settled at all, are more likely to be resolved by elucidation and persuasion on the spot, than by calling in the gendarmerie or by applying the comparable pressure of external public opinion.

The opponents of the Bauhaus did not stop at labeling its work expressionistic. Expressionism was equated with Communism. The supporters of the Bauhaus were labeled as trouble-makers, and the Bauhaus charged with harboring Bolsheviks and Spartacists. A strongly Spartacist brochure, the opponents contended, had even been circulated in the Bauhaus. Other accusations of a similar tenor were made. Gropius hastened to point out that political activities within the Bauhaus were strictly forbidden; the pamphlet in question was not only quite harmless but had been printed and distributed to all art schools by the recruiting office of the central German government. Gropius also refuted the other, equally groundless, charges. But denials of patent fabrications serve little purpose when those who contrive them and those who embrace them are not concerned with the truth. In this case, the object was the closing of the Bauhaus (the same tactics were to be used against the Bauhaus in Dessau).*

Another tactic in the campaign against the school was to accuse the students of offenses against propriety and morality. The Bauhaus students, their critics declared, were deliberately slovenly in their dress and went out of their way in their deportment in general, thereby showing their contempt for the citizens of Weimar.

On the subject of costume, Gropius remarked that these needy students, many of whom were subsisting on twenty or thirty marks a month and had suffered through a five-year war, could not be expected to arrive in Weimar with an impeccable wardrobe. As for affronts to townspeople, these were rare exceptions and could not be taken as the rule. More sensational was the charge, made by a *Landtag* delegate, that men and women students had been seen bathing naked together in the River Ilm. The story lost a measure of credibility when the delegate, who regaled his colleagues with it in a plenary session, refused to divulge the name of the landlady who claimed to have observed these goings-on.[4]

In their tirades against the behavior of the students, the denouncers singled out the "foreigners" (by whom, for the most part, they meant persons of Jewish extraction) as especially arrogant in their demeanor and inconsiderate of the sensibilities of the residents of Weimar. It was claimed that there were large numbers of these foreign students and that they were tyrannizing the rest of the student body and attempting to run the school in accordance with their own notions. To the statements concerning the makeup of the student body, Gropius replied that this consisted of 208 Germans of the Reich and twenty Germans from Austria, Bohemia, Hungary, and the Baltic countries. The Weimar Ministry of Culture (at that time, 1920, still Social Democratic), reporting the results of an investigation conducted by it into charges which had been leveled at the Bauhaus, asserted that it was manifestly impossible for the seventeen Jewish students at the school to seize control and to tyrannize the more than two hundred Aryans enrolled there. In the *cause célèbre* of the reactionary master student, Hans Gross, who had allegedly been abused by his fellow students and suspended by Gropius for pro-German remarks made by him at a public meeting, the findings of the ministry absolved the students and the director of all blame.[5]

The opponents of the Bauhaus held one powerful trump card: money. Everybody knew, when a nationalist delegate to the Weimar

---

*The accusations against the "situation" at the Bauhaus, including the attitude of the students and the content of the curriculum, were presented to the Ministry of Culture (Weimar) on December 30, 1919, in the form of a petition signed by various members of the community, including artists [see Notes]. The Ministry investigated issuing an undated report (prior to July 9, 1920) in 1920. In his remarks to the provincial legislature on July 9, 1920, Gropius refuted the allegations, re-affirming the essential goals of the Bauhaus and its essentially apolitical nature.

parliament spoke movingly of the sad condition of the streets of the city and the plight of the needy in poverty-stricken Thuringia, that this meant he hated the Bauhaus and would vote against funds required for the annual support of the disreputable institution. Weimar could not afford luxuries when people were homeless and starving, contended the delegate, as if, well-fed though he was, he couldn't bear to see others suffer, especially if it was to provide funds to support a project that was as dangerous as it was foolish. It was useless to point out, as Gropius tried to do, that the Bauhaus, if given the chance to develop its potential, could help invigorate the crafts and industries of Thuringia by furnishing them with new ideas, or that the effect would be to bring far more revenue to the state than it cost to maintain the school. To the foes of the Bauhaus this was just so much pie in the sky, whereas the money it was taking out of their pockets was a painful reality.*

Moreover, since they felt they were paying for the Bauhaus, the conservative burghers of Weimar, falsely claiming to represent the entire populace, demanded a voice in the determination of the policies of the school, which signified the right to say what should and what should not be taught there. Gropius, in reply, denied that the payment of taxes gave them the privilege of meddling in the internal affairs of the Bauhaus. The democratic system permitted them to participate in political and economic decisions; it did not allow them a voice in cultural matters, especially in those of art. To resolve aesthetic problems by majority vote would be stretching the democratic principle too far. How could a public "for whom art serves as entertainment and diversion, as the embellishment of an unspiritual existence, for whom it is a matter of taste and luxury . . . ," how could such a public possibly pass a sound judgment on art? The authorities in the field agreed, he said, that to entrust the supervision of art to the people would mean the destruction of art.

To subject art to political control is disastrous. It is at least as senseless as placing politics in the hands of artists, as the Arbeitsrat für Kunst and the Novembergruppe dreamed of doing at the end of World War One. As past president of the Arbeitsrat für Kunst, Gropius could well have concluded, after observing the dismal failure of attempts by his organization and the Novembergruppe to educate the masses in the things of the spirit, that art was and would always remain the province of a small minority of the people, and that these persons of understanding would have to make the decisions affecting it, if it were to survive.

Another major source of opposition to the Bauhaus ironically came from the craftsmen of Weimar. Their grounds were, above all, economic. These people feared that the school, with its workshop production, constituted dangerous competition for them—

*In 1920 the state's subsidy to the Bauhaus was RM 164,000.

despite their judging the objects made at the Bauhaus to be out-landish and impractical. They extolled the fruitful working rela-tionship which van de Velde had established between his school and the crafts and industries of Thuringia. The only kind of reaction Gropius succeeded in arousing in those same quarters was bitter antagonism. He had been, from the outset, outspoken in his as-sertions that handwork in Weimar was in a state of decline and required, for its recovery, the infusion of new ideas which he and his school were willing and able to administer.[6] Thus the hoped-for link between the Bauhaus workshops and the workshops of the city was never forged. Hildegarde Brenner, attempting to pin down the reason why the Bauhaus was forced out of Weimar, says:

They [documents still existing in Weimar] leave no doubt that the very handwork circles whose representatives, as so-called masters of handwork, together with the so-called technical masters, directed the famous work courses, stood behind the expulsion.[7]

Even though politics and art are fundamentally different in na-ture, it will surprise no one to learn that in all the wrangles which took place over the Bauhaus, the sides were drawn up strictly in accordance with political persuasions. The parties of the left (for example, the Social Democrats) supported Gropius; those of the right (particularly the People's Party, forerunner of the National Socialists) opposed him. The conservatives as a bloc rejected the Bauhaus and its radical aesthetic tendencies; the liberals accused them of playing politics with the school. The conservatives then charged the liberals with mixing politics and art when they lent their united support to the Bauhaus. Under the circumstances, the fortunes of the Bauhaus depended not upon its virtues or lack of them but upon the political makeup of the parliament. So long as the left-wingers were in the majority the school was relatively se-cure; when the parties of the right took over control in 1924, its days were numbered.

The passage of its budget in 1920 gave the Bauhaus a breathing spell of three years until the legislature, egged on by recurring defamatory speeches by certain delegates such as, above all, those of the insidiously clever arch-conservative, Dr. Emil Herfurth, de-manded that the Bauhaus demonstrate its right to continued ex-istence through an exhibition of its work.[8]

the 1923 exhibition

Neither Gropius nor the masters favored an exhibition at this time because they felt that the Bauhaus was not ready to step before the public. But confronted by the necessity of making an exhibition, Gropius, born propagandist that he was, determined to put on a big show. The exhibition was scheduled to start on August 15, 1923, and run through September 30. The Bauhaus masters and students became engrossed in preparations for the extravaganza. Nothing like this had happened before. The exhibition "50 Years Bauhaus," which toured the world in 1969 and aroused much interest, inasmuch as it displayed the mummified remains of a defunct institution, did not touch the Weimar show of 1923. Gropius invited everybody he could think of to attend the big show and many of them did, especially during the Bauhaus Week (August 15–19) which started it. These action-packed five days deserve

Postcards advertising the Bauhaus Exhibition of 1923

particular attention, and in describing them I will follow the official program which I discovered in Gropius's files.

The week started with the lecture by Gropius entitled "Art and Technology, a New Unity," (see page 67) a thesis to which certain Bauhaus masters, most of whom were painters, strongly objected. The activities of the second day opened, in the afternoon, with a lecture by Kandinsky called "Concerning Synthetic Art," and in the evening, Schlemmer's *Triadic Ballet* was performed in the German National Theater in Weimar.

On the morning of the third day, the distinguished Dutch architect Oud, invited for the occasion, gave a slide lecture called "The Development of Modern Architecture in Holland." According to the Dutch reporter Augusta de Wit,[9] writing in the *Nieuwe Rotterdamsche Courant* of August 29, 1923, Oud demonstrated conclusively that the Dutch were far ahead of the Germans in the

J.J.P. Oud

Walter Gropius and Adolf Meyer, city theater in Jena, remodelled, 1922

development of modern architecture. (Gropius later invited Oud to compile a volume on Dutch architecture for the series of Bauhaus books.) On the evening of the third day, the *Mechanical Ballet* was performed in the Jena City Theater, which Gropius and Adolf Meyer had remodeled in 1922. The guests went to nearby Jena and returned by train. In the newspaper article mentioned above, de Wit reports on the *Mechanical Ballet* and the performance which followed it:

This idea of "mechanization of movement" that was exhibited in the *Triadic Ballet* found an even stronger expression in the *Mechanical Ballet*, which we saw in the Jena City Theater. In this case, a "circus" of M. Breuer's was performed by two figures, set together out of long, rectangular, triangular, and broad wood planes, which literally had neither head nor tail but which, nevertheless, gave the impression of two riders trotting toward each other, rearing up, and exchanging blows. They alternately drove each other to flight and then returned to resume the battle. Finally, they made peace with each other. The audience laughed and applauded.[10]

But then came the musical part of this week of varied performances and it was apparently of such great distinction as to elicit universal approval.

[Next] came a concert, at which Busoni, appearing for the first time after a long illness, was present at the performance of six of his pieces (six piano compositions). Egon Petri from Berlin executed them for the first time; and, on the same occasion occurred the initial performance of Hindemith's *Marienlieder*, sung by Beatrice Lauer-Kottler from Frankfurt.[11]

On the last day of the week came the crowning event, the matinee, with a performance of Krenek's *Concerto Grosso*, with Hermann Scherchen conducting, and the second German performance of Stravinsky's *The Soldier's Tale*. Walther Scheidig reported:

Stravinsky traveled expressly from Paris to Weimar in order to hear his composition. He remembered these days, because he made the acquaintance of Busoni in Weimar and learned to respect him upon whom he had previously looked as a sworn opponent of his artistic creation. . . . [12]

The close of it [the Bauhaus Week] was the [Japanese] lantern parade, Sunday evening, starting at the Bauhaus and skirting the edge of the park, Goethe's beautiful creation, until it reached the Armbrust in the Schützengasse in the heart of the old town. The lanterns, fantastic in form and color, had recently been used by the Bauhaus youth to pay homage to Johannes Schlaf—the poet could be seen marching happily in the midst of his admirers.

Finally, at the end, a colored screen play was performed (the reflected-light plays of Ludwig Hirschfeld-Mack). Colors which moved in accord with a fuguelike, flowing music and which kept changing—[13]

And then chairs and tables were moved aside and the young people and many older ones danced until daybreak and then went home with faces beaming with happiness.[14]

The official program I have also lists, in considerable detail, the various features of the exhibition, which was parceled out among four buildings in Weimar. Part 1 of the big show was to be seen in the two buildings of the Bauhaus, the Main Building and the

Workshop Building; Part 2 was held in the *Landesmuseum* on the Museum Square; and Part 3 took place in the experimental House on the Horn, designed by Muche, executed by the architectural office of Gropius and furnished by the Bauhaus workshops, with the coöperation of German industry.

Left Oskar Schlemmer, mural painting in the workshop building, Bauhaus, Weimar, 1923

Right Oskar Schlemmer, wall relief in the stairhall of the workshop building, Bauhaus, Weimar, 1923

Left Oskar Schlemmer, ceiling relief in the stairhall of the workshop building, Bauhaus, Weimar, 1923

Right Joost Schmidt, relief in the main building, Bauhaus, Weimar, 1923. Stucco and glass

Under Part 1 were found *Raumgestaltungen* (examples of the creative shaping of space), Products of the Workshops, Theoretic Works, an International Exhibition of Architecture, Posters and Photography, and a room for the sale of Bauhaus products.

The last item listed under *Raumgestaltungen* was the office of the Bauhaus director, "decorated" by Gropius. Mies van der Rohe, commented on this about three weeks before his death on August 17, 1969 (he had evidently attended the Bauhaus Week of 1923):

No, we were opposed to a certain direction which Gropius took. The fifth anniversary of the Bauhaus took place in Weimar in 1924 [*sic*]. The main celebration was held in Jena. There was a theater there which Gropius had built or remodeled—built, I believe (no, remodeled). He did this with Adolf Meyer. We were rather disappointed and we said, "That is so strange, it is all so decorative, like the *Wiener Werkstätten* [Vienna Workshops]." We were thinking especially of Gropius's writing desk [Mies may have meant his magazine case]. He had a meander band on both ends, not inlaid but built of solid wood—not a decoration, the whole thing was a piece of decoration. Then he had a lighting contraption with a few wires, etc.—light tubes. In any case, we decided that if one doesn't watch out, the thing will go in the wrong direction. Then we brought out the magazine *G*. The *G* stood for *Gestaltung*. [The nearest English equivalent of this word is "creation."] This was a word we wanted to have. You can do anything you want with our architecture but *Gestaltung* is something very particular. That is not fiddle-faddle, not design. And, actually, the same difference holds between the Pan-Am Building in New York and our buildings, which are constructed.[15]

The International Exhibition of Architecture consisted, in the main, of large and small photos, drawings, and blueprints of buildings. Two typewritten sheets, listing the German works in the show, start out, unblushingly, with forty-six plates depicting work done by Gropius with Adolf Meyer.[16] These are followed by six plates showing the House on the Horn and the proposed development on the Horn. Then, under "Germany" are listed three plates of work by Hans Poelzig, five by Bruno Taut, five by Erich Mendelsohn, five by Hugo Häring, five by Max Taut, four by Mies van der Rohe, and three by Mart Stam. (In view of the fact that Stam was Dutch, he shouldn't have been included among the German architects.) The grand total of illustrations of works by German architects shown in the exhibition was seventy-three, of which forty-six were by Gropius and Meyer and twenty-seven by all the other German architects.

The International Exhibition of Architecture also included works by Wright (America), Lönberg and Holm (Denmark), Le Corbusier (France), and also buildings by Dutch, Russian, and Czech architects. However, I have no record of the extent of the coverage of the work of these architects.

Part 2 consisted of an exhibition of paintings and sculptural works by Bauhaus masters and students.

Part 3 involved the display of Muche's famous building. Gropius, apparently, was opposed to the building of the house and washed his hands of all responsibility for it. Walther Scheidig says the house was forced upon Gropius by student adherents of Muche, who insisted on executing a design made by the latter. Muche's plan was carried out by Adolf Meyer and Gropius's architectural atelier. The house was square and had a sizable, centrally placed living room completely surrounded by the other necessary rooms. The living room was higher than the peripheral spaces and was lit by clerestory windows. It was fitted out with furniture, rugs, and lighting fixtures made in the Bauhaus workshops; but building equipment and accessories available on the market were employed wherever possible.

Following the exhibition, it appeared that the Bauhaus would have a period of renewed activity and productive work. Such illusions were shattered when, in an election in March 1924, the reactionary parties of the right wrested control of the Thuringian legislature from the left-wing parties which had supported the Bauhaus. That sealed the fate of the school, and its demise at Weimar was only a matter of time. In September of 1924, the Thuringian Ministry for Public Instruction (*Volksbildungsministerium*) can-

Herbert Bayer, director's office designed by Walter Gropius at the Bauhaus, Weimar, 1923

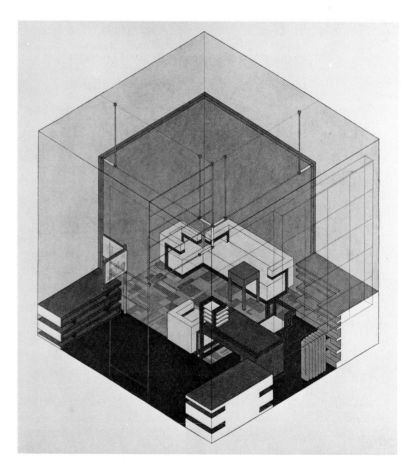

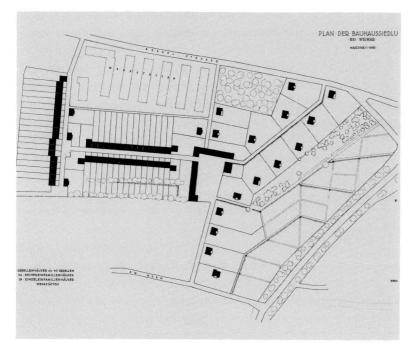

Walter Gropius, site plan of the Bauhaus housing settlement in Weimar, 1922

celed the contracts of all the Bauhaus teachers and employees as of the end of March 1925.

A flood of public protests followed this action. Articles appeared in newspapers and magazines throughout Germany, pleading for the preservation of the unique school. Even van Doesburg's adherents, who had previously been critical of the Bauhaus, called for its retention.* The *Kreis der Freunde des Bauhauses* (Circle of Friends of the Bauhaus), which had been founded in the spring of 1924, also remonstrated against the measures taken by the Weimar government. Though the board of trustees of the Circle included personalities of European reputation, such as the architects Behrens, Poelzig, Berlage, and Hoffman; the painters Marc Chagall and Oskar Kokoschka; the composers Adolf Busch, Edwin Fischer, and Arnold Schönberg; the writers Gerhart Hauptmann, Franz Werfel, and Herbert Eulenberg; and the scholars Albert Einstein and Joseph Strzygowsky, the Weimar authorities remained stolidly unmoved by the Circle's appeal, as it did, indeed, in the case of the other numerous representations.

Gropius and the masters announced to the public press on December 26, 1924, their decision to dissolve the Bauhaus with the expiration of their contracts on April 1, 1925, and the Weimar government accepted the declaration even though, in actuality, the director and masters of a state institution had no authority to dissolve it.

*Dearstyne does not indicate in his manuscript what form this support from van Doesburg's adherents took.

The Bauhaus had become so famous (or, possibly, notorious), thanks to the highly effective proselytizing of its director, that, following its dissolution in Weimar, several German cities, including Frankfurt-am-Main and Dessau, in the north-central state of Anhalt, offered to take it over. The invitation of Mayor Fritz Hesse of Dessau was far and away the most favorable, and Gropius and the masters decided to accept it. So the director, the teachers, with the exception of Marcks, and most of the students removed to Dessau where the school, housed at first in temporary quarters, started a promising new career on April 1, 1925.

THE PRELIMINARY
COURSE

6

**the
three phases
of the
preliminary
course**

When I joined the Bauhaus in 1928, Albers was in charge of the preliminary course. Every student entering the Bauhaus had to take his *Vorkurs* which lasted six months. The 1919 outline of studies has nothing to say of this course because it had not yet been inaugurated. By the time the Bauhaus catalog of July 1922 appeared, however, it was in full swing, though the description of it is brief:

> *Preliminary Course.* Duration: one-half year. Elementary instruction in form together with exercises in materials, in the special workshop for the preliminary course. Result: admission as apprentice to a workshop.

In his essay "Idee und Aufbau des Staatliches Bauhauses Weimar", ("The Idea and Organization of the State Bauhaus in Weimar"), which appeared in 1923, Gropius describes at much greater length the objectives of the preliminary course:

> Texture was one of our major subjects of study, for it brought us closer to an understanding of our materials. We made scales of texture from hard to soft, and we drew it—the kind of *trompe-l'oeil* illusionism that the layman values so highly was done only in the early part of the course, and the final test was collage. For collage tested our creativeness, our sense of form, and our feeling for the combination of different textures.[3]

And in a letter written by Schlemmer to his friend, Meyer-Amden in 1921, shortly after he had started to teach at the Bauhaus, he relates, with a touch of irony, an anecdote about Itten:

Itten gives "analyses" in Weimar. He projects pictures and the students are supposed to draw this or that in them which is essential, mostly the movement, the chief line, curve. Thereafter he refers them to a Gothic figure. Then he shows the weeping Mary Magdalen of the Grünewald altar. The students strive to puzzle something essential out of its great complexity. Itten sees these attempts and thunders, "If you had any feeling for art, you would not draw in the presence of this representation of weeping which is so sublime that it could be the weeping of the world, you would just sit there, dissolved in tears." So saying, he slams the door![4]

Early on Itten gained a potent influence at the Bauhaus, an influence which he exercised for a long time. Not only was he Gropius's right-hand man, but, as Schlemmer wrote in his diary on June 23, 1921, "Itten _is_ Gropius. . . . " Gropius finally realized that his chief minister was usurping more and more of his authority, and a power struggle ensued. In one of his letters Schlemmer described the position of the two men at the time:

Itten has succeeded in having his course made compulsory and he is the only one who has. He holds the essential workshops in his hand and harbors the not insignificant, the admirable ambition to put his stamp upon the Bauhaus. He has been working at this, indeed, as long as it has existed (three years). Gropius, still the only one to be thought of as director (the teachers, the "Council of Masters," reached its full strength only half a year ago) let Itten do as he pleased because he himself was too much involved with organization and administration. At present Gropius, who now openly resists Itten's monopolization, thinks that Itten must be put back inside his proper bounds, which Gropius sets as within the pedagogical field. So there is a duel between Itten and Gropius, and the rest of us have been asked to decide its issue.[5]

Johannes Itten

Accepted candidates enter the preliminary course first. This lasts for half a year and serves as an introduction to the entire range of the main teaching. Practical and theoretical work are interwoven with each other and progress simultaneously. Their aim is to release the creative powers of the student, to help him understand the nature of materials, and discern the basic principles of creative work. Concern with style movements of any sort is consciously avoided. Observation and representation, to make clear the need for an identity of form and content, define the limits of the preliminary course. The most vital task is the unfettering of the individual, his emancipation from dead convention, in order to pave the way for personal experience and perception and make him aware of the limits which nature has set to his creative powers. Collective work is therefore not essential in the preliminary course. Subjective and objective observation are cultivated side by side, the investigation of abstract principles as intensively as the interpretation of objective things. The teaching itself can be a very great stimulus to this.

Above everything else we shall seek to recognize and accurately evaluate each person's proper medium of expression. The creative potentialities of different individuals are variously delimited. For one person, rhythm is the primary means of expression; for a second, light and shade; for a third, color; for a fourth, materials; for a fifth, sound; for a sixth, proportion; for a seventh, objective or abstract space; for an eighth, the relation of one of these to another or of both to a third or fourth.

All of the work in the preliminary course is done under the guidance of an instructor. It possesses artistic quality only to the extent that any expression of an individual which is fundamental and based on principle can form the groundwork of that peculiar creative discipline which we call art.[1]

Unknown, light and shade of rhythmic form, preliminary course

The preliminary course was actually created by Itten. Gropius visited Itten's art school in Vienna, (called, simply, the *Ittenschule*), was impressed with him and his teaching methods, and subsequently invited him to teach at the Bauhaus. He became the second of Gropius's original masters, Feininger being the first. Itten scrutinized applicants closely and sometimes made it difficult for even talented students to get in. Helmut von Erffa relates how he had to submit to an unorthodox probationary examination:

E. Mögelin, "Plastic Representation," preliminary course

His [Itten's] influence was strong among the students—it was not easy to get oneself accepted for his preliminary course which prepared one for the workshops, but after we had had an interview with Gropius, we still had to be passed by a kind of one-man student council. I remember my trepidation as I was led into the room, whitewashed and totally bare except for a huge black wooden cross on one wall. On a simple iron bedstead sat a haggard young man in a monk's habit. His cheeks were hollow, his eyes burned feverishly, and he was one· of Itten's most trusted pupils—"Really a saint," my companion whispered. He looked me over while my companion stood in respectful silence, then he said something in an ecstatic singsong voice and nodded. He had seen none of my drawings and barely heard me utter a word, but I had passed the test and was accepted. "The master has complete trust in his intuitive judgment," my companion explained after we had left the room.[2]

Von Erffa also wrote about Itten's teaching:

The teaching methods that Itten used in those early days, and which were partly his invention, are now widely used in the United States—

though with local modifications. He made us feel and experience whatever we drew, and, in fact, he wanted us to feel and experience every daily event, however trivial, as profoundly as possible. He made us draw a thistle so that it would really prick you; we had to experience its sharpness and prickly character. . . .

The struggle between Itten and Gropius seems to be yet another example of the continuing conflict between progress and principle, between the material and the spiritual. Gropius came out on top, as Schlemmer relates in a letter written to Meyer-Amden in June 1922:

I wrote you about the Itten-Gropius duel. This at one time reached such a pitch that it seemed to be a matter of one or the other. Meanwhile things appeared to have been settled amicably. Itten had to surrender some of his authority, Gropius's reason for this being the new appointees and their share of operations. Gropius extended his influence all the more by this. Itten withdrew visibly from his teaching, from the workshops to his own work. He began to paint again from nature and also easel pictures . . . He is taking soundings in Switzerland in order, if the circumstances warrant it, to remain there and leave the Bauhaus. Possibly he will issue an ultimatum—perhaps not even that any more. It would unquestionably be a loss to the Bauhaus. He is the most capable of us pedagogically and he has a marked talent for leadership. I feel only too keenly the lack of this in me. Furthermore, if Gropius no longer has the strong opposition of Itten, he will be the much greater danger.[6]

Moholy-Nagy took charge of the *Vorkurs* in 1923 after Itten's departure from the Weimar Bauhaus. Moholy was a constructivist in his painting, his sculpture, and his thinking, and his students were encouraged, in the basic course, to do constructivist geometric sculpture. These so-called exercises were composed of bars and blocks of wood, strips of metal and glass, wire, string, etc.; spatial sculpture in which a minimum of solid material was used for the purpose of setting up space relationships. In these works it was the voids which counted rather than, as in the case of traditional sculpture, the masses. Problems of asymmetrical balance, both physical and visual, played an important role in these constructions so that they had a dynamism lacking in conventional sculpture. These exercises related to much 1960s "hollow" spatial sculpture and, for that matter, to the spatial geometric painting by Moholy himself. He believed that such studies were a useful preparation for the understanding of spatial relationships in architecture, and his preliminary course was carefully calculated to develop a sensitivity to visualization of space.

M. Téry-Adler, analysis of Giotto painting, preliminary course

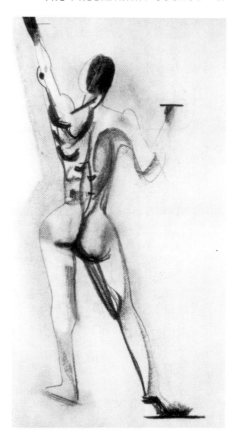

Ida Kerkovius, life drawing, preliminary course

K. Auböck, plastic material study, preliminary course

N. Wassiljeff, construction of tin cans, preliminary course

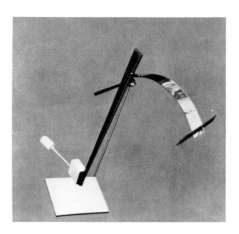

Object from Moholy-Nagy's preliminary course

L. Leudersdorff, split tree trunk, preliminary course

Jon Naar, *Josef Albers*, 1967

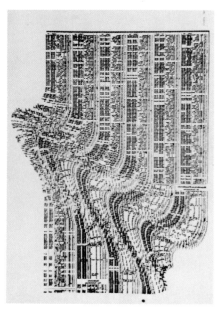

Warped newspaper sheet made in Albers's preliminary course

When Gropius resigned Moholy left the Bauhaus as well, in the spring of 1928, and Albers became director of the preliminary course, a position he retained until the closing of the Berlin Bauhaus in 1933. Albers had started teaching his preliminary course in Weimar as a supplement to Moholy's, under whose authority he stood. Then in Dessau he became a fully-fledged instructor. From 1925 until 1928 he taught the first semester of the *Vorkurs* while Moholy conducted the second. His Weimar course concerned itself mainly with material studies. To acquaint his students with the uses of materials, he visited, with them, a number of craft workshops—box-, chair-, and basket-makers, fine cabinetmakers and carpenters, coopers and wheelrights. He also conducted such tours in Dessau, taking us, among other places, to the Schultheiss-Patzenhofer brewery. We also went to see a wallpaper factory, where we observed the printing of wallpaper from rollers impressed with various designs. Our guide informed us that these rollers were shipped to the United States after the patterns had become outmoded in Germany.

Albers was my first teacher, as I mentioned earlier. He had an insistently inquiring mind and a dry sense of humor. To me, fresh out of Columbia's School of Architecture, he was an exciting influence. He didn't require us to draw in minute detail the five orders of architecture; they were never so much as mentioned in his class. He didn't set us to copying, in charcoal, plaster reproductions of classic sculpture, possibly because the Bauhaus boasted none of these; he didn't have us make elaborate watercolor renderings of grandiose and painfully symmetrical imitations of French and Italian Renaissance buildings; he didn't ask us to digest the writings of Vitruvius, Vignola, or Palladio; in fact, he emphasized the uselessness of reading anything (except possibly his own articles).

What Albers did was to seat us at long tables in the workshop wing of the Bauhaus and confront us with some unlikely materials such as wire, wire mesh, paper, corrugated cardboard, sheet metal, match boxes, newspapers, or whatnot. We were supposed to do something with these—just *basteln*, or play around with them, to see if we could make something out of them or discover something about them. Sometimes we constructed things of paper or corrugated cardboard; sometimes the things we made were objects with some aesthetic content. Whatever we produced, Albers appraised it for what it was worth, without reference to established art canons. The course was a voyage of discovery on, as yet, an uncharted sea, and we discovered values in unexpected places.

Once I wound a coil or wire around a pop bottle; somehow the relationship of the materials, wire and glass, and of the forms, coil and cylinder, seemed good, and Albers praised it. Another time I cut and bent a sheet of cardboard into an animal-like form and again he liked it. Albers was generous in seeking out the merit in whatever we did and he was usually able to find some value, great or small, in it and to draw a kernel of truth from it. Toward the

Coil of wire around a beer bottle. Arranged by Howard Dearstyne in Albers's preliminary course

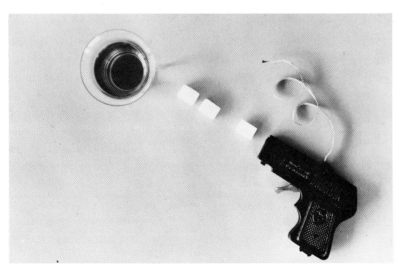

Eduard Ludwig, composition, arranged in Albers's preliminary course

close of each class period we put our more successful objects on display and discussed them so that we all learned from the work of the others. As a matter of fact, language played only a minor role in the class, luckily for me, with my meager knowledge of German, doing was what counted. Nonetheless, I remember certain things which Albers said, because even in German they impressed me, such as that in mathematics two plus two always equals four but in the realm of the spirit two plus two had to add up to five or more. Then, again, he admonished us to make much out of little because there is virtue, if not art (a word he didn't use), in economy. According to Albers:

Economic forms are the result of function and material. The study of the working material naturally precedes the perception of function. We therefore begin our investigation of form with the study of materials.

. . . Inventive construction and pioneering observation are developed—at least in the beginning—through undisturbed and uninfluenced, that is, unprejudiced experimentation which, at first, amounts to aimless playing with material . . .

Experimentation takes precedence over study and a playful beginning develops confidence. We do not start, therefore, with a theoretical introduction; in the beginning we are concerned only with materials.

In order to achieve the closest contact with materials by way of the fingertips, the use of tools is limited in the beginning. In the further course of the teaching the possibilities of application become more and more restricted; the commonest methods of working are noted and, since they can no longer be discovered, they are banned. For example, in the outside world (in the crafts and industry) paper is employed, for the most part, lying flat and glued, the edge is almost never used. This is a reason for us to use paper standing up, uneven, plastically mobile, two-sided and with the edges emphasized. Instead of gluing it, we tie it, pin it, sew it, rivet it, that is, fasten it in other ways and we also investigate its capacity to withstand tension and pressure. . . .

Study for the displacement of black and white bars in a plane. Made in Albers's preliminary course

Thus, the treatment of materials is intentionally different from that on the outside, though not basically so. The purpose is not to do things in other ways but, rather, not to do things as the others do them. This means not to imitate but, rather, to search by oneself and to learn how to discover for oneself—constructive thinking.

To give preference to such materials or building elements whose use or application is nonexistent or whose treatment is unknown encourages self-reliance. For example, building with corrugated cardboard, wire mesh, matchboxes, gramophone needles, and razor blades. . . .

The relationship of effort to effect serves as the criterion of accomplishment. This underscores one of the main aspects of the teaching: economy. Economy in the sense of frugality in the expenditure of material and work and their best possible utilization in relation to the effect achieved. . . .

Briefly summarized, the inductive teaching method practiced here attempts to develop responsibility and discipline in respect to oneself, the material, and the work, to equip the student, for the determination of his choice of a profession, with the recognition of which areas of work and which classes of materials are most compatible to him. It seeks training in flexibility on the broad basis. It leads to economical form.

We must as students and teachers once more learn with and from each other (in competition, which elevates), otherwise teaching is sour bread and bad business.[7]

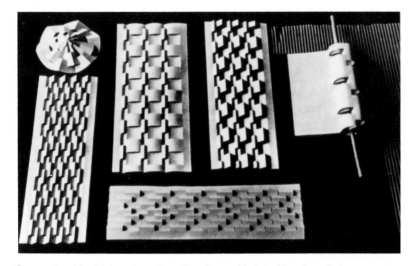

Paper cut and bent into various decorative shapes. Made in Albers's preliminary course

I have translated what I believe are the most pertinent of Albers's remarks. After the passage of almost fifty years (they were written in 1928), they no longer sound like the clarion call to creative action they once seemed to be. I now question the efficacy of building things out of gramophone needles and razor blades and wonder whether it is always necessary to do things in a way others don't. Albers's statement that there is a virtue in doing things in a way others don't is misleading because it suggests that people have unthinkingly overlooked useful potentialities in various materials and have neglected to try out new methods of joining them—although certain important discoveries have been made, to be sure, more by accident than design.

On the other hand the optical illusions of the third dimension obtained with two-dimensional means, as well as Albers's later studies of the interaction of juxtaposed colors, could doubtless serve a useful purpose in the fine arts. Indeed, today I find the most interesting *Vorkurs* work that which relates to painting and the other arts, such as the study in the displacement of alternating bars of black and white shown in *Bauhaus 1919–1928* and the basically similar one in which the type columns of a newspaper sheet have been warped out of alignment.

Mies van der Rohe, also, evidently felt that Albers's basic course was too little directed toward the study of architecture, the field which concerned him most. On becoming director he reviewed the subjects being taught at the Bauhaus in Dessau and whatever it was that Mies told Albers, it is certain that he greatly wounded the latter's feelings. He went out of his way to mollify the injury by a show of camaraderie. "*Josefchen*," said he, throwing his arm over Albers's shoulder as they walked together toward the master houses, "come have a drink with me." (This was the substance of what Mies said, though the precise wording may have been different.) Whether or not they had the drink, Albers's ruffled feathers were smoothed out and he even agreed to teach, at Mies's behest, a class in freehand drawing, along with his *Vorkurs*.

Albers remained with the Bauhaus until the end in 1933. He was one of the Bauhaus masters to go to the United States, where he continued to teach his preliminary course at Black Mountain College and elsewhere. And it is Albers's version of the basic course which has been imitated by emulators of the Bauhaus through the world.

IV

AN EXAMINATION OF THE WORKSHOPS

Upon the satisfactory completion of the work of the preliminary course, a student was admitted to one of the workshops. The Bauhaus statutes of July 1922 set forth at considerable length the responsibilities he shouldered when he entered it:

Admission to a workshop depends upon the personal qualifications of the candidate and upon the quality of the independent work done by him in this trial half-year in the preliminary course. The accepted apprentice can choose his own workshop, though he must take the question of space into consideration and receive the permission of both of the workshop masters.

Apprentices who, after passing the preliminary course, have entered a workshop, must conclude an indenture of apprenticeship with the Chamber of Crafts. The trial period in the workshop lasts one semester. Only after he has successfully completed the trial period is the apprentice looked upon as enrolled, and he now pledges himself explicitly to complete the course of instruction in the Bauhaus workshop.

Upon expiration of the legally prescribed time and fulfillment of the legal requirements, apprentices can apply for admission to the journeymen's examination and journeymen to the master's examination. The examinations are taken before the Chamber of Crafts. Examinations, independent of these, are also given by the Bauhaus Council (Bauhaus journeymen and junior masters), whose requirements, in question of form, go beyond those of the public journeymen's and masters' examinations. The Bauhaus masters establish regulations for these examinations.

Every junior master, journeyman and apprentice is obliged to obey the statutes and the house regulations.

Craft instruction and instruction in form constitute the foundation. No apprentice or journeyman can be excused from either of these.

Every accepted apprentice and journeyman is permitted to attend, along with his own, the courses of the other form masters and, with the consent of his masters, to obtain technical or aesthetic advice from other masters.

Every apprentice and journeyman working in a shop is required to discuss continually every single object made in the workshop, both before and during its production, with each of his masters, with the workshop director, that is, and with his master in form theory.

It is only in this way that an amalgamation of artistic and manual work can be achieved.

7

**the
furniture
workshop**

Gropius was in charge of the furniture workshop (*Tishlerei*) from the beginning, its products being so indispensable an adjunct to architecture. He designed a number of pieces for his office in the Weimar Bauhaus, which were executed by students. Although he contributed little to the development of modern furniture, which sets him apart from certain other distinguished modern architects who devoted much effort to its design, such as Behrens, van de Velde, Wright, Mies, and Le Corbusier, he did not need to be a furniture designer in order to be an effective critic, for he amply demonstrated that he could teach almost anything in the realm of art. Hilberseimer once said of him, in regard to the contribution made to their joint enterprises by Adolf Meyer and other of his collaborators, that he was able to draw the best out of those who worked with him.

When considering the objects produced in the furniture workshop in Weimar (or, for that matter, any of the workshops there) one should bear in mind that, though the students were required to submit to the guidance of their form masters, they were forbidden to imitate them. In a letter to the *Journal of Architectural Education* Gropius wrote:

> Starting the Bauhaus as its responsible director, I had come to the conclusion that an autocratic, subjective approach must block the innate budding expression of differently gifted students, as the teacher, even with the best intention, imposes the results of his own thought and work on him. I convinced myself that a good teacher must abstain from handing out his personal vocabulary to his student, but should

rather let him find his own way even via detours; that he should encourage the growth of independence in the student, and vigorously destroy his imitative reactions, or at least make him aware that he tries to harvest on foreign soil.[1]

Magazine case designed by Walter Gropius

Marcel Breuer

Marcel Breuer, wood chair, 1922

As a theory, Gropius's "objective" teaching method had a disarming plausibility about it; in practice, it did not work. The Bauhaus students did, in fact, depend upon their masters—or, if not their own, then upon other masters—and the products of the Weimar furniture workshop bear a striking resemblance to each other.

Far from displaying the kind of self-sufficiency required to justify Gropius's objective teaching method, the students, naturally enough, drew inspiration from the works of the leading artists of their day, both inside and outside the Bauhaus. De Stijl principles, for example, were very influential at the Weimar Bauhaus. Its influence can be seen in every lineament of the pieces turned out in the furniture workshop, to say nothing of the work of the other studios. The emphasis, in the case of the Weimar furniture, can scarcely be said to have been placed on function, but rather on form. In this fusion of art and handwork, the pursuit of form for form's sake is all too evident. The Bauhaus designers conceived the object of use, whether a chair, table, desk, or cabinet, as an abstract composition of planes, cubes, rectangular volumes, or a combination of these. This conception of furniture design was held by everyone in the early years of the school, from the director down through the ranks of the students.

The Bauhaus furniture designers went astray when they sought to give form, willfully, to their ideas. There is every evidence in their works of mixed motivation, of an impatience with the mere fulfillment of function, and a desire to endow their objects of use with the more exalted attributes of fine art.

Breuer, the most prolific of the furniture makers in Weimar, became director of the *Tishlerei* in Dessau. He retained this position until the spring of 1928, when he joined the Great Exodus that carried Gropius, Bayer, and Moholy-Nagy from the Bauhaus into voluntary exile. Albers, a considerable furniture designer himself, became form master of the workshop upon Breuer's departure. He held this position in addition to teaching the *Vorkurs*, when I entered the Bauhaus in 1928.

Breuer first stepped into the limelight in Dessau with his design of an armchair of tubular steel. Practically everybody in Germany in those days was a cyclist, and Breuer is said to have hit upon the idea of making a chair of steel tubing from the contemplation of the structure of his bicycle. He also designed built-in cabinets and free-standing furniture for Gropius's master houses in Dessau. The cabinets, with sliding doors of either glass or wood, were made in the Bauhaus furniture workshop. In the case of Kandinsky's house, he evidently felt that he had to do something special, something which would relate in character to the artist's work, for he says:

> Our dwellings need not have any distinct "style" but they should reflect the individuality of the occupant. The architect creates only half of the dwelling, the person who lives in it the other half.[2]

Kandinsky, at the time, was in the midst of his "geometric" period; so Breuer designed a "geometric" dining room suite for him. Kandinsky had, among other valued mementos of his homeland, some antique Russian furniture which, he said, went very well in his modern living room, since the pieces were well designed. What he thought about Breuer's dining room table and chairs, which were not, I can only surmise; but he made no excuses for them when Madame Kandinsky served tea and cakes to me in their dining room over fifty years ago.

Breuer described furniture thus:

> A piece of furniture is no willful form but, rather, a necessary component of our surroundings. In itself impersonal, it derives its meaning only from the manner in which it is used, which is to say, in the framework of a total plan.[3]

Breuer, the creator and promoter of the tubular steel chair, never succeeded in designing a really good-looking piece. His second armchair comes closest, and while his chairs look efficient they are stiff and ungraceful. It remained for Mies van der Rohe to create, in 1927, the first handsome tubular steel chair, his famous "cantilever" chair in which the seat and back are suspended from two semicircles of tubing which form the only supports. Mies made several versions of this, differing in size and proportions, to serve various uses—armless dining room chairs, a larger model with armrests, and, of course, the low, ample, and armless "MR" chair, the most elegant of them all. The latter was upholstered in either roll and pleat cushions or cane, and the two former chairs in cane. The tubing came in three different finishes—lacquer, nickel, and chromium plating. They also make more legitimate use of the structural material. Breuer's chairs, at least before the advent of Mies's cantilever chair, were built up of solid wood and they could have been executed in that material. Mies's tubular chairs utilize, as Breuer's original chairs did not, the tensile capability of steel. They are also more comfortable because the resilience of the suspended tubing gives them a kind of springlike action resembling, in some sense, the back-and-forth motion of a rocking chair.

No metal furniture was made at the Bauhaus during my time there. When Breuer left, the tubular furniture left too. What I saw

Tubular steel "MR" chair designed by Mies van der Rohe

Takehito Mizutani, wooden stool, 1926

when I was a student in the *Tischlerei* under Albers's directorship was the making of wood furniture—for instance, chairs, tables, desks, cabinets. One of the best pieces turned out there was a bentwood chair by Albers himself. This was set together on four slender lengths of wood, bent in such a way as to form the arms and legs and the supports for the cushioned seat and back. The four wood members were held together by a pair of metal rods which were screwed to them. The chair could be disassembled to facilitate packing and shipping.

Another notable piece was a wooden stool with a fabric seat designed and executed by Takehito Mizutani, a student. It consisted of four wooden spokes or legs inserted on the diagonal into a kind of pierced wooden hub which held them securely in position. The upper ends of the legs, in turn, were mortised into two horizontal wooden rods between which the fabric seat was stretched. To apply the principle to a stool, however, was a distinct innovation.

A number of experimental wood chairs were made in the Dessau workshop using cushions or webbing for seats and backs and also bent plywood, which was unusual at that time. The best-looking chair and probably the most comfortable of them all was the one by Martin Decker, with a back and seat of plywood, and an elegance of form.

Decker was an ardent Social Democrat and once tried to inveigle me into marching with a group of his political associates through the streets of Dessau. I refused to do this and, indeed, during my six years in Germany I sedulously avoided any and all political activity. I never attended a single Hitler rally during the two years I lived in Berlin, though I must confess I listened, on occasion, to his rousing radio tirades.

There are amusing sides even to ruthless dictatorships; as watchful as the tyrants are, they are unable to prevent little hairline cracks from developing in the political monolith. The Nazis celebrated flag day once each year. I had to laugh when, on one such day, with each house bedizened with swastika flags, an organ-grinder went down our street innocently cranking out Sousa's *The Stars and Stripes Forever*. It is doubtless not widely known that Hitler once tried out a tubular steel reclining chair. I have proof of this in the form of a picture postcard that was presented to me some years ago by Hilberseimer. The picture actually shows the Führer, with a puzzled look on his homely visage, stretched out in just such an unseemly chair. According to Hilberseimer, Thonet, the firm which manufactured the chairs, tricked Hitler into sitting in one, photographed him in it, and then, for publicity reasons, circulated the photo far and wide. The Nazis, so skilled themselves in the uses of propaganda, saw through the stratagem and banned the further distribution of the picture, but Hilberseimer had procured

Adolf Hitler, sitting in a Thonet chair

a copy. It is understandable that the Nazis, who so consistently eschewed the new and embraced the old, should not want their leader to become "Breuerized".

One striking innovation achieved at the Bauhaus was in the construction of the chair leg. Of the six chairs seen on page 101, three of them, the first two in the top row and the first in the bottom row, have an unusual leg construction. The legs of these three pieces are made of relatively thin (approximately three-quarter-inch-thick) slats. These thin legs are connected by equally thin U-

Six wood chairs, made in the furniture workshop,
Bauhaus, Dessau

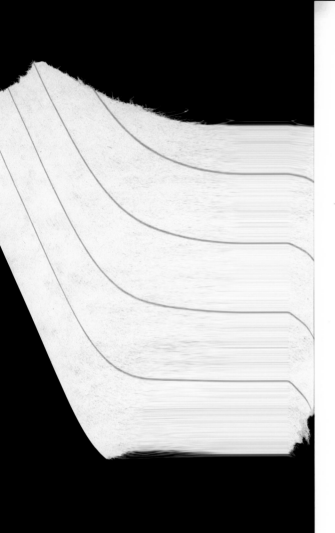

shaped wood braces, attached to the legs by screws. The braces, whose vertical members run nearly the length of the legs, serve as stiffeners. This braced framework, replacing the customary solid wood construction, made the chairs surprisingly lightweight, without sacrificing strength. I never learned who invented this construction, and no mention of it or its author is made in any of the Bauhaus books, though furniture employing this structural system is frequently shown. This unusual and successful construction was employed at the Bauhaus in Dessau, particularly during the regime of Hannes Meyer, for chairs, stools, tables, and desks. I even used it for the legs of an improved extension table which I made.

This lightweight leg construction was one of the few viable inventions of the Bauhaus cabinetmaking shops. Like the substitution in the balloon frame of light studs and joists for the massive posts and beams of medieval house construction, this replacement of the heavy wood members of traditional furniture design by thin staves resulted in a saving of materials and a reduction of the weight of a chair or a table.

I used this, let us call it "Hannes Meyer" leg construction, in the

Howard Dearstyne, extension table made in the furniture workshop, Bauhaus, Dessau

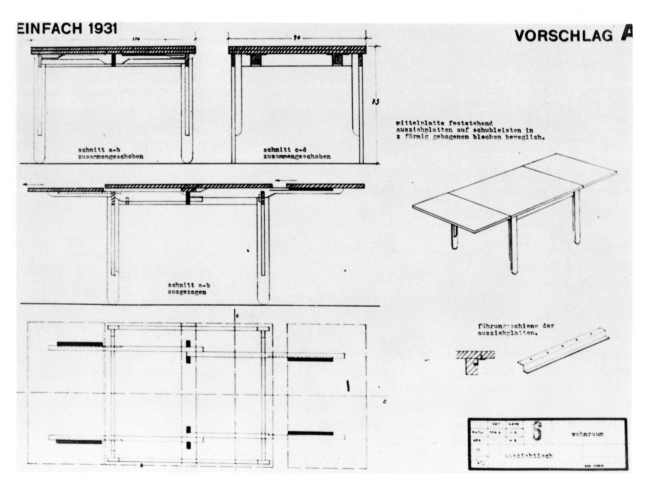

design of my extension table, which I executed in a quarter-size model during my term in the *Tishlerei*. The leg construction was only incidental, however, the virtue of the table being that it remedied a defect in the traditional German extension table. This was different from the American variety. The German type had a main panel or top which covered the area of the table frame. Two leaves, each half the size of the main top, slid under this on runners and actually sustained it. To enlarge the table, one pulled out the leaves and the main top dropped down to their level with a bang. It was my object to eliminate this bang and I succeeded in doing it by means of a device which eased the main top down gradually when the leaves were pulled out. If I had had Breuer's business acumen, I might have been able to market the table; but this and other furniture of mine never got beyond the workshop.

Josef Albers, chair

Another piece which I designed in the furniture workshop (but did not execute) was a tubular metal rocking chair. Such chairs have since appeared on the market, but I feel confident mine was the first. I also experimented with the treatment of quarter-inch pine plywood to bring out the decorative quality of the grain, long before this kind of emphasized-grain wood was on the market as wall paneling. What I did was to gouge away the soft wood with a wire brush, a procedure which left the hard wood intact and in low relief. Then I lacquered the surface, which rendered the grain still more prominent because the hard wood took on a deeper tone. I suspect that the soft wood could have been etched away much more readily by sandblasting, which, no doubt, was the method used to produce the commercial paneling.

I did other remarkable things in the *Tishlerei*, such as piecing together a "picture" out of selected wood grain patterns. This elicited general admiration, but somehow I was never invited to hang it beside works of Kandinsky or Klee. I also made a *hocker* or stool of cherry wood, with "Hannes Meyer" legs and a seat of *eisengarn*, a very tough fabric. This was my initial attempt at furnituremaking after I had learned how to handle the hammer, the chisel, the bucksaw, and the plane, to make mortises and tenons and to cut dovetail and even hidden dovetail joints. In consequence of my experience, I am bound to confess, since this is a frank and true account, that I sliced up an entire cherry log before I managed to get enough pieces of the required length and thickness to produce the flimsy *hocker*.

Alma Buscher, baby commode, 1924

Marcel Breuer, living-room table

During the directorship of Mies van der Rohe the furniture workshop was very much as before. It was not until after the Bauhaus period that Mies and Walter Peterhans considered stamping chairs and other furniture out of plastic, a pioneering idea at the time. Under Mies everything was subordinated to architecture, including furnituremaking, metalworking, and wall painting, and their re-

Marcel Breuer geometric chair for Kandinsky's diningroom, 1926

spective workshops were combined, in name, at least, into an *Ausbau* or interior design department. This was directed first by Alfred Arndt, a former Weimar student turned instructor in Dessau, and later, after 1932, by Mies's professional and pedagogic collaborator, Lilly Reich.

As far as I can recall, no furniture was made at the Bauhaus in Berlin during its brief existence. Weaving was continued there on looms lent by the city of Dessau; to the best of my belief, no woodworking or metalworking machinery was acquired in that way, and Mies was in no position to purchase it.

The greatest single accomplishment of the Dessau workshop (this was, strictly speaking, not of the workshop because it was done outside of the Bauhaus) was Breuer's invention of the tubular steel chair, but with the exception of some pieces by Breuer, which have lately been revived, no Bauhaus furniture has stood the test of time and continued in production.

8 the print shop, typography, and advertising art

The Bauhaus print shop was not a typographical printing shop but, rather, a studio. In it both students and masters made prints from a variety of materials—woodblocks, etching plates, and lithographic stones. While the Bauhaus was not conceived, of course, as a center for the propagation of the fine arts, unsurprisingly, considering that its staff was composed almost entirely of artists, it became one. There was no regular instruction at Weimar in "the useless arts," but the private activities of the masters on those lines naturally inspired many of the students to follow them. All the masters, including the sculptor Marcks, were graphic artists, and competition arose between them and the students for use of the limited facilities of the print shop.

Feininger, Gropius's first appointee, was form master. He was a distinguished graphic artist, and a master of the woodcut. Since the time, early in 1919, when he had asked Feininger to do the symbolic woodcut for the first Bauhaus proclamation, Gropius had made repeated demands of his time. In 1921 Feininger wrote:

> I am very busy designing script for the lettering of the portfolios—for days to come I can't think of doing anything besides. As I took it upon myself to do this work I have to carry it through. The responsibility for the completion of the "Masters of the Bauhaus" portfolio has been placed into my hand, and lastly, it is also a creative work, achieved to serve our mutual cause.[1]

Obliging though he was, Feininger finally baulked at doing further graphic work for the "mutual cause." A few days later he wrote that "not everything should be done by my hand."

Feininger also served as a mentor to the Bauhaus students, a role he took very seriously. In a letter of June 1919, he wrote:

These consultations with students are among the affairs uppermost in my mind. I often ponder on the way of establishing a working relationship with students. I think I have it now: leading and helping them along, talking freely to them and exchanging thoughts and ideas. I feel strong and rich. I am convinced that I can contribute to their development without forcing them into something foreign to their nature. The trust they place in me is very wonderful.[2]

In another letter from the same period, he wrote:

At the request of the students, I put up a show of selected graphic works of mine . . . obviously it was a good idea . . . the *necessity* of the way I look makes itself evident. The students can see clearly that, also without working in a classroom, one is able to learn, investigating and analyzing, and how I have gone to work to maintain the tension between nature and the work of art.[3]

Feininger exerted a strong influence on the community at the Bauhaus by the mere fact of his presence:

[His] noble and modest nature was very reserved. Though he, to all appearance, scarcely participated in the teaching, his demeanor and his own accomplishment served as a constant example. He spread the atmosphere of concentration and meditation which is essential to creative life.[4]

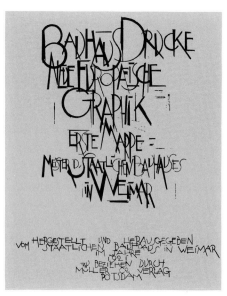

Lyonel Feininger, title page of first portfolio, *Masters of the State Bauhaus in Weimar*

I have a clear recollection of an exhibition of his work arranged by my student friend Christof Hertel at the Bauhaus in Dessau in 1929. One of the major characteristics of his woodcuts is the strong use of line. It distinguished them from the works created during the flowering of German woodblock printing in the fifteenth and sixteenth centuries, which were almost chromatic, and also, for that matter, from the woodcuts of the expressionists, also exuberant colorists who revived the tradition in the twentieth century.

I have followed Feininger's work with interest during the forty-odd years which have elapsed since I saw his one-man show at the Bauhaus, and later the great exhibition of his work at the National Gallery in Berlin in 1931. At times, standing before his work, I have had the feeling that whatever steps he had taken to modify the naturalism of his subject matter, the picture still remained naturalistic, a kind of architectural rendering, whether the subject was buildings or an illustration.

His graphic work became progressively an art of elimination, of extreme economy of means, and he eventually pushed this economy to its limit. His woodcut, *The Cathedral*, which appeared on the cover of the first Bauhaus proclamation in 1919 (see page 40), is a composition of straight lines, verticals and diagonals chiefly, in which broad strokes of black, in the manner of the expressionists, predominate. A significant change had taken place by the time of his woodcut of 1923 (opposite). The main subject of this work is also a church, but it has been abstracted almost to the point of unrecognizability. The strong diagonals and heavy black bars of *The Cathedral*, which lend it a dynamic character, have here given way to "bundles" of short, tranquil lines. Only two strong accents remain, a black horizontal band at the base and a vertical black bar following the line of the steeple. These form the framework of the picture. Before, the positive, powerful blacks produced a compacted whole; now the negative whites permeate and loosen up the entire composition. The result is an airiness, a spatial effect lacking in the *Cathedral*. I compared these two works to indicate the direction Feininger took in his woodcuts, his etchings, his watercolors, and, for that matter, in many of his oils.

By the time of his exhibition in 1929, his woodcuts had become sparse arrangements of a few straight lines. Feininger's predecessors, in cutting the wood block, had retained more of its surface than they had whittled away. He excised almost all of it, leaving only what he required to create the illusion of space. It is evident that he sought, in these works, to evoke a sense of spaciousness and depth; he accomplished this by suggestion:

Lyonel Feininger, church, from Bauhaus *Master's Portfolio*. Woodcut

> It seems to me of utmost importance to become more simple. Again and again I realize this when I come to Bach. His art is incomparably terse, and this is one of the reasons that it is so mighty and eternally alive. I must avoid becoming entangled and fettered in complexities. In one respect, perhaps, my work may be considered of significance: its passionate quest for strictest delineation of space without compromising.[5]

Feininger's characteristic way of transmuting his subject matter to make it into a picture is illustrated in his painting *Gelmeroda IX*, of 1926, typical of his mature work. As was so often the case with his village scenes, a church flanked by lower buildings constitutes the central motif. The artist has rendered the building shapes nearly abstract by resolving them into overlapping planes of color. He has treated the sky as a series of translucent rectilinear planes of colored light, superimposed one upon the other. The planes of the buildings and those of the sky merge to form a unified pictorial structure with a predominantly vertical accentuation, an aspiring quality. Feininger's forms, reduced to planes of light, have become nearly weightless, and the result is a gracefully monumental space composition with melodic overtones.

Lyonel Feininger, *Sailing Ships*. Woodcut

Lyonel Feininger, *Gelmeroda IX*, 1926

Rudolf Baschant, 1922. Etching

A number of the most active student printmakers, naturally, came under Feininger's tutelage. One of these, Hirschfeld-Mack, developed such proficiency in printmaking that he was entrusted with the making of the covers for the *Masters of the Bauhaus* portfolio, "using his special technique with the roller." Hirschfeld-Mack was the first Bauhaus apprentice to become a journeyman. His works ranged from painting and lithography to toys and the famous "reflected light plays," of which he was coinventor.

The works of a number of other graphic art students of Feininger's can be seen in the Busch-Reisinger Museum at Harvard. It has some etchings of Rudolf (Rudi) Baschant, which tend toward the fantastic, and of Johannes Driesch, which are down-to-earth. There are also linoleum cuts—blocky expressionistic "portraits"— by Reinhard Hilker and, executed in the same technique, a rather tragic-looking nude *Madonna with Child* by Heinz Borchers. Among the best prints are some sensitive animal woodcuts by Karl Peter Röhl.

Röhl apparently became a convert to constructivism when the proselytizing van Doesburg turned up in Weimar. I have a copy of the journal *Mecano*, edited by van Doesburg, which seems to prove this. This paper, which called itself "a journal for spiritual hygiene, mechanical aesthetics, and neo-Dadaism" was printed on both sides of a single sheet of calendered paper and folded like a map. One side of my copy is greenish-blue and the issue is designated as "No. blue 1922." It carries text in four languages and reproductions of art works, among which are two cuts by Röhl. One of these is a constructivist abstraction, composed of circles, squares, and rectangles. His second work bears the superscription, *Thistle Seer/Dedicated to the Bauhaus*. It depicts, on the right, an innocent-looking nude gentleman, equipped with a halo and holding a thistle. On the left, facing him, is a figure made up wholly of geometric shapes. A line of text at the right reads, "Confrontation of the natural and the mechanical man in Weimar in the year 1922." The man with the thistle, of course, represents Itten. The mechanical man, in his stiff-necked rigidity and black garb, was intended, I am sure, to be the effigy of van Doesburg himself, since it so accurately suggested the monolithic immobility of his views and even his appearance (he wore black shirts). Thus the cartoon symbolized the internal state of affairs—the conflict of ideologies—which obtained at the Bauhaus in 1922.

Since the Bauhaus was a school, it may be argued that the facilities of the print shop should have been devoted first and foremost to the work of the students. However, at least from 1921 on, the ambitious projects of the instructors claimed the attention of the technical master, Carl Zaubitzer, and the form master, Feininger, and engaged the available hand presses. These projects

Reinhard Hilker. Wood or linoleum cut

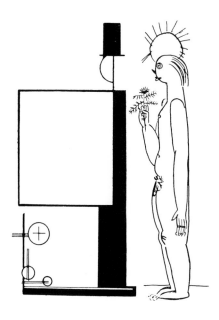

Karl Peter Röhl, *The Thistle Seer.*

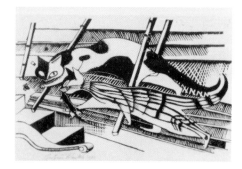

Gerhard Marcks, *The Cats*, from the portfolio *Masters of the State Bauhaus in Weimar*, 1921. Woodcut

Wassily Kandinsky, from his portfolio *Kleine Welten (Little Worlds)* ca. 1922. Color lithograph

were the printing and publication of a series of portfolios of graphic works by the masters of the Bauhaus and the leading modern artists of Germany and Europe. They were the first significant publications of the Bauhaus and proved to be one of the most lasting achievements of the school.

Appropriately, the first portfolio, issued in 1921, was devoted to Feininger's work and carried twelve of his woodcuts. This was followed by other collections of graphic works by individual Bauhaus masters: Kandinsky's *Kleine Welten* (*Little Worlds*) portfolio, consisting of twelve plates (four etchings, four lithographs, and four woodcuts), printed in 1922 for distribution by the Propylaen Verlag; a portfolio of ten woodcut illustrations by Marcks to Karl Simrock's translation of the Norse epic, *Das Wielandslied der alten Edda* (*The Wieland Song of the Old Edda*), first publication of the then (1923) newly established Bauhaus Press; and a portfolio of graphic works by Schlemmer, published by himself. A collection of eight woodcuts, lithographs, and etchings by the Bauhaus masters (the so-called *Meistermappe*), consisting of prints by Feininger, Kandinsky, Klee, Marcks, Muche, Moholy-Nagy, Schlemmer, and Schreyer, was published by the Bauhaus Press in 1923.

The most ambitious of all the Bauhaus graphic art printing ventures, undertaken with Müller and Co. as publisher, was the series of portfolios known as *Neue europäische Graphik* (*New European Graphic Art*). As originally conceived in 1921, the series was to consist of five portfolios of graphic works by the leading contemporary artists of Europe; unfortunately, only four of the portfolios were completed.

The grand plan for the five portfolios had a practical as well as an educational basis. The Bauhaus, as always, was short of money and it was hoped that the sale of the portfolios would improve its finances. The plates from which the prints were pulled were contributed gratis by the makers. It is a testimony to the sense of solidarity which existed among the artists of Europe, of so many divergent trends, that they were willing thus to come to the aid of the Bauhaus. The scheme, unfortunately, failed to have the expected financial success. Only 110 copies of each portfolio were printed, and though these were enthusiastically received, the proceeds from their sale were disappointing, largely because of the instability of the German currency at the time of their publication.

This idea of aiding a good cause through the voluntary contribution of art works did not die at the Bauhaus with this attempt, however. When, in the late 1920s, Christian Zervos, publisher of *Cahiers d'Art*, fell into financial difficulties and appealed to his artist friends for help, Kandinsky conceived the plan of putting together a rescue portfolio of works by himself, Paul Klee, and other artists, and asked me to take orders for it on one of my return trips to the United States. But the S.O.S. portfolio never came into being;

Zervos evidently found funds elsewhere to enable him to continue his work.

The job of creating the title sheets, tables of contents, and other incidental text of the portfolios fell to Feininger. The lettering was carved from woodblocks and the introductory pages were printed, as any other woodcuts, on the hand presses. The Bauhaus portfolios were bound, wholly or in part, in parchment. I am fortunate enough to own one of these, the *Kleine Welten*, which has a design of Kandinsky's impressed on the cover. If they were all as handsome as this one, they were luxury items indeed. This work was done in the Bauhaus bookbindery, privately operated by Otto Dorfner. I am not acquainted with whatever arrangements the Bauhaus made with Dorfner for the preparation of the portfolios, but they evidently worked very well!

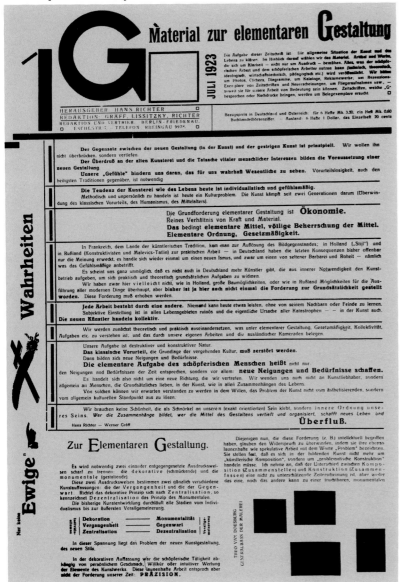

Cover of the first issue of *G*

The Bauhaus possessed only hand presses for graphic art work so that it was compelled to farm out its typographic printing. In so doing it was dependent upon the typefaces commercially available in Weimar and elsewhere. These were so limited in variety as to inhibit radical experimentation in typographical design.

With the scarcity of modern typefaces, one could hardly have expected the first publication of the Bauhaus, the famous proclamation, to be revolutionary in anything, except, perhaps, its content. It was embellished, indeed, with Feininger's excellent woodcut, and it was printed in Roman type, but there was nothing in the least remarkable about its layout. It was not until the *Satzungen, Staatliches Bauhaus in Weimar* (*Statutes, State Bauhaus in Weimar*) were issued in July 1922 that any attempt was made at typographical innovation.

These statutes or bylaws, printed by the Utopia Press in Weimar, consisted of six pamphlets, 7 7/8" x 11 1/2" in size and horizontal in format. Each pamphlet dealt with a particular phase of the school's curriculum or organization and was distinguished from the others by being of a different color. The type was sans serif Gothic and was printed in both black and colored inks. There was a main cover page, and part titles for each pamphlet. These carried titles in neat blocks of uppercase lettering, along with Schlemmer's newly designed Bauhaus seal. The text was set double column in uppercase and lowercase type, punctuated by subtitles in large boldface capital letters. It is quite evident that an attempt was made to render the *Satzungen* both readily legible and pleasing to the eye. We may look upon this as a transitional stage in the development of Bauhaus typographical design, since the bars and other printers' devices which later came to characterize it were lacking and since the type remained discreetly horizontal throughout.

The new look in Bauhaus typographical design was inaugurated by Moholy-Nagy, who arrived at the school early in 1923. Moholy, it could be argued, was a pioneer once-removed: his innovations in his chief fields of activity, painting, photography, and typographical design, could be traced to others—to Malevich and El Lissitzky (painting); to Man Ray (photography); and to de Stijl artists (typography and layout).

Moholy was brought to the Bauhaus because Gropius felt that constructivism (then in ascendancy at the school) should have its representative on the teaching staff and to appoint van Doesburg was out of the question. (See page 65). He was a controversial choice, arguing, for instance, the supremacy of photography over painting. The clearest presentation of this thesis is found in his article "Ismus oder Kunst" ("Isms or Art"), published in 1926:

Cover page, *Satzungen* (by-laws) of the Bauhaus, Weimar, July 1922. The seal is by Oskar Schlemmer

Whether a representation is plastic, linear, painterly, black and white, colored, photographic, or is made in some other way is theoretically unimportant. Today it goes practically without saying that one is

Moholy-Nagy, photo of dolls

bound to favor a mechanical-technical method of representation, with all of its associated phenomena, to a tedious manual optical representation. The situation of photography is, therewith, clearly defined. The creative representation of the nature-bound, the fantastic-Utopian, the dreamlike and the surrealistic, even in the case of accidental achievements, has been carried so far and demonstrated so unequivocally that similar attempts with manual means can only in the rarest cases attain an equally convincing effect. In this contest, the photographic process, because of its boundless representational potentialities, will emerge victorious. Only fetishistic worship of "handwork" can contradict this statement. For he who is able to abstract the planar projection of a "holy" hand from that of a "soulless" machine and to perceive behind them the creative powers of the makers, it will be impossible for the brush to compete with the camera. The fact that the results of photography—for the viewer—are of such unprecedented richness and have pressed far forward into the realm of clarity, precision, fullness of light, of the immateriality and yet reality of the representation, compels us to assert that the delineating painter would do well to concentrate his talents on this process which, of all representational procedures, is most capable of development, the most versatile and the most splendid.[6]

I recall having had an argument in Dessau with Fritz Kuhr, one of the "influential" students, over this eminently controversial subject. Though Kuhr himself was a painter, he maintained that painting was an obsolete art and that photography would supersede it. Photography involved more than the mastery of a mechanical technique, he contended, and in proof of this he told me that he had taken a dozen pictures of a burnt match before he got the precise effect he sought. I was a photographer then and I am one still and yet, at the time, I defended painting.

Moholy was always provocative, as a person and in his views. In typography as well as photography he sought new techniques. Taking his cues from Kurt Schwitters and the Dadaists and van Doesburg and de Stijl, Moholy-Nagy sought to give "visual validity" to the printed page, in order to make it better serve its basic function of communication. Here, as in other fields of the arts, he and the other Bauhaus designers attempted to introduce reforms or innovations. They tried to improve the visual presentation of language, not its structure. They played with unusual combinations of type, illustrations, signs, and symbols, turning the printed page, intended first and foremost to convey information, into a game of aesthetic checks and balances. They tried to increase the legibility of type by devising new alphabets (Albers, Herbert Bayer, Joost Schmidt) but these, though ingenious, were as difficult to read as the old German type. They sought, in the interest of simplicity, legibility, and economy, as they claimed, to do away with one of

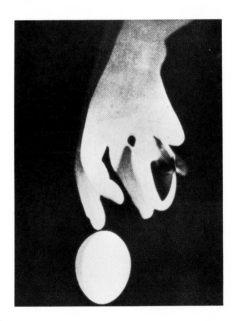

Man Ray, *Hand with an Egg.* Photogram

the time-honored cases of the typesetter's font and proceeded to print everything in small letters ("the Bauhaus prints small and talks big," as the saying went in those days) but the elimination of capital letters, so beloved by the Germans and, indeed, so useful when taken in moderation, proved to be a fruitless experiment.

In an article entitled "Zeitgemasse Typographie. Ziele, Praxis, Kritik" ("Modern Typography. Aims, Practice, Criticism"), Moholy explains the need for typographical reform:

The old handwritten codices and even the first typographical works utilized to the full the contrasting effects of colors and forms (initial letters, script in several colors, colored illustrations). The wide diffusion of the printing process, the heavy demand for printed works, hand in hand with the economical and profitable utilization of paper, the small format, cast type, monochromatic printing, etc., have transformed the type page of the old printed works, so lively and rich in contrasts, into the gray of later books with its, for the most part, decidedly monotonous effect.

This dullness of our books has certain disadvantages. In the first place, it renders a clearly perceptible organization of the text difficult, despite the possibility of a basic organization through division into paragraphs. Secondly, it tires a reader far more quickly than does a printed page composed of contrasting colors and tonal values. Thus, in spite of a fundamental technical transformation in their manufacture, the majority of our books today have advanced no farther in their typographic-optic-synoptic form than Gutenberg's production. . . . The situation is much more favorable in the case of newspapers, posters, and displaying printing, because typographical development has taken place almost exclusively in these fields.[7]

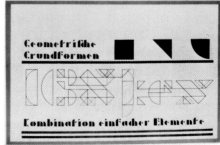

Josef Albers, design for stencil lettering

He then proceeds to discuss ways of livening up contemporary printing by means of lines, bars, circles, squares, crosses, etc., photographic illustrations, and color. He continues:

An essential aspect of typographic order is the harmonious organization of the surface, of the invisible but nevertheless clearly felt, tension-charged linear relationships which, in addition to an equilibrium obtained through a symmetrical distribution of the parts, admit various asymmetrical possibilities of balance. Today, in contrast to the static-concentric type of equilibrium in use for hundreds of years, we are seeking to produce a dynamic-eccentric equilibrium. In the first case, the typographic subject, in the central disposition of all of its constituent parts, including the peripheral, is comprehended at a single glance. In the second case, the eye is led step by step from one point to another, in the course of which the awareness of the relationship of the individual parts must not become lost (posters, display work, book titles, etc.).[8]

The title page of the book *Staatliches Bauhaus Weimar 1919–1923* indicates the direction design was to take. In this, the conventional "static-concentric" placement of the type (that is, the grouping of horizontal lines of letters about a central vertical axis) gives way to an asymmetrical arrangement in which the letters of the title form three "nested" right angles pointing toward the upper left. The strong diagonal movement thereby generated is held in check by a more or less centrally located square composed of the dates, "1919" and "1923." The letters are sans serif capitals, some of them solid and some built up of parallel lines. The large upright letter "B" serves as the vertical leg of the uppermost angle, while lines of letters placed on their sides form the corresponding verticals of the other two angles. Letters here constitute the only typographic tools; no bars or other printing devices have been used. The composition, without question, is dynamic. The letters have been forced to play a role for which they were not conceived to make an abstract pattern. Whatever aesthetic advantages this may have, their capacity to perform their basic function of conveying information has hardly been increased.

Moholy-Nagy, title page of *StaatlichesBauhaus in Weimar*

The title page just discussed, by comparison with later typographic works by Moholy, could be said to be a rather mild example of "dynamic-eccentric" page layout. The announcement designed by him to herald the publication of the first eight Bauhaus books, however, exhibits both the dynamism and the eccentricity characteristic of his mature style. It consists of a single sheet with printing on both sides. The face introduces the books and gives their authors and titles. The back lists some thirty other books which are in preparation.

In composing the two sides of this prospectus, Moholy used all the visual devices he could. The message to be communicated is nearly overwhelmed and the result is lumbering and heavy-handed. The announcement, to be sure, falls into the category of advertising "art." But Moholy strove to give a comparable "optical validity" to the pages of the Bauhaus books themselves. The type used in these books, which were planned in Weimar and published after the move to Dessau, is squat and heavy, and the text is punctuated, in the interest of easy readability, with dots, bars, and other printers' adjuncts. A comparison of the composition of Moholy's announcement, sandwiched, as it is, between the pages of the book, with the layout of the letter, is illuminating. It reveals the forthright nature of his typographical design and explains why his approach has been largely ignored or rejected by modern designers of fine books.

Moholy-Nagy set the pace in typography at the Bauhaus. He introduced de Stijl principles of layout into the school, and he also started using photomontage or, as he called it, *Fotoplastik*. As he explained it, this technique harkened back to the old days of the

IM VERLAG
ALBERT LANGEN MÜNCHEN
erscheinen die
BAUHAUSBÜCHER
SCHRIFTLEITUNG:
WALTER GROPIUS und **L. MOHOLY-NAGY**

Die Herausgabe der Bauhausbücher geschieht von der Erkenntnis aus, daß alle Gestaltungsgebiete des Lebens miteinander eng verknüpft sind. Die Bücher behandeln künstlerische, wissenschaftliche und technische Fragen und versuchen, den in ihrer Spezialarbeit gebundenen heutigen Menschen über die Problemstellung, die Arbeitsführung und die Arbeitsergebnisse verschiedener Gestaltungsgebiete Aufschluß zu geben und dadurch einen Vergleichsmaßstab für ihre eigenen Kenntnisse und den Fortschritt in anderen Arbeitszweigen zu schaffen. Um eine Aufgabe von diesem Ausmaße bewältigen zu können, haben die Herausgeber bestorientierte Fachleute verschiedener Länder, die ihre Spezialarbeit in die Gesamtheit heutiger Lebenserscheinungen einzugliedern bestrebt sind, für die Mitarbeit gewonnen.

SOEBEN IST DIE ERSTE SERIE ERSCHIENEN:

8 BAUHAUSBÜCHER

			Abbildungen	PREIS steif brosch.	i. Leinen geb.
1	Walter Gropius,	INTERNATIONALE ARCHITEKTUR. Auswahl der besten neuzeitlichen Architektur-Werke.	101	Mk. 5	Mk. 7
2	Paul Klee,	PÄDAGOGISCHES SKIZZENBUCH. Aus seinem Unterricht am Bauhaus mit von ihm selbst gezeichneten Textillustrationen.	87	Mk. 6	Mk. 8
3	Ein Versuchshaus des Bauhauses.	Neue Wohnkultur; neue Techniken des Hausbaues.	61	Mk. 5	Mk. 7
4	Die Bühne im Bauhaus.	Theoretisches und Praktisches aus einer modernen Theaterwerkstatt.	42 3 Farbtafeln	Mk. 5	Mk. 7
5	Piet Mondrian,	NEUE GESTALTUNG. Forderungen der neuen Gestaltung für alle Gebiete künstlerischen Schaffens.		Mk. 3	Mk. 5
6	Theo van Doesburg,	GRUNDBEGRIFFE DER NEUEN GESTALTENDEN KUNST. Versuch einer neuen Ästhetik.	32	Mk. 5	Mk. 7
7	Neue Arbeiten der Bauhauswerkstätten.	Praktische Beispiele neuzeitlicher Wohnungseinrichtung.	107 4 Farbtafeln	Mk. 6	Mk. 8
8	L. Moholy-Nagy,	MALEREI, PHOTOGRAPHIE, FILM. Apologie der Photographie, zugleich grundlegende Erkenntnis abstrakter und gegenständlicher Malerei.	102	Mk. 7	Mk. 9

Die Reihe wird in schneller Folge fortgesetzt.
IN VORBEREITUNG:
BAUHAUSBÜCHER

W. Kandinsky:	Punkt, Linie, Fläche
	Violett (Bühnenstück)
Kurt Schwitters:	Merz-Buch
Heinrich Jacoby:	Schöpferische Musikerziehung
J. J. P. Oud (Holland):	Die holländische Architektur
George Anthell (Amerika):	Musico-mechanico
Albert Gleizes (Frankreich):	Kubismus
F. T. Marinetti und	
Prampolini (Italien):	Futurismus
Fritz Wichert:	Expressionismus
Tristan Tzara:	Dadaismus
L. Kassák und E. Kállai (Ungarn):	Die MA-Gruppe
T. v. Doesburg (Holland):	Die Stijlgruppe
Carel Teige (Prag):	Tschechische Kunst
Louis Lozowick (Amerika):	Amerikanische Architektur
Walter Gropius:	Neue Architekturdarstellung ● Das flache Dach ● Montierbare Typenbauten ● Die Bauhausneubauten in Dessau
Mies van der Rohe:	Über Architektur
Le Corbusier-Saugnier (Frankreich):	Über Architektur
Knud Lönberg-Holm (Dänemark):	Über Architektur
Friedrich Kiesler (Österreich):	Neue Formen der Demonstration Die Raumstadt
Jane Heap (Amerika):	Die neue Welt
G. Muche und R. Paulick:	Das Metalltypenhaus
Mart Stam	Das „ABC" vom Bauen
Adolf Behne:	Kunst, Handwerk und Industrie
Max Burchartz:	Plastik der Gestaltungen
Martin Schäfer:	Konstruktive Biologie
Reklame und Typographie des Bauhauses.	
L. Moholy-Nagy:	Aufbau der Gestaltungen
Paul Klee:	Bildnerische Mechanik
Oskar Schlemmer:	Bühnenelemente
Joost Schmidt:	Bildermagazin der Zeit I
Die neuen künstlichen Materialien	

Die **BAUHAUSBÜCHER** sind zu beziehen einzeln oder in Serien durch jede Buchhandlung oder direkt vom

VERLAG
ALBERT LANGEN
MÜNCHEN Hubertusstr. 27

Bestellkarte liegt diesem Prospekt bei.

BAUHAUSDRUCK MOHOLY DIN C5

Moholy-Nagy, announcement of the Bauhaus Books

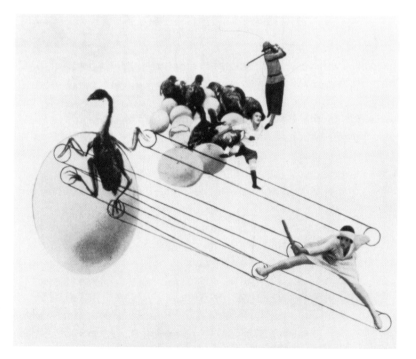

Moholy-Nagy, *Once a Chicken, Always a Chicken*.
Photomontage

camera when a photographer, given the job of making a group picture of persons who, for one reason or another, had to be photographed individually, resorted to cutting out the single portraits and pasting them together against a trumped-up backdrop, thus achieving the desired ensemble. Dadaists also made such compositions of cut-out and pasted-up photographs, but they used them to surprise and shock the public. Moholy combined cutout photographs with hand-executed lines and geometric forms and achieved striking and unusual effects.

Moholy was quick to exploit the potential of montage in advertising. Though there was no formal instruction in advertising design in Weimar, as there later came to be in Dessau, a number of students experimented with it under Moholy's guidance. Chief among these were Bayer, Schmidt, and Arndt, all of whom became

Herbert Bayer, cover for Bauhaus magazine, 1928

teachers in Dessau. Bayer, who had some architectural experience, took the lead in designing display kiosks, towers, and pavilions, utilizing light, smoke, and sound as auxiliary sales inducements. In these projects he strove for novel and striking forms, creating structures which could hardly be claimed to be architecture but which might still be used in a poster. All three designed posters and other printed advertising matter. In this field where "customer appeal" was the paramount consideration, no holds were barred, as they sometimes were in book layout, so that the use of all kinds of typographical "additives" to lend "visual validity" to some humdrum cause was sanctioned.

In the days of the Bauhaus in Weimar, the persuasive power of the female figure to promote sales of anything from toothpaste to dog food had not yet been exploited; so the Bauhaus designers used abstract visual stimuli, especially geometric forms in Mondrian-like arrangements. In other words, they impressed art into the service of profit. Malevich, in his Bauhaus book, *Die Gegenstandslose Welt* (*The Non-Objective World*),[9] edited by Gropius and Moholy-Nagy, and designed by the latter, had some scathing things to say about such practices, which were repugnant neither to Gropius nor Moholy. Small wonder that the editors, in a prefatory note which was purposely omitted from the English translation, expressed their disapproval of the position taken by the book.[10]

Malevich realized that although living conditions change, human beings do not, in any fundamental way; and art, the objectification of our profoundest feelings, also remains essentially the same.

"Practical life," like a homeless vagabond, forces its way into every artistic form and believes itself to be the genesis and reason for existence of this form. But the vagabond doesn't tarry long in one place and once he is gone (when to make art serve "practical purposes" no longer seems practical) the work recovers its full value.[11]

9 the pottery workshop

When the Bauhaus moved to Dessau, Gropius decided not to continue the pottery workshop even though it had been extremely successful in making contact with industry. His decision is hard to understand considering that Bauhaus ceramics came to be looked upon as one of the outstanding achievements of the school, second only to the products of the weaving studio.

The Bauhaus had a pottery shop in the first place because pottery was a traditional craft in the Weimar area. Physically the workshop was not a part of the Bauhaus proper. Gropius merely took over an existing pottery in Dornburg, a hill village some distance from Weimar, and placed Marcks, his third appointee, in charge of it. Marcks had worked with Gropius at the Werkbund Exposition in Cologne in 1914, and Gropius evidently felt that he could count on him to support his Bauhaus program: Muche speaks of him as "Gerhard Marcks, the sculptor, who best personified Gropius's conception of handicraft teaching and the role of workers in building construction."[1]

Osborn, reviewing the Bauhaus exhibition of 1923, wrote:

> At the same time, very able work is being done in ceramics, even though the solutions in this field are not so surprising. Marcks sits with his students in the isolation of Dornburg, up the Ilm River, and models pots, jugs, and vessels of all sorts with a lively feeling for form. New types have been created, not all such as to arouse enthusiasm, but many of them convincing and capable of further development. Connections have already been established with industry and these are to be further extended.[2]

Gerhard Marcks

Gerhard Marcks, tile for an oven in Potters House, Dornburg

Marcks was a kind of primitive with archaic leanings. He shared something of the native person's anthropocentric point of view, so that when he made a pot or inspired the making of a pot, it acquired a sort of personality, either human or animal, which our strictly functional utensils lack. There is an affinity with the objects made by the Mayas and Incas, those preeminent artist-potters. There are, to be sure, among the pieces turned out by Marcks and his students, no Indian warriors, ball players, or portrait heads, no pot-bellied dogs intended as containers for liquids. Nevertheless one can almost detect a transmuted Mayan warrior in Otto Lindig's water jug, and Theodor Bogler's "coffee machine" is surely an Inca chieftain in disguise. This is doubtless what Schreyer alludes to when he says:

The activity of the pottery shop was almost invisible to us in Weimar, for the pottery, with Gerhard Marcks as form master and Max Krehan as technical master, was located in Dornburg, between Jena and Apolda. We Weimar people recognized, always with astonishment, how Marcks, in his plastic works, succeeded in shaping earthen vessels for the hidden postures of the human soul. Under the eyes of such a master, even the plates, pots, and pitchers of the pottery became, as it were, living beings to which we had, so to speak, a personal relationship.[3]

Theo Bogler, plaster model of teapot designed for mass production

Gerhard Marcks, *Drummers*. Woodcut

Marcks was also a talented woodcut artist. The Bauhaus portfolio *Edda* [see page 110], was illustrated by ten of his works in this medium. As one might expect, his woodcuts share many of the characteristics of his sculpture. Ludwig Grote included more than a dozen of these, made by Marcks in his Weimar years, in his exhibition "The Painters at the Bauhaus," held in Munich in 1950. He wrote in the catalog that "The woodcuts by Marcks, which were printed in the Bauhaus print shop, were developed out of the technique and material and have a harshness and power peculiarly their own." The titles of the exhibited woodcuts suggest Marcks's concern with human activities and animals: *Cat Hunting a Bird; Witch; Ox-Driver; Goatherd; Jacob and Esau*. To Marcks, as to Schlemmer, man remained the measure of all things and the ever-recurring subject of his art. Perhaps the reason Gropius never restarted the pottery workshop lies in the character of his colleague. As Muche wrote of him:

I decided in favor of the Bauhaus, but really not so much because of its program as the people who were there, for Marcks, who was especially close to Gropius, also impressed me by his upright and clean-cut humanity. His art and his artistic convictions were different from ours, because we believed that in following the abstract path we were on the trail of the elements which would become decisive for the Bauhaus. Gerhard Marcks was the opposite pole to us. Who but he would have had a human constitution strong enough to enable him to persevere, alone and by himself, during the often heedless breaking out of the bondage of handicraft and the ardent turning to the development of new formal beauty through the functions of machines. . . . [4]

10 the weaving studio

The weaving studio, or *Weberei*, was the only workshop from van de Velde's Arts and Crafts School which survived World War One except for the bookbindery, which was the private undertaking of Otto Dorfner. The credit for preserving it goes to Helene Börner, who was a teacher of weaving under van de Velde. When the school closed, Börner continued the weaving studio under her own management but when the Bauhaus started she offered to provide the necessary looms. Thus work in the weaving studio began much earlier than that in the other workshops.

Klee was briefly made form master, then Muche succeeded him with Börner as its technical director. What became of her I cannot say. She did not, evidently, accompany the Bauhaus to Dessau because her Weimar student Gunta Stölzl became technical director there and later, form master. Muche had been Itten's assistant in the preliminary course before he became head of the weaving studio. Considering his experience, it would have been logical to turn the preliminary course over to him when Itten left the Bauhaus in 1922. In fact, he remained head of the *Weberei* until 1927, when circumstances compelled him to resign. Muche, was, with Moholy-Nagy, the youngest of the masters of the Weimar Bauhaus (both born in 1895). He had studied painting in Munich and later in Berlin where Herwarth Walden had given him four exhibitions between 1916 and 1919; he also taught in the Sturm art school between 1916 and the time he went to the Bauhaus.[1] Muche has this to say about his responsibilities as head of the Bauhaus weaving studio and his attitude toward actual participation in the work:

I lived and worked solely for the Bauhaus. I gave up everything else, even painting. As form master, I directed the weaving studio for years. I allowed myself to become entangled in the problems of buying and selling, workshop, industry, and production. My form vocabulary of abstract painting turned into fantasy and, in the hands of the woman weavers, into Gobelins, rugs, and stuffs.

I promised myself that I would never in my life with my own hand weave a single thread, tie a single knot, make a single textile design. I have kept my word. I wanted to be ready for painting because I knew that I would one day return to it.[2]

His dedication, however, helped make the weaving studio one of the successes of the 1923 exhibition. Writing about the exhibition, Osborn singles out for special commendation the creations of the Bauhaus weavers:

Georg Muche

Benita Otte, wall hanging

The handwork activity now (after Itten's departure) became more decisive, purer. An abundance of admirable works by the students demonstrates this. Above all in the textile art. That is the pride and the great success of the Bauhaus. A thorough acquaintance with materials and techniques forms the basis. Instruction is given in dyeing, in the treatment and potential uses of the various fabrics. And here, uninfluenced by any precedent, the modern way of devising and freely organizing decoration, of filling surfaces, achieves genuine triumphs. "Designs" play no role but, rather, the reality of the studio work. The Orient has taught us how the fantasy of the eye, in the case of textiles, operates most appropriately, but these experiences are applied here from a quite different point of view. In the single-family dwelling shown in the exhibition (we shall speak of this again), we are delighted by Agnes Roghé's rugs for the mistress's room—lovely, graceful textile compositions—and the one for the children's room by Benita Otte who, with unusual sensitivity and a naive approach, has created an article of use which charms one like a Klee rendered in fabric. Forgotten peasant techniques are here applied in original ways. Pieces woven tone in tone exploit the fascination of modern surface ornamentation.[3]

Four years after issuing his proclamation Gropius had not lost sight of his object of incorporating the fine arts into architecture. But craftsmanship had now given way to technology and the artist was to become an industrial designer. Greatly to his credit, Muche voiced his opposition to it publicly in a very perceptive article entitled "Bildende Kunst und Industrieform" ("Creative Art and Industrial Form") in which he exposed the fallacy in Gropius's new program:

Art cannot be bound by utility. Art and technology are not a new unity. They remain, in their creative values, essentially unlike each other. The boundaries of technology are determined by reality. Art cannot realize its value except by setting an ideal goal. Contrasts coincide in its domain. It comes into being remote from any technical connection in the Utopia of its own reality.

An artistic form element is a foreign body in an industrial product. A connection with technology makes art into a useless something or other—art which alone can afford a view beyond the boundaries of thought into the great limitless realm of creation.[4]

The article was tantamount to open revolt against Gropius's policies. It is significant, also, that his article appeared in the same issue of the school magazine in which the newly completed Bauhaus building in Dessau and two of the masters' houses were featured. In his discussion of architecture in the essay, he asserted that contemporary buildings, though having the appearance of modernity, were in fact technologically obsolete. He thus attacked, by implication, Gropius's vaunted new structures.

In 1924 Muche visited the United States, presumably to study

Georg Muche and Richard Paulick, prefabricated steel house, 1926

"American beauty" at first hand—the beauty of tall office buildings and other engineering structures such as grain elevators, factories, and bridges. Though a painter, Muche had already tried his hand at architecture. It was he who had designed the model house displayed at the 1923 Bauhaus exhibition in Weimar, as has been noted, (the famous House on the Horn). His observation of American technology inspired him to further architectural experimentation, for in 1926, with the help of the Bauhaus student Richard Paulick, he erected, at the edge of Gropius's housing settlement in Dessau-Törten, a dwelling of prefabricated steel beams and panels. This, he said, could readily be enlarged or decreased in size to bring it into conformity with the changing needs of the family. The house was a pioneering work, but despite these excursions into the realm of architecture, Muche was fundamentally a painter and remained so.

This was the beginning of the end of Muche's career as a Bauhaus teacher. He had evidently succeeded in alienating both his colleagues and the students at large. It was the defection of the weavers, however, that made his position untenable. Schlemmer, in a letter of April 16, 1926, to his wife, describes their efforts to oust Muche:

Klee will hold no classes this summer. The weaving studio, nevertheless, wishes to have "formal instruction." Thereupon Gropius requests Muche to give this to the weaving studio. The latter rejects Muche's instruction and—two flies with one swat—declares Muche to be "dispensable for the workshop." The memorandum was, it seems, in a very blunt tone. Gunta took no part in it; it stems from the weaving studio alone. The studio is extremely determined. It has the student body behind it and views this as a crucial test of whether or not it still has any voice at all.[5]

About two weeks later (May 1, 1926), Schlemmer, again writing to his wife, continues his account of the uprising in the weaving studio:

Meeting yesterday. Five minutes in advance of this a declaration of the student body, to the effect that it stood unanimously behind the cause of the weaving studio, was delivered. Muche wished to find out the attitude of the masters "before he came to a conclusion." Kandinsky, Moholy, Breuer condemned the form of the weaving studio attack. The others said nothing, at least nothing in Muche's favor.

Today the weaving studio and the student representatives are invited to meet with us and the impropriety of their action will be made clear to them. They are so furious that it probably will end very badly for Muche. Gropius remains very objective toward both sides.[6]

Paul Klee, attrib., tapestry, c. 1922

I do not know what the immediate cause of the student outburst against Muche was, but Gropius and the Bauhaus masters only gave him lukewarm support at best, and Muche found it expedient to resign, leaving the school about a year later.

Muche and Schlemmer remained in Germany during the hegemony of the Brown Terror, while most of the other Bauhaus masters left it. The mental torture inflicted by this sadistic regime killed Schlemmer. Muche somehow managed to survive and to pursue his work even at the end when his once-great nation was being blasted into ruins. His friend, Schreyer, had this to say of his remarkable tenacity of purpose:

> Alone of those in Germany, Georg Muche, who since 1938 has been director of a master class at the Textile Engineering School in Krefeld, has succeeded in continuing the practical and pedagogical work of the Bauhaus. He was now the leading artist of the international textile industry in Krefeld and, nevertheless, through his great fresco works, he also carried an architecture problem of the Bauhaus, the decorated wall, to an independent solution.[7]

Helene Jungnick, tapestry, 1921–1922

Gunta Stölzl, 1927

Muche's position was filled quite naturally by Stölzl. Stölzl had been a weaving student under him in Weimar. She distinguished herself there and had been made technical director of the studio when the Bauhaus moved to Dessau. Now she combined the two functions of technical master and form director, a position she retained until October 1931, when she was required to resign, under Mies van der Rohe's directorship of the school, for reasons that had no bearing on her competency as a weaver or teacher of weaving. Rather she was a sacrifice by a harassed Bauhaus director to the mean-minded prejudices of the parochial community in which the school had sought an uneasy and precarious refuge. As the Weimar debacle had already demonstrated and as subsequent events were here soon to prove, it is fruitless to attempt to appease an appetite which, once aroused, as Shakespeare said, "grows on that it feeds on."

Stölzl created many fine textiles in Dessau, and when design of fabric samples for machine duplication became the cardinal aim, she and her associates cheerfully reoriented their efforts to further this. Woven pictures gave way to yard goods, but yard goods so satisfying in their texture, pattern, and color that one could only rejoice that these beautiful textiles, instead of becoming the unique possessions of a privileged few, were now being made available to the public at large. Examples of Stölzl's "functional" fabrics may be seen in the Busch-Reisinger Museum at Harvard, and one may also study there textiles by Otti Berger, one of the most gifted of the Bauhaus weavers, who entered the school in 1927.

Agnes Roghe, yard goods, 1923-1924

Gunta Stölzl, tapestry, 1927–1928

When it became known that Stölzl was to leave the Bauhaus an entire issue of the school magazine, edited by Albers, was devoted to her and to the work done under her in the *Weberei*. The magazine, reflecting the prevailing stringency, was reduced to eight pages; but along with the text, they carried four fine photographs of textiles by Peterhans, head of the photographic department, one by my exuberant classmate Josef Tokayer, and another by Erich Consemüller, whom I can no longer recall.

Stölzl's article, bearing the title "Die Entwicklung der Bauhaus Weberei" ("The Development of the Bauhaus Weaving Studio"), one of several she wrote, describes the changing character of weaving at the Bauhaus:

Gunta Stölzl, Fabric for wall, with a mixture of cellophane

Weaving is an old craft which has evolved principles upon which even the mechanical loom must still build today. A high degree of handicraft dexterity, skill, and understanding must be acquired, and these are not, as in the case of tapestry, to be nourished by imaginative power or artistic feeling. The coming to grips with the flat loom had, as its natural result, the limitation of materials, the restriction of color, the tying of the form to the weaving process. The use of a material, on the other hand, limits and determines the choice of the elements. Conclusions about function are always dependent upon the conception of life and of living. In 1922–23 we had an idea of living fundamentally different from that of today. Our materials could then still be poems fraught with ideas, flowery decoration, personal experience! They also quickly met with approval outside the walls of the Bauhaus with the public at large. They were the most easily understood and, thanks to their subject matter, the most ingratiating of those wildly revolutionary Bauhaus creations.

Gradually a change took place. We began to sense how pretentious these independent, unique pieces were—tablecloths, curtains, wall coverings. The richness of color and form became too licentious for us; it did not adapt itself, it did not subordinate itself to living. We tried to become more simple, to discipline our means, to use these in a more straightforward and functional way. Thus we came to yard goods which could directly serve the room, the living problem. The watchword of the new epoch was "models for industry."[8]

It is my recollection that Anni Albers was in charge of the weaving studio for a while following the resignation of Stölzl, although Wingler says it was Berger who carried this responsibility. Whether Albers was acting head or not is a matter of little consequence because her tenure of that position could have been only brief. My chief reason for mentioning her here is that of all the Bauhaus weavers, she is best known in this country, having taught weaving for a number of years at Black Mountain College.

The legitimate inheritor of Stölzl's job as head of the weaving workshop was Reich, Mies's assistant for interior design at the Bauhaus. To the best of my knowledge, Reich was not a weaver but she was quite evidently conversant with textiles; and had apparently been a dress designer before she became associated with Mies in Berlin. A notice which appeared in the November 1925 issue of *Die Form* under the heading of "Communications of the Werkbund" supports this:

> *Courses in instruction.* Our member, Miss Lilly Reich, intends this winter to set up in her workshop a private course for a limited number of technically advanced women students. The course will deal chiefly with the execution of individual articles of clothing, but will also include dress pattern design, embroidery, etc. Interested persons can obtain further information by inquiring directly of Fräulein Lilly Reich, Frankfurt a. Main, Fahrgasse 43.[9]

Reich was the last director of the weaving studio. She assumed the position in January 1932, three months after Stölzl's departure. When the school was closed in Dessau in the fall of the same year, the city authorities permitted Mies to transport the looms to his new Bauhaus in Berlin. There Reich continued the work of the studio until the final shutdown of the institution in 1933.

11

the
stained
glass
workshop

It is easy to see why Gropius included a stained glass, or glass painting, workshop (*Glasmalerei*) in the Bauhaus at Weimar. In a program based upon the ideal of medieval handicraft and aiming at the creation of a great, complex structure which would embrace all of the arts, as did the Gothic cathedral, stained glass had an important place.

From its inception, the form master in the stained glass workshop was Klee. However, nearly all the extant work is by Albers. These works differ from Gothic stained glass windows in that they consist of nonfigurative patterns composed entirely of colored squares and rectangles. In them, the influence of the Bauhaus, or better, that of de Stijl, is evident, because Albers had not previously worked in this rigorously geometric manner. Luckier than Kandinsky with his mural painting, Albers had received a number of commissions for "painted" windows in Berlin and Leipzig. The designs he executed for the Ullstein printing establishment in the former city and the Grassi Museum in the latter consisted wholly of rigorously ordered horizontal bars of color, and these set the pattern for the flashed glass painting upon which he concentrated in Dessau. An art more sparing in its use of the pictorial means than this could hardly be imagined; yet, much later, Albers achieved a still further reduction in compositional elements in his disconcertingly simple paintings of superimposed squares. Albers, typically, confined himself to rigidly controlled arrangements of horizontal and vertical bars in the two colors which the technique afforded. He evidently loved glass and courted the discipline which its use imposed; he might well have continued working in that medium, if a number of his

Josef Albers (and the Bauhaus stained glass workshop), stained glass windows for the Ullstein factory

precious but fragile works had not been broken by careless handling in transit when he came to the United States in 1933.

I have encountered in my lifetime many things which were difficult to grasp. For the most part they are things which could be apprehended only through intuition. This, I suppose, is what made it so difficult for me to understand Klee when I was his student in Dessau. I took his course in aesthetic theory in my second, third, and fourth semesters at the Bauhaus. I am sure that my inadequate understanding of German, at the time, and particularly in the beginning, aggravated my difficulty. Klee's lectures in aesthetic theory were as baffling to me in their rigorous matter-of-factness as his paintings in their secret depth and mystery. He presented to us students, in a dry and unemotional manner, exercises of a mathematic-geometric nature, drawing diagrams on the blackboard with both hands, which he could use equally well. We copied these drawings and the illustration shows a page from the notebook I kept in his class. It was quite startling to have this to put before us in an aesthetics class. At the time, I didn't fathom Klee's purpose. Looking back on this now, I judge that he felt it desirable to

A page from the notebook kept by Howard Dearstyne in Klee's lecture course on aesthetic theory

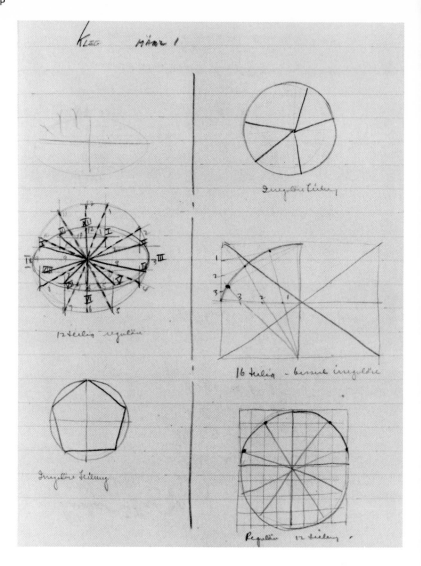

encourage us to temper our dreams with reason. In actuality, knowing that the intuitive aspects of art cannot be taught, Klee found
it useful to establish a rational groundwork upon which art could
be constructed. He explains this clearly enough in the *bauhaus*
article below.

Klee felt it necessary, especially during Hannes Meyer's directorship of the Bauhaus in Dessau, when logic and function were
heralded as the all-sufficient bases for the work at the school, to
point out the limitations of construction as an avenue to creation.
Since this statement reveals the depth of Klee's insight, I will present it in full:

We construct and construct yet, for all of that, intuition continues to
be a good thing. One can accomplish much without it, but not everything. One can work long and do many and diverse things, essential
things, but not everything.

Josef Albers, stained glass window in red

When intuition is combined with exact investigation, it accelerates the progress of this exact investigation so that it forges ahead. Exactness winged with intuition is, timewise, superior. Since exact investigation is, however, exact investigation, it can get along without intuition if the tempo doesn't count. It can do entirely without it. It can remain logical, can construct itself. It can boldly bridge the gap between one thing and another. In the ups and downs of events it can preserve an orderly mien.

There is also plenty of room for exact investigation in art, and the gateway to this has stood open for some time. What was already done for music before the end of the eighteenth century, has at least been started in the plastic arts. Mathematics and physics provide the instrument for this in the form of rules respecting limits and deviations. The necessity here of dealing, first of all, with functions and not with the finished form is a salutary thing. Algebraic, geometric problems, mechanical problems are training steps directed toward the essential, the functional, as opposed to the emotional. One learns to see behind the facade, to seize a thing by the roots. One learns to recognize what flows beneath it, learns the previous history of the visible. Learns to dig deeply, learns to uncover. Learns to verify, learns to analyze.

One learns to have little respect for the formalistic and learns to avoid taking over finished things. One learns the particular way of advancing in the direction of critical backward penetration, in the direction of earlier things out of which later things grow. One learns to rise early in order to become familiar with the current of history. One learns obligatory things on the way from the causative to the actual. Learns digestible things. Learns to organize movement in accordance with logical connections. Learns logic. Learns the organic.

The effect is a loosening-up of the tension in respect to the result. Nothing overstrained, tension the inside, behind, beneath. Means only innermost. Inwardness.

That is all very good and yet something is missing; in spite of everything, intuition cannot be replaced altogether. One documents, proves, supports, one constructs, one organizes—good things. But one doesn't succeed in totalizing.

One was industrious but genius is not hard work, as a very erroneous common saying goes. Genius is not even partly hard work just because men of genius have also been industrious. Genius is genius; it is a gift, without beginning and without end. It is generation.

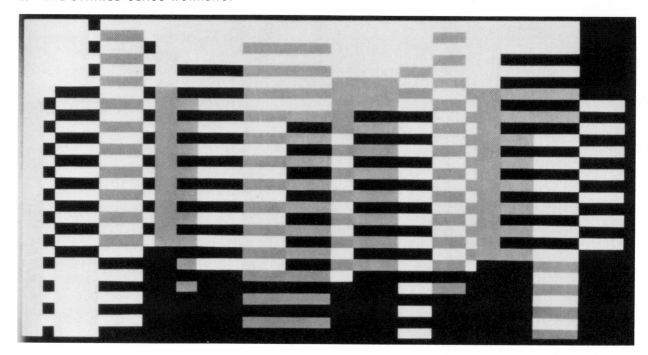

Josef Albers, flashed glass painting, 1928

One doesn't teach genius because it is not average, because it is a special case. It is hard to deal with the unexpected. And yet it is as leader, in person, always far in advance. It springs ahead in the same direction or in another direction. It is perhaps even now in a region about which one thinks little. For genius is, in respect to dogmas, very often heretical. Has no principle except itself.

Let the school remain silent about the concept of genius, with a conscious side glance, with tactful respect. Let it keep it as a secret in a locked room. Let it keep a secret which, if it were to issue from its concealment and being, perhaps, illogical and foolish, could mislead.

That would mean revolution. Bewilderment through surprise. Indignation and banishment—out with the synthesizer! Out with the totalizer! We are against it! And then the hail of abusive words— Romanticism! Cosmology! Mysticism!

So, finally one would have to summon a philosopher, a wise man! Or the Great Dead Ones (are they really dead?). One would have to hold classes on holidays, outside the school complex. Outside under trees, near animals, along streams. Or on mountains in the sea.

There would be problems to give, such as the construction of a mystery. *Sancta ratio chaotica!* Pedantic and ridiculous! Yet this would be the problem if construction is looked upon as everything.

But let us calm ourselves; construction doesn't mean everything. The fortunate thing is that we, through the cultivation of exactness, laid the foundation for a specific science of art which includes the big unknown X. Virtue out of necessity.

The school lives—long live the school![1]

Klee labored all his life to achieve a synthesis of the outer and the inner, of nature and human nature, of nature and art, of pictorial form and content. However, he became weary of combating Hannes Meyer's doctrine that construction is the sum of everything and accepted a professorship at the Academy in Düsseldorf in 1931, the year after he wrote the above piece. I recall saying to my socialist fellow-student Decker, a disciple of Meyer's, when we in Dessau learned of Klee's impending departure, "You people have driven Paul Klee away with your barren functionalism," but he merely shrugged off the accusation. And then, in 1933, almost, as it were, in fulfillment of his prophecy, came the revolution, the indignation, the hail of words of abuse, and Klee was banished to his native Switzerland.*

During his ten years of teaching at the Bauhaus in Weimar and Dessau Klee was forced to clarify his own ideas on art, to enable him to communicate with his students, and, for that matter, with the public.[2]

One is forced to draw upon a whole bookshelf of works in order to explain Klee and his teaching.[3] I sometimes wish he had remained as transparent and uncomplicated an artist as gentle old Feininger, who did not, like Klee, go seeking out the origin of things. Though I had taken a number of art courses before going to Germany, I was unprepared for this kind of search for the ultimate. One of Klee's students, a contemporary of mine at the Bauhaus, understood him better:

At the Bauhaus in Dessau, the three painters, Feininger, Kandinsky, and Klee, occupied an entirely different position from the one I had expected. . . .

Klee gave instruction and conducted painting classes as did Kandinsky; but he was neither hated nor attacked. He lived like a strange being in the rationalistic and political world of the Haus. His withdrawal was respected.

To outward appearances Klee's teaching was quiet, almost silent. He would enter the room and immediately start to talk or illustrate

*Finding much in Klee's work to which they could object, upon their assumption of power in 1933, the National Socialists forced him to flee Germany. Klee took up residence in his native Switzerland.

Paul Klee, *Afraid on the Beach*, 1929. Pen

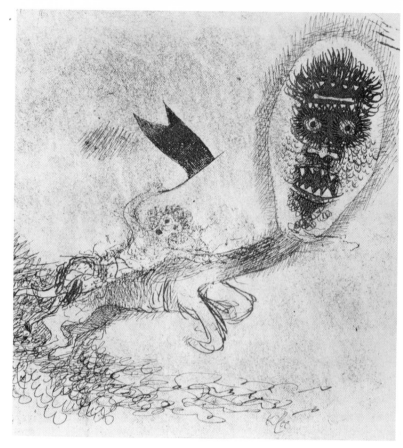

Paul Klee, *Demonic Ride*, 1925. Pen

on the blackboard. Often with both hands at once. His reserve and remoteness tended to accentuate the impact of his speaking. In case of some disturbance, he could become quite provoked, even angry.

In his course Klee presented a genesis of forms and colors. The ideas he developed were so general and basic that, beyond being fundamentals for prospective painters, they also served as foundations for students from every department of the Haus.

Life is grasped in its origin and its survival through change. The potentialities and powers of nature are taken into account, also the means conceived by man to exploit the given facts of nature. From the point, a concept, an intangible, motion or expansion creates the relative shape of a visible point, namely, the line and plane. The fundamental geometrical and free forms are analyzed, their nature examined. The hidden powers of forms are recognized, their possibilities are developed, the combination of forms into rhythmic groupings, into structures, is made clear in the projected world of geometry as well as in the free forms of nature. All powerful is the principle of economy, i.e., the minimum but most lucid application of means for the achievement of the maximum results. Contact with nature must be maintained, but our interests no longer lie in imitation. We now work with an understanding of nature, her laws; we create like nature. Anything created by man, even if it be purely imagined, nonmaterial, is nevertheless subject to laws identical with or similar to those developed by nature. Only in this way can a creation today remain "human," only so does it not lose itself in inhuman, unemotional and dead speculations.

As one entered, the house was very quiet. In contrast to other masters of the Bauhaus, old furniture, highly polished and seemingly inherited, was very much in evidence. The largest wall in the studio was painted black and was hung with new and half finished paintings. The room was arranged for students. Chairs stood in a semicircle and in the center of it, in front of two or three easels was an old rocker. We sat behind Klee who quietly swayed in his rocking chair. Our pictures completed during the week stood on the easels. As a matter of principle we painted at home, independent of instruction. Each brought his pictures to painting class for discussion.

Klee inspected the paintings in perfect silence. Then he suddenly started to talk, not about the excellencies or deficiencies of a work, but about general problems of painting which he saw in our canvases. He developed an exhaustive analysis and demonstrated things which our talent created subconsciously and brought clarity into the world of our imagination. He often taught us to see our paintings for the first time. Criticism of a work was latently present in these remarks but it was rarely stated openly and as a result, was sensed that much more intensely.

After these discourses, at times giving the effect of monologues, we continued to talk and smoke around a big, gray, glazed clay pot which was placed in the circle. The relationship between Klee and his students is more precisely given in a remark he once laughingly made: that we really should not be paying tuition, but that he, the teacher, should be paying us for he felt that the stimulation he received from us was far in excess of that which he gave.[4]

Paul Klee

Another article was written by my Bauhaus friend and fellow-student, Hertel, as a tribute to Klee as he was about to leave Dessau for Düsseldorf:

The pedagogic work of Paul Klee at the Bauhaus consisted in the *Demonstration of his Theory of Forms* [in the second and third semesters] and in the *Analysis of Pictures* [in the painting class].

Klee's theory of forms, which continues to be further developed and which exercises an ever greater influence on his creative work, is as

Paul Klee, *Historic Scene*, 1930. Pen

many-sided and as endless as life itself. It is the result of a rich, creative life. Like a magician, as it were, with glance, word and gesture—utilizing all three expressive possibilities with equal intensity—he transformed, for us, the unreal into the real, the irrational into the rational. Things which existed only in feeling became graphically determinable. We learned to see that the primary forming [*Gestaltung*] of the plane [with the ideal means] is not a matter of the simplest deliberation but, rather, of the deepest experience. We saw the genesis of forms which were, at one and the same time, both real and fantastic to an unprecedented degree. We learned to draw functional sketches for creation [*Gestaltung*].

Klee's methodology was exactly scientific but, at the same time, truly Klee-like, touching at once "on the nearest" and "on the farthest." This did not prevent him, when he deemed it necessary, from making side springs and taking bypaths—for us, in the beginning, these seemed roundabout—in order to reveal to us most clearly the diversity of the life of forms.

Klee's pedagogy was actually never instruction in the most primitive sense, whereby the "teacher" lectured and the "student" learned. The full extent of this structure of ideas and experiences, which is the systematized image of life in its entire vastness, was grasped only by those who were able to share the feelings and experiences.

In the beginning it was not always easy to follow him with understanding. Yet we gradually came to realize that this person here— Klee—was talking to us about life. We were permitted, with him, to experience the development of human existence in its entire capriciousness. We raced with him through tens of millenia. Klee made us again participants in primordial experiences which, until then, had only been mechanically drilled into us. Was it a "pre-creation festival" [as a charming drawing of Klee's of 1914 is called] which he prepared for us? There was nothing that he did not mention.

Klee likewise had his method of procedure in the painting class, yet he was never bound by this. Most often he started by discussing the question of format. From there, he proceeded to the real scene of

Josef Albers (and the Bauhaus stained glass workshop), stained glass window in the house of Dr. Otte in Berlin

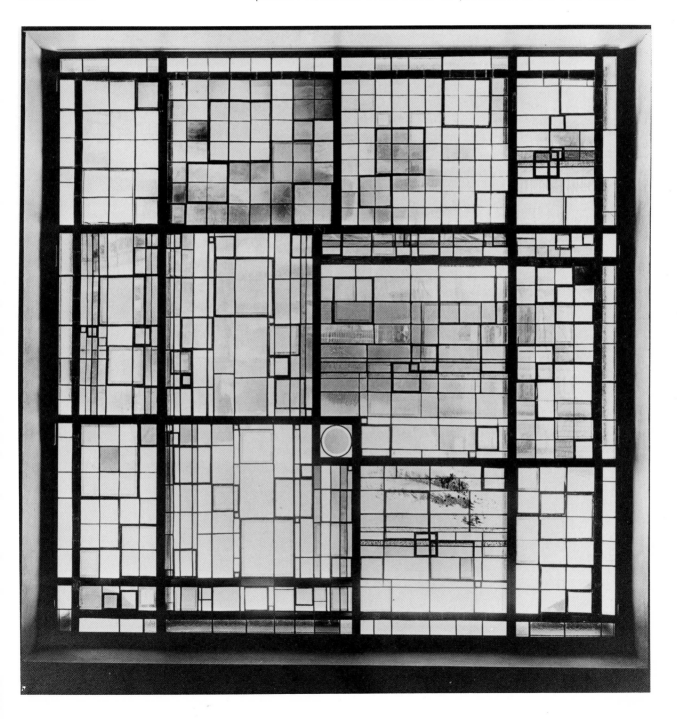

the action and then to the action itself, to that which took place on the scene. Until then, the discussion had been purely formal. Now the expressive values of the forms came into their own. It was almost unbelievable and only to be explained as intuition, the way Klee taught the painters actually to see their pictures for the first time. Klee examined the pictures for a short while and then began to talk, pausing briefly from time to time—"creative pauses"—and speaking like a seer. He saw everything. And he told us everything. The question is, did we understand everything?

These formal-optical investigations open up to our consciousness new, broad fields. Things of whose existence we were not even aware enter our consciousness and produce their effect. Ancient experiences which, through thousands of years of habit, had been forgotten, become, once more, new, powerful experiences and penetrate to the depth of our consciousness and move us. Empty words, blunted conceptions again become living experience. Areas of knowledge which, until now, had been the exclusive domain of the mind, are now experienced through the senses. Klee thus pointed out to us ways into the future (but not "seductive goals," to which no ways lead) and, consequently, he accomplished pioneer work. He extended and deepened our consciousness and the circle of our experience. . . . He clarified elementary things in order to arrive at life-representing, conscious creation.[5]

There are two prerequisites for success in translating works from the German, or, for that matter, any other foreign tongue. First, one must understand what is being said in the original text; and second, one must have a respectable command of the language into which the work is being rendered. In the case of Hertel's article on Klee, it is not his handling of German which makes the translation difficult but, rather, the subject he is discussing, Klee's philosphy. The concepts are elusive and hard to understand. Klee made a valiant attempt to elucidate shadowy things, but such things cannot readily be clarified. He was one of the genuinely great artists of this period, perhaps of all time.

12

**the
wall-painting
workshop**

The wall-painting workshop (*Wandmalerei*) was set up in 1920 with Schlemmer as form master. When the workshops were reorganized in 1922, Kandinsky was invited to take it over. Thus, it was not until April 1924 that the program for the workshop was drawn up and submitted to the Bauhaus faculty.

Kandinsky was appointed form master of the *Wandmalerei* as the next best way of utilizing the talents of a painter in a school which frowned upon easel painting and had no studio for it. The mural paintings executed by the students on the wall of the Weimar Bauhaus were, as far as they have been recorded, all abstracts, which suggests that Kandinsky's influence was very strong. Moholy-Nagy, an abstractionist of the El Lissitzky school, had arrived at the Bauhaus by this time and doubtless too made his influence felt because the murals seem to lean toward Russian constructivism.

The sole example of mural work by Kandinsky which I have seen was in the small music room which he did for the Berlin Building Exposition of 1931. He covered the three walls of the room (the fourth was left open) with glazed ceramic tile bearing the abstract forms of his geometric period. Kandinsky was a great lover of music, so it was appropriate for him to do a music room, although I wondered at the time about the acoustical properties of tile sheathing. His ceramic murals hung there as a kind of protest against the blank, undecorated walls of the other rooms in the exhibition. The starkness of these was unrelieved except for a sprinkling of framed pictures, curtains, rugs, and upholstery materials by means of which the architects sought to alleviate the effect of their white plastered interiors. The music room is listed in the catalog of the 1931 Berlin Building Exhibition (page 170). Instead of a description of the project such as those which accompany the listings of most of the other architectural works in the show, there appears an unsigned essay (surely written by Kandinsky) explaining the function served by paintings in buildings:

In the course of the great "revision" of building materials, mural painting was thrown overboard as an unessential (i.e., harmful) appendage. The barren wall appeared to be a definitive solution of the wall treatment of rooms of every kind. This solution stems, basically, from a superficial attitude toward painting which, supposedly, has served and can serve no other purpose except that of ornamentation. A viewpoint such as this took only the external aspect of painting into consideration.

In reality, however, painting is not decoration but, rather, a kind of tuning fork. Rooms in which numbers of persons are to assemble for some *inner* purpose, which, that is, are not constantly used and by the same people, must have the special capacity for "attuning" these people inwardly for this purpose, of influencing them, so to speak, "purposefully." Painting is able to do this. It is almost superfluous, in this connection, to mention that the ordinary run of living rooms cannot tolerate "fixed" painting. One of the essential aspects of such rooms is the possibility which they offer of changing and varying them.[1]

Wassily Kandinsky at work

Kandinsky was a profound student of color and realized that if color was to be applied to architecture, its physical characteristics had to be understood and the techniques of its application mastered. This much was fundamental, the least one had to learn. Being a painter who exploited the psychological potentialities of the medium, he was fully aware of what color could do to architecture. He knew that it could reinforce form and alter it. His proposal to the Bauhaus faculty included the study of both the physical properties of color and its psychological ramifications:

The wall-painting workshop is distinguished from all the other workshops of the Bauhaus by the fact that one cannot, with color alone, produce any objects.

Of the various powers possessed by color, the one which most concerns the Bauhaus is that which enables color to change a given form, so that out of the given form another arises.

Two basic cases are possible here:

1. The concurrence of the color with the given form, whereby the effect of this form is enhanced so that a new form is created, and
2. The conflict of the color with the given form, whereby this is transmuted.

One or other of these two powers must necessarily be employed whenever color is applied to form.

The power likewise possessed by color to shape a given space in these and other ways is one of the most important things to be taken into account in coping with the problems of the Bauhaus.

This especially complex and difficult problem can only then be solved to some extent when a systematic program is introduced into the wall-painting workshop. Two separate problems which encompass the nature of color in the sense used in the wall-painting workshop are relevant here:

1. The chemical-physical properties of color—its material substance.
2. The psychological characteristics of color—its creative powers.

Two kinds of problems are bound up with those two points:

1. Technical problems—the use of different physical properties, various pigments and vehicles, application of color.
2. Speculative experimental projects of an analytic and compositional nature—design and creative development of surfaces and space treatment.[2]

Herbert Bayer (left wall) and Rudolf Paris (right wall), murals in the wallpainting workshop of the Bauhaus, Weimar

Nothing outstanding took place in the Weimar *Wandmalerei*. A few odd jobs were undertaken, such as painting the interior of the theater in nearby Jena, painting the rooms of the House on the Horn for the exhibition of 1923, and some other things; but by and large the workshop was a financial disappointment.

Wall-painting during the early years of the Bauhaus was predominantly picture painting. (A parallel can be drawn here between the character of the work in the wall-painting workshop and that done in the weaving studio: the weavers, at that time, were making pictures in cloth.) In Dessau, however, both paint and textiles surrendered their independence and came to play an ancillary role in architecture, contributing chiefly the humanizing influence of texture and color to the total work. The person entrusted with carrying out Kandinsky's proposed program was Hinnerk Scheper, a wall-painting student of Kandinsky's in Weimar. He was appointed to direct the workshop in Dessau in 1925.

Scheper had already been trained in wall-painting at the Arts and Crafts Schools of both Düsseldorf and Bremen before he entered the Weimar Bauhaus in 1919, and he continued his wall-painting studies there.

With the exception of a year and a half (1929–1931) which he spent in Moscow as a consultant to the Soviet government in the use of color in architecture, Scheper directed the *Wandmalerei* until the final dissolution of the Bauhaus in Berlin in 1933. He was no writer like Kandinsky; indeed he left behind very little in the way of quotable material. I do recall his telling us, after his return from Russia, how he had been called upon to refurbish Stalin's apartment in Moscow. In those days (the late twenties and early thirties), the Russian Communists imported many German architects and planners to assist them in the design of new buildings and laying out new cities. The fact that they put up so many dryly unadorned, strictly functional structures at that time is one of the reasons why the Nazis later came to stigmatize anything resembling these and, indeed, all the architecture of the so-called "international style," as "communist." Stalin changed the Soviet image. He decided that what the people needed was monumental buildings to impress them with the glory and might of the new order. He reintroduced classic colonnades, pediments, and other trappings of the architecture of the czars. Scheper, entrusted with the redecoration of Stalin's dwelling, had an enviable opportunity to observe the kind of furnishings, knickknacks, and bric-a-brac that appealed to Stalin's crude sensibilities. He told us with a grin that the latter's taste was that of a *petit bourgeois*.

Scheper was an altogether good-willed and amiable person, around whom no controversies raged such as those stirred up by more contentious men, Itten, van Doesburg, and Hannes Meyer. A complete master of his craft of wall painting, his quiet demeanor helped to convey this to his students. No clique of malcontents

Hinnerk Scheper, 1928

Josef Maltan and Alfred Arndt mural in the workshop building of the Bauhaus, Weimar

ever raised a cry demanding that "Scheper must go," as they did (in Dessau) in the case of Muche. Scheper was also immune from such attacks because the things he taught were not the subject of dispute. One could, if so inclined, accuse Albers and Kandinsky of "playing around" with form and color (Klee's retiring presence more or less exempted him from such reproaches). To some, art was an immoral occupation in a time of stringency such as Germany was passing through. In Scheper's case, though, no stigma was attached to the use of color in buildings, paint being viewed as a necessity.

Scheper's curriculum in the wall-painting laboratory was full of things such as "the technical composition of the painting ground," "the study of all known painting techniques of the past," "the fundamental principles of color harmony," "the practical application of the new techniques discovered in the experimental workshop," "projects for color schemes for given architectural models, plans, and elevations," "poster work," "knowledge of tools, erection of scaffolding, the making of stencils and cartoons, working drawings, perspectives, models," and "taking dimensions, preparing estimates, bookkeeping." He carried fully to realization the program which Kandinsky proposed. It should be emphasized that this program embraced what should have been the real objective of the teaching: not to make mural painters of the students but to acquaint them with the appropriate uses of flat color in architecture.

Even though I didn't absorb all this, I am sure I must have learned much about color under Scheper's guidance. The most poignant recollection I have of my activity in the wall-painting workshop centers about trying my hand at the application of plaster to one of the shop walls. Scheper neglected to warn his protégés of the dermatological dangers of working with wall-finishing materials, so I have reason to lay my subsequent discomfort at his door. I contracted a case of eczema from contact with the plaster and had to wear white cotton gloves over well-salved hands, which set me apart from my less elegantly dressed Bauhaus friends for a considerable period.[3]

Scheper and his students were fortunate enough to have the opportunity of putting their understanding of paint techniques and color to the test on actual building projects. Gropius's great new Bauhaus building and the four nearby masters' houses were to be painted. The job, logically enough, was turned over to the *Wandmalerei*. The stucco exteriors of these buildings were not the subject of any unusual psychological or aesthetic experimentation. Following the mode which prevailed in the modern architecture of that day, they were painted almost entirely in the flat white. Gropius and Scheper preferred to preserve the boxlike character of the structures by painting their walls a uniform color. The interior of the Bauhaus building was likewise done largely in blank white,

Wallpainting workshop of the Bauhaus, Dessau. Werner Drewes (center), Hermann Fishcher (right), person in foreground not identified

though some unobtrusive departures from the prevailing monotone were permitted in the public areas—entrance hall, auditorium, and cafeteria.

The color treatment of the interiors of the masters' houses was left to the discretion of the occupants; here some color experimentation was attempted by Breuer and Moholy-Nagy, assisted by the students of the wall-painting workshop.

Scheper and his students also did painting jobs for outside clients. They were called upon to "decorate" several public buildings in Dessau, the *Folkwang* Museum in Essen, a hospital in Münster, the Institute for Vibration Research (*Schwingungsforschung*) in Berlin, and a number of other structures. These projects were executed in blank color; mural painting was excluded from the instruction and practice of the *Wandmalerei* under Scheper in Dessau.

The most notable achievement of the workshop was the development of a line of Bauhaus wallpapers. The method of finishing a plaster wall by covering it with patterned paper rather than paint had not been taken into consideration in the *Wandmalerei* until the Rasch wallpaper firm in Bramsche, near Osnabrück, brought the subject up and offered the Bauhaus a contract for the design of wallpapers suitable for modern use. The covering of a wall with some decorative material other than paint was nothing new; the creation of wallpaper at the Bauhaus was. It was looked upon as a legitimate project, and we set ourselves to work on it. (Albers, it will be remembered, while teaching his famous preliminary course, served, at that time, as form master of the cabinetmaking shop where I was working. He took a group of us incipient wallpaper designers on a field trip to a wallpaper factory in the Dessau area in order to familiarize us with the method of manufacture of the material.)

I went about carving some more-or-less abstract shapes in pieces of linoleum and making prints from these in various colors. I was enthusiastic about my designs until Hannes Meyer, director of the Bauhaus at the time, examined them and remarked sarcastically that they looked like something an American might be expected to do. A few days later, I happened to turn one of these pieces of linoleum over and discovered that the fiber network of the burlap backing formed a satisfying texture. I pointed this out to a fellow student, saying that it might make a suitable wallpaper pattern. Taking this cue, he made an impression from the back of the piece of linoleum and turned it in as his idea. Subsequently, this became one of the designs in the Bauhaus wallpaper line. To this day, I am a little incensed that I never received my proper share of glory from this. In any event, the royalties made their way into the coffers of the Bauhaus.

Arndt, like Scheper a former student at the Weimar Bauhaus, directed the wall-painting workshop during the latter's absence in Russia and was initially in charge of the big wallpaper operation. Scheper might have been expected to urge the use of flat colors in these papers. But he recognized that such wallpaper is easily soiled; and that if this had been what the Rasch people wanted, they would have had no need to ask the Bauhaus to assist them. Obviously they didn't want blank paper, and just as obviously, they weren't looking for elaborate, pronounced designs. The market was already glutted with these. What they wanted were papers with simple, unobtrusive patterns which, when on the wall, were scarcely apparent to the casual glance but nevertheless lent the papered surface textural warmth and richness.

We had a few wallpapers in those days, such as our oatmeal paper and, for that matter, our ceiling papers, which were intended to give some life to the ceiling plane without attracting undue attention to themselves. These papers served a purpose similar to that of the Bauhaus papers. But one had to comb the sample books then, as today, to find anything reasonably acceptable. That wallpapers of the Bauhaus sort were long overdue was indicated by the fact that they were an immediate success. The Rasch Brothers sold some three million rolls of the various patterns and colors during the year they first appeared on the market. In fact, since they were free of stylistic implications, Rasch wallpapers were the only Bauhaus product that weathered Nazi domination and the war. The Rasch people must have realized large profits from the sale of these wallpapers, and they acknowledged their indebtedness to the Bauhaus in 1962 by underwriting the publication of Wingler's book about the school. Much credit is due this enlightened firm for its sponsorship of the Bauhaus wallpapers and for enabling Wingler to bring out his valuable work.

As a matter of personal interest rather than historic importance, Scheper came to my rescue in the summer of 1932. The occasion was the big do-or-die exhibition which was to be reviewed by the Nazi emissary, Paul Schultze-Naumburg, to determine the fate of the Dessau Bauhaus.* Mies van der Rohe, then director, was naturally intent upon putting the school's best foot forward in this critical situation, so he carefully selected the work to be shown. I had just completed my *Diplomarbeit* (thesis project), a restaurant pavilion designed for a lakeshore site near Dessau, and Mies had earmarked it for exhibition. I drew an elevation of the building on watercolor paper with the intention of rendering it in color. Mies, knowing that I was no renderer, suggested that I get Scheper to do it for me. When I put the proposition to Scheper, that long-suffering, helpful man dropped his own work to make a tempera rendering of my project. The rendering did nothing toward saving the Bauhaus, for the Bauhaus could not have been saved at that juncture by the coöperation of Titian himself. But I will always be grateful to the maker of it. I am proud, furthermore, still to possess an architectural plate representing the collaboration of Scheper and myself.

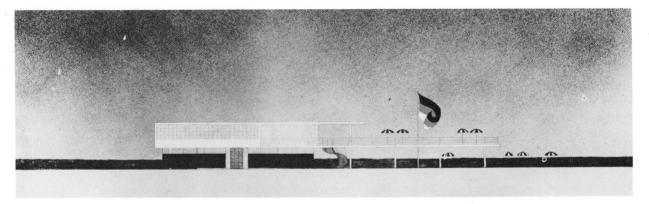

On a last note, while no mural painting was done by the students in Dessau, many of the students tried their hand at easel painting since the urge to paint pictures was not easily suppressed among the Bauhaus people. Easel painting, always an extracurricular activity at the Bauhaus, enjoyed a kind of unofficial sanction in Dessau, where Kandinsky and Klee held weekly painting classes in which they criticized the canvases brought in by the not-to-be-intimidated student painters. Thus, however much Gropius excoriated easel painting, Hannes Meyer ridiculed it, and Mies van der Rohe ignored it, it continued to flourish to the bitter end.

Howard Dearstyne, Bauhaus thesis project, beach house with club facilities, 1932. Rendered by Hinnerk Scheper

*In 1928 Paul Schultze-Naumburg, an architect, landscape architect, and critic, published *Kunst und Rasse*, one of the more influential treatises of this time to identify art with theories of racial supremacy. The appeal of Schultze-Naumburg's argument for purposes of National Socialist propaganda was immediate and lasting.

kandinsky

Mies van der Rohe once said to me of Kandinsky, "Er ist ein hoch-intelligenter Mensch." Literally translated, this means, "He is a highly intelligent person," but the English version lacks the impact of the German. What Mies intended to say was that Kandinsky was "a supremely intelligent person." I heartily agreed with this; I have never encountered an individual of deeper insight than Kandinsky. I was, indeed, lucky to have been accepted by him and to have been, as it were, sponsored by him. I took his course in aesthetic theory in the winter of 1928–1929, my very first semester at the school, and attended his weekly painting class for the subsequent seven semesters of my sojourn in Dessau. I continued to attend his *Malklasse* at the Bauhaus in Berlin.

Kandinsky's course in analytic drawing was not so easy to understand, now that I look back upon it. According to a Dessau reporter, who signed himself "*p*," Kandinsky, in his "Jubilee" lecture, said that the course had, as its purpose, to teach the students to experience objects as living beings, a not unreasonable project in his view since, to him, everything about us was alive. But he was speaking figuratively. What he meant was that we were to observe the forces, the stresses, the tensions between objects and groups of objects. To him each complex, stripped of its objective connotations, consisted of a system of forces, attracting, repelling, moving in various directions or remaining immobile, a system which, in a work of art, had to be in equilibrium. In this sense, the elements constituting such a complex were alive, since movement and the power to exert force and to resist force were attributes of living things.

Strictly speaking, of course, inanimate objects, "dead" things, live only in our imagination. But, in the anthropocentric realm of art, this ostensible life is tantamount to life itself. What counts is not what is, but what seems to be. Art, Kandinsky believed, could be looked upon as a visual deception, a sort of legerdemain perpetrated to make people see into things that do not exist, that intangible, invisible things, the things of the spirit, are, or should be, more important to human beings than the earth, the sea, the sky, and all that in them is.

As with Klee's teaching, Kandinsky's was a distillation of his own creative activity. In his paintings he cast aside the irrelevant baggage of the objective world and composed with essences, with forms which were the visual symbols of forces. He believed, as I do, that such intrapictorial contests between attracting and repelling energies, unadulterated by associational considerations, can have a deeply moving effect.

I still possess four plates, executed in black ink and watercolor, which I made in Kandinsky's class in analytic drawing. These are

Wassily Kandinsky, 1938

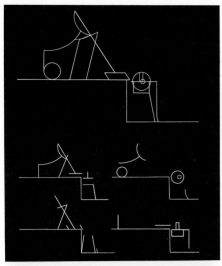

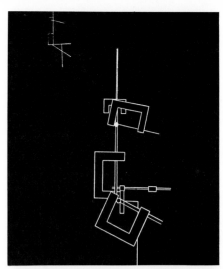

Top left Kandinsky course in analytical drawing. total subject. *Below* four different constructive variations obtained by eliminating individual parts

Top right Kandinsky course in analytical drawing. *Beginning of Problem*. Relationship of similar individual objects in large format. *Above left* R. L. Kukowa, concise drawing of construction

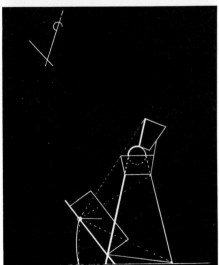

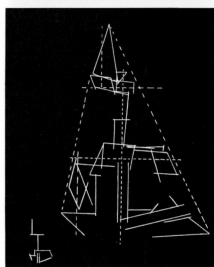

Bottom left Kandinsky course in analytical drawing. *Stage 2*. Objects recognizable, chief tensions indicated by color, important stresses by heavier lines. Starting point of constructive art. *Above left* Erich Fritzsche, abbreviated diagram.

Bottom right Kandinsky course in analytical drawing. *Stage 3*. Objects completely translated into energy tensions. Complicated construction with displacement of individual parts, major construction indicated by dotted lines. *Below left* Fritz Fiszmer, diagram.

abstractions, so-called, or, more accurately, simplified representations of groups of objects selected from the equipment of the furniture workshop and set together in more or less balanced arrangements. These drawings are not without merit, but they should be classified as exercises rather than incipient art works.

Kandinsky described his analytic drawing course as follows. The four drawings to which he refers, made by four different students, accompany his text and, since they were chosen by him, doubtless accurately reflect the objectives of the various phases of the problems presented by him.

The students set up the still lifes themselves, right from the beginning. The first problems in analytic drawing are:

1. The subordination of the total complex to a simple, large form which must be exactly drawn within limits established by the student himself.

2. [Delineation of] the form character of individual parts of the still life, viewed by themselves and in relationship to the others.
3. Representation of the total composition in the most concise possible diagrammatic form. (See illustration 2.)

Gradual transition to the second stage of the problems which, briefly stated, consist of the following:

1. Exposure of the forces discovered in the composition and their representation by linear forms.
2. Emphasis of the main forces by broader lines or, later, colors.
3. Indication of the constructive network with the starting point or focus (dotted lines). (See illustration 4—objects clearly indicated: saw, grindstone, pail.)

Third stage:

1. The objects are viewed exclusively as energy-tensions and the composition is restricted to complexes of lines.
2. Diversity of compositional possibilities: clear and veiled construction. (See illustration 3.)
3. Exercises in the greatest possible simplification of the total complex and of the individual forces—brief, exact expression.

The instruction and its methods are outlined in these brief words only in a very general way. More possibilities and requirements than have been touched upon here are considered in many individual problems. For example, can the main subject be investigated on the basis of very diverse subordinate forces—significance of individual elements with their weight, center, form character, etc. (See illustration 1. Above is the total subject and below, four different constructive accentuations.)

The following remains to be noted:

1. The drawing instruction at the Bauhaus is training in observation, exact seeing, and exact delineation, not of the external appearance of an object but of its constructive elements, their law-abiding forces-tensions, which can be discovered in given objects and their law-abiding construction. It is training in clear observation and clear reproduction of relationships, in the case of which two-dimensional phenomena become an introductory step to the spatial.
2. The drawing instruction is founded upon a method similar to that in the other branches of my teaching and which, in my opinion, should be the method in all other areas (See my article, "Kunstpädagogik," in this issue.)[4]

I must confess that I found Klee's exposition of the nature of the work in his analytic drawing class difficult to understand. Undoubtedly, as Herbert Read says of Klee's Jena lecture,[5] it is not any inadequacy in the presentation which makes the ideas hard to grasp but, rather, the intrinsic difficulty of the subject itself. Kandinsky tried to teach us to look beneath the surface of the visual world, in order to uncover those essences which constitute the immaterial but absolute reality which is the province of art.

Schreyer, in his book *Erinnerungen an Sturm und Bauhaus* quotes Kandinsky as having said, in a conversation with him:

> I see the kingdom of the spirit moving upward in the light and I will proclaim it, as far as I can, with my art. I therefore paint no pictures of Christ; I don't paint the Son of Man, who can be represented in human form. The Holy Ghost cannot be portrayed objectively but only nonobjectively. That is my aim; to proclaim the light of the Light, the flowing light of the Godhead, the Holy Ghost. . . .[6]

Wassily Kandinsky. Woodcut

I am suspicious of the authenticity of Schreyer's reports considering that he quotes, verbatim, conversations which he allegedly held with various people thirty-some years before his book was written. I look upon his book as generally unreliable, but have to confess that his quotation of Kandinsky's religious views is in substantial accord with the latter's own statement of these, except that Kandinsky would never have used the grandiloquent language attributed to him. Kandinsky set out his thoughts in his autobiography, *Rückblick (Looking Backward)*. I have yet to read anywhere so profound and so beautiful a statement of the relation of art to religion as he presented in his book.

Kandinsky wrote *Rückblick* for the catalog of an exhibition of his work which was held in the Sturm Gallery in Berlin in 1913. In it he tells of his early life and of the experiences which shaped his personality. The part which concerned me however, falls at the end of the book and has to do with the relationship of art and religion. I noted with interest that Hilberseimer, that hard-shelled unbeliever, had underlined many of the passages in the copy he gave to me and from which I quote:

> Art is in many ways similar to religion. Its development does not consist in new discoveries which cancel the old truths and stamp them as erroneous (as, apparently, happens in science). Its evolution takes place through sudden flashes, resembling lightning, in explosions which, like fireworks, burst in the heavens, strewing about them whole "bouquets" of variegated stars. These flashes reveal, with brilliant light, new perspectives, new truths which are basically nothing

other than the organic development, the organic further growth of earlier wisdom, which is not annulled by them but which, rather, as wisdom and truth, continues to live and create. The trunk of the tree is not rendered superfluous by this new branch. Would the New Testament have been possible without the Old? Is it conceivable that we would now stand on the threshold of the "third" revelation if it had not been for the second? It is a ramification of the original tree trunk, in which "everything begins." And this branching out, the further growth and the further complication which often cause perplexity and despair, are stages necessary to the attainment of the mighty crown; the steps which, in the last analysis, shape the green tree.

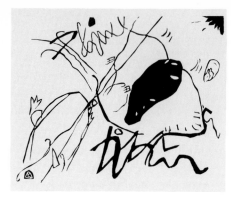

Wassily Kandinsky. Woodcut

Christ, by his own words, did not come in order to overthrow the old law. When He said: "It was said to you . . . and I say to you . . . " He thereby transmitted the old material law in the form of his spiritualized law: the people of His time, in contrast to the people of the time of Moses, had become capable of understanding and experiencing the laws, "thou shalt not kill," "be not immodest" not only in the direct, material sense but also in the abstract sense of sins conjured up.

The value of fact, in Christ's scales, is placed not on the external, hard act but, rather, on an inner, flexible one. Here lies the root of the further revaluation of values which, without interruption, and even today, continues slowly to be fruitful and which, at the same time, is the root of the inwardness that we are also gradually achieving in the realm of art. In our time, in a strongly revolutionary form. I have finally, in this way, reached the point where I have come to feel nonobjective painting to be not a negation of the entire earlier art but, rather, an extraordinarily important, fundamental division of the single old trunk into two main branches, the ramification of which is indispensable to the creation of the crown of the green tree.

I have felt the truth of this, more or less clearly, from time immemorial, and I have always been disturbed by statements that I wished to overthrow the painting of the past. I never found such an overthrowing in my works: I felt in them only the internally logical, externally organic, inevitable further growth of art. Gradually I became conscious of my earlier feeling of freedom and, thus, gradually, the inconsequential demands which I had made of art fell away. They retreat in favor of one single requirement: the requirement of *inner* life in the work. At this point, I noted, to my surprise, that this requirement stemmed from the same basis that Christ set up as a basis for moral qualification. I observed that this view of art is Christian and that, at the same time, it harbors within it the elements necessary to the reception of the "third" revelation, the revelation of the spirit. . . . [7]

Kandinsky continues by saying that the elimination of the object in painting makes it necessary for the observer to develop a sensitivity to "the inner experience of the purely artistic form." He goes on to speak of the benefit to the artist of being able to appreciate works by others and he says, in respect to these:

> So far as I am concerned, I love every form which has arisen, of necessity, from the spirit and which was created by the spirit. Contrariwise, I hate every form in which this was not the case.[8]

He concludes by saying:

> I have many things for which to condemn myself but to one thing I have always remained true—the inner voice, which has determined my objective in art and which I hope to follow to the final hour.[9]

Kandinsky, *Composition No. 8*

Kandinsky never relinquished his adherence to the faith of his youth. The Russian Orthodox faith conditioned his entire artistic career, which was a never-ending quest of the spiritual, of the inner truth behind external appearances. To him there was no difference between the aims of religion and the aims of art. They were, as he said, both parts of the same great tree. He thought of himself as contributing to the "third revelation" as Christ had conveyed the second. We don't think of artists as holy men simply because we are unaware of the correspondence between art and religion. This is our shortcoming.

The last friends whom my wife and I saw in Europe before our return to America were Wassily and Nina Kandinsky. Kandinsky presented us with a print, inscribed to us, but he also gave us a magazine, likewise inscribed. The magazine was issue No. 14 of *Sélection*, published in Antwerp in 1933. This was, at that time, a fairly recent issue, since Kandinsky dated his inscription "Paris 13 VII 34." This number of the magazine, devoted entirely to Kandinsky, contains reproductions of many of his graphic works, three articles about him, and a number of *homages* (short laudatory pieces). The authors of these were Christian Zervos, Willi Baumeister, Michel Seuphor, Alberto Sartorius, Jan W. E. Buys, Diego di Rivera, André de Ridder, Elizabeth Luther Cary, and Galka E. Scheyer.

Some years later, in 1946, I wrote a piece not as an *homage*, but as an attempt to explain the nature of his painting. The original pen and ink script has many scratched-out passages and it appears to have been written at a single sitting:

The frequently expressed belief that nonobjective art is divorced from the world proceeds from a failure to understand its essential significance. All art expresses some phase of human experience. Sometimes the objective element predominates and the external world is

Werner Drewes, prismatic, 1930

Max Enderlin, untitled, 1931. Wood or linoleum cut

Mejschke Bahelfter, still life, 1930–31. Monotype. (Bahelfter later changed his name to Moses Bagel.)

presented in a more or less factually exact way. Sometimes the subjective predominates and, as in the case of the Expressionists, Surrealists and primitive artists, the world is presented as the artist "feels" it, not as he "sees" it and, consequently, the realistic appearance of things may be radically distorted. In any case, it is the thing lying behind the forms, the meaning of which the forms are only the carriers, that counts—the essential final effect of the picture. It is the same with experiences in life—what matters is not the experience per se, but its effect upon us. How and what we feel about it matters, not what, as a matter of scientific fact, happens.

Kandinsky, like artists in general, sought to express in his paintings his feelings concerning specific experiences or to put upon canvas his human reaction to forces at work in the world about us. To this end, he used symbols as largely divorced of representative significance as he could make them. It was, so to speak, the composing with those essences which might be perceived *behind* the form in representative painting. He knew that no line or form could be drawn which did not carry some abstract meaning and that every color had its psychologic effect quite aside from any association with specific forms in the world. He proceeded to compose with these "abstract" forms and colors or, rather, with their psychologic effects, to reproduce on canvas the essence of the experience which he had had.

A reading of Kandinsky's book *Point and Line to Plane* will go far to initiate one into the nature of the approach he took to painting. He discusses throughout the "feeling" significance of the basic elements of painting—point, line, and plane—making some reference to color, although a thorough treatment of this lies beyond the purpose of the book. He discusses the change in the effect with the change in the

shape of the form—point or line or plane—or the change in the effect of forms brought about by various interrelationships. He discusses the forms divorced from any representational association. But it is significant that throughout, in describing their character or effect, he ascribes qualities to them possessed by things in the external world. He refers to an "obstinate" line or a "laborious" tension or the "indifferent" center or the "breathing" of the ground plane. It appears that, having stripped the visual form of his elements of their naturalistic connotations, he proceeds to personify them. It is evident from this that Kandinsky does not seek to deny the world and its experiences since even to him, his forms have characteristics in common with human beings, natural forms, and natural forces. It is reasonable to conclude that he sought, by cleansing his form of extraneous matters, to present his experience of the world in a more unequivocal form.

What Kandinsky sought, in another and purer way, was to present to us his experiences of the world. I remember his saying to us in his painting class in the Bauhaus-Dessau, that many of his paintings had, as their basis, some specific personal experience. As a concrete example, he referred to a recent painting as having been inspired by the experience he had had while crossing the railroad overpass connecting the Dessau suburb in which the Bauhaus was situated with the town. As he neared the center of the bridge, a slowly moving locomotive stopped beneath and, without warning, blew a blast of smoke up through the planking of the bridge. He transferred the essential effect of this experience upon him to the picture.

The type of experience set down in the picture just discussed was characteristic of the type of thing Kandinsky sought frequently to express. We are all conditioned by the interplay of physical forces in the world about us. A deep-lying sense of the working of these forces is present in all of us. Kandinsky presented in many of his pictures comparable conflicts of such forces—the forces ranging the world, gravity, repulsion, attraction, etc.—brought upon the immaterial plane of the canvas to work their effects by suggestion. He heightened these contests of physical forces and elevated them to the level of profound spiritual experiences.[10]

13 the sculpture workshop

By the time I arrived, the sculpture workshop had been ended. Initially there were two sculpture workshops at the Bauhaus in Weimar, the workshop for stone sculpture and the workshop for wood sculpture. Itten was, in the beginning, artistic director of the former and Muche, for a short time, of the latter. When Schlemmer arrived in 1920, he became form master of the wall-painting workshop, but after the reorganization of the Bauhaus workshops in 1922, Kandinsky took over; the stone and wood sculpture ateliers fell to Schlemmer. In 1925 Schmidt was made form master, and he continued to direct the combined workshop until it closed in 1928.

It is impossible to distinguish, in style and evident intent, certain of the studies done in Itten's preliminary course from some of the works done in the sculpture workshops, where the acknowledged objective was to produce works of art. Hermann Müller's "plastic representation," a composition of horizontal and vertical rectangles of plaster of paris, can as surely be called sculpture as Kurt Schwerdtfeger's relief composition of horizontal and vertical lines and rectangles of glass and gypsum. Both pieces are equally successful as works of art; and both derive unmistakably from van Doesburg.

One of Schlemmer's major projects was not sculpture, in fact, but wall painting. In what amounted to a practical demonstration of one of the main tenets of Gropius's program, the consolidation of architecture and the arts, Schlemmer decorated the entrance vestibule and stairhall of the workshop building. The project was proposed by Schlemmer as a feature of the Bauhaus exhibition in

1923. Whatever their quality, and however much they were admired in liberal quarters, the murals enjoyed only a brief existence. In 1930, seven years after their creation, they were destroyed on the order of Schultze-Naumburg, then director of the architecture school which succeeded the Bauhaus in Weimar (Weimarer Kunsthochschule).

Stone sculpture studio in the Bauhaus, Weimar

Oskar Schlemmer, mural painting in upper part of stairhall of workshop building, Bauhaus, Weimar

 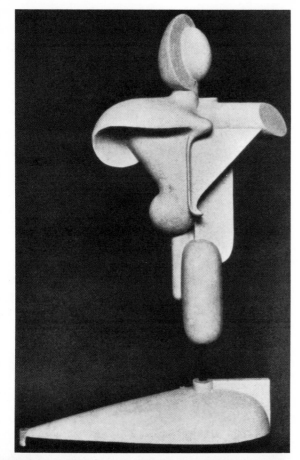

Oskar Schlemmer, front and side views of *Abstract Figure*, 1921. Plaster of paris

Oskar Schlemmer. Pen and brush drawing

Oskar Schlemmer, *Space Dance*, performed at the Bauhaus in 1927 by Werner Siedhoff.

The only piece of Schlemmer's sculpture that I have seen (it was still at the Bauhaus in Dessau when I was there) was a severely geometrized human figure of plaster of paris, elevated above a base of the same material, which formed part of the composition. This figure had an almost baroque feeling of movement, so that it was a sort of inanimate first cousin of the masked, costumed, human figures of Schlemmer's ballets.

The truth is that Schlemmer was chiefly a painter and a theater composer. He clung doggedly to one theme, "Man in Space." His painted figures are mannequins, dummies, wooden and half-human, not, of course, because he was unable to paint realistically, but because he strove to achieve, through the avoidance of all particularity, a monumental result. He shunned naturalism and sought a controlled two-dimensional art, devoid of the fortuitous and shorn of easily grasped, easily pleasing effects. There are still examples of his easel painting and his graphic work surviving. Only a few of his canvases are in the United States; his best-known picture in this country is *The Bauhaus Staircase*, painted in 1932 and now in the Museum of Modern Art, depicting a series of figures ascending the main staircase of the Dessau Bauhaus, (see illustration p41).

The destruction, in 1930, of his Weimar murals and reliefs did not deter Schlemmer from trying again. In an entry in his diary dated June 22, 1931, he speaks of having completed "wall treatments" for the Folkwang Museum in Zwenkau, and in the Berlin Building Exhibition. The "wall treatment" in Zwenkau, a village near Leipzig, was a composition of wire rather than a painting, and photographs of it still exist. Schlemmer describes this work in a letter of July 22, 1931, to Baumeister:

The wire sculpture or, better, "metal composition" or figural composition of various metallic wires, consists of three figures. A large figure holds a smaller one in its hand. At the right side of the wall, in relation to the first, is a five-meters-high metal profile of a face. The figures project about eight centimeters from the wall, whereby, in changing light, changing shadows are cast, in the manner of a sundial.[1]

As to the nature of Schlemmer's "wall treatment" for the Berlin Building Exhibition of 1931, I visited the exhibition, but I do not recall seeing his murals. (His name appears in the official catalog in a list of artists who participated in an exhibition entitled "Creative Art and the Art of Building.")

The best-known works of the wood-carving workshop were the decorative panels made by Schmidt for the stairhall of Gropius's log house in Berlin (the Sommerfeld House). The inclusion of these wood carvings in the Sommerfeld House was hailed as a demonstration of Gropius's principle of the integration of the arts and architecture. Of course, the house itself represents a major departure in Gropius's development of a modern architecture. Whereas Gropius's Fagus factory of 1911 and the Machinery Hall and Administration Building of the Werkbund Exposition of 1914 were in so many respects ahead of their time, the Sommerfeld House of 1921 seems to be a throwback to a pre-twentieth century point-of-view.

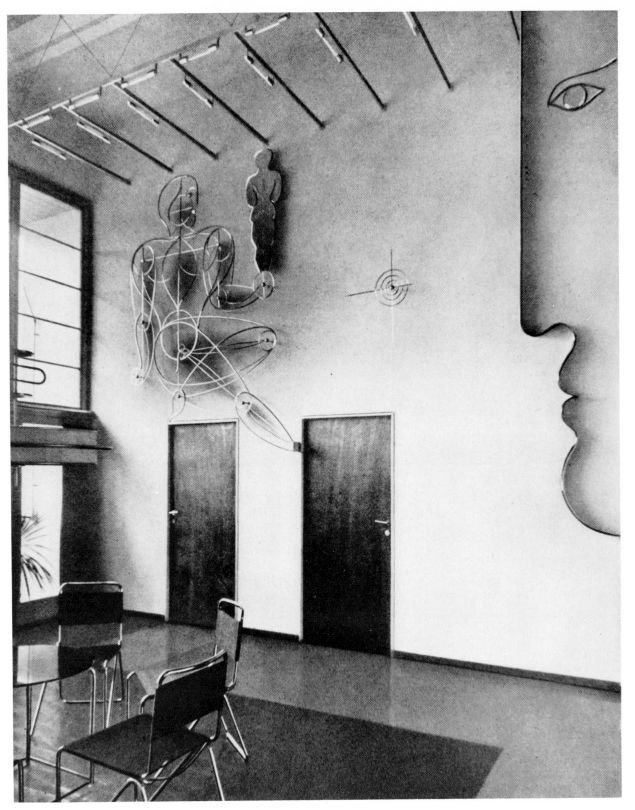

Oskar Schlemmer, wire sculpture in residence of
Dr. Raabe in Zwenkau, 1931

Joost Schmidt, carved stair-railing in Sommerfeld House

Lili Gräf, chest of pearwood

Although the sculpture course was no longer offered by the time I arrived at Dessau, I did have Schmidt as a teacher for lettering. But I found his classes tiresome. All his alphabets were in block letters and had to be constructed with a T-square, triangle and

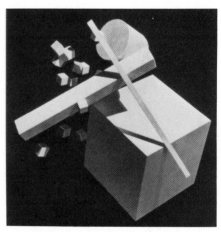

Exercise with woodcutting tools by Heinrich Busse

Two plates from Joost Schmidt's sculpture workshop. *Top* loose order

compass. They made no demands on either the intellect or the spirit.

Among the few other notable works of architectural sculpture which Schmidt executed were his stucco reliefs for the vestibule of the main Bauhaus building. The four stucco reliefs, like Schlemmer's murals, became part of the 1923 exhibition. Schmidt's remodeling of the vestibule required the removing of a statue of Eve by Rodin, and this caused a storm of indignation. Schmidt's reliefs were short-lived, being moved by prearrangement in 1924, and Eve was presumably restored to her central position. Schmidt's works were in place just long enough for the exhibition visitors to admire them and for photographs to be taken for future Bauhaus books and catalogs.

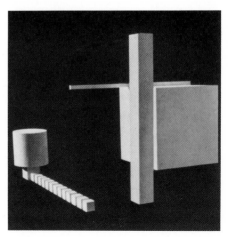

Bottom one of many possible orderly arrangement of same objects

14

the bauhaus theater

The dramaturge, poet, and painter Schreyer was invited to the Bauhaus in the summer of 1921 to set up a theater workshop. Schlemmer, who had joined the Bauhaus in December 1920 but who was also working on the scenery and costumes for two one-act plays to be performed in Stuttgart, wrote from nearby Cannstatt on May 16, 1921:

This morning express letter saying Gropius had arrived. Met him at 10 o'clock in the Marquardt Hotel—we talked a lot. We came down, after I had excused myself at the theater, and I showed him the costumes for the ballet. Their solidity pleased him very much. Would fit in very well, he thought, with what Lothar Schreyer wants to do. He [Gropius] is theater-minded, interested in costume-making and the like at the Bauhaus.[1]

A month later Schlemmer, writing this time from Weimar, again refers to Schreyer and the projected state workshop:

Because of our economic depression we won't be able to build, possibly, for a long time to come. There is a lack of great projects for the utopian fantasies of the moderns. But there is a place for them in the theatrical world of illusion. We have to be satisfied with substitutes and make out of wood and pasteboard what we are not permitted to build in stone and iron. It may be that Gropius felt somewhat the same way; he has called to Weimar a poet and theatrical artist, Lothar Schreyer, who set up a *Kampfbühne* (*Battle Theater*) in Hamburg, so that we will now get the theatrical slant here, something of which I heartily approve. Henceforth the theatrical will have an important place in the discussions.[2]

Early the next year, in a letter to Meyer-Amden, Schlemmer gave his friend an inkling of his doubt about the correctness of Schreyer's approach to the theater:

> Incidentally, a gate is slowly being opened for the theater at the Bauhaus. Through it has entered Schreyer, poet and painter at the same time, but in a "sacral" vein. To me remains, filling in, so to speak, the dance and the comic which I gladly embrace, that is, without jealousy.[3]

Schlemmer was too sincere and modest a person to do more than suggest, even to so close a friend as Meyer-Amden, that he would have been happy to have had the job for which, unaccountably, another man had been chosen.

Schreyer, as he liked to put it, "came out of" Herwarth Walden's Sturm gallery in Berlin. (It is interesting that all of the Bauhaus artists, with the exception of Marcks had, at one time or another, exhibited their works in the pioneering art gallery of that extraordinarily keen-sighted and fearless connoisseur.) Schreyer's relationship with Walden was very close. He had been, for more than twelve years, one of his best friends and collaborators in the various Sturm enterprises. He became editor of Walden's magazine *Der Sturm*, which waged an unceasing and uncompromising battle against reactionary art and purblind art critics, published trailblazing works of poetry, music, and the drama, and championed, with unerring insight, the as yet unrecognized and unacclaimed leaders of modern painting and sculpture. Walden also entrusted to him the management of the Sturm theater which, because of the unsettled state of affairs in postwar Berlin, was moved to Hamburg, where it became the *Kampfbühne*. As playwright, scene designer, and director, Schreyer staged eight radically new and controversial works, among which were three of his own, *Kindsterben* (*Child Death*), *Mann* (*Man*), and *Kreuzigung* (*Crucifixion*). Schreyer explained his theatrical aims, which were the same objectives he tried to achieve at the Bauhaus, as follows:

Lothar Schreyer, 1956

> Like my Berlin friends, I sought, in the theater, the unified work of art in which all the creative resources of the stage, that is, word, tone, movement, color-form are elevated to the totality and unity of a self-contained art form. In this aim lay the contrast between us and the contemporary theater. This contrast was social as well as artistic.[4]

He continued:

> Just as every performance of the Sturm theater was a mystery play—one of the twentieth century—so is every verbal art work of the Sturm a mystery text, a pronouncement either of God or against Him. And the Sturm poetry, like the Sturm art, also has a religious basis and it has this even when—and these are, of course, only exceptions—it is aesthetic. It is almost always a striving for the divine.[5]

Oskar Schlemmer and crew on the rooftop of the Bauhaus in their Triadic Ballet costumes

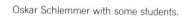

Oskar Schlemmer with some students.

Oskar Schlemmer

Left Lothar Schreyer, *Death Picture of the Man*

Lothar Schreyer, figure for *Moonplay*

Still later in his book, Schreyer spoke of the objectives of the Bauhaus theater workshop and managed to convey the erroneous impression that he and Schlemmer collaborated in the work there:

Our theater workshop sought to serve the revelation of the hidden spiritual world in the midst of the cosmic powers. Oskar Schlemmer and I were form masters of the theater workshop. We needed no technical master. Oskar Schlemmer and I were, in respect to our expressive aims, very different natures, so that the workshop had the most varied possibilities. Oskar Schlemmer had brought his famous

Triadisches Ballett (*Triadic Ballet*) along with him to Weimar and we carried out, with masks which we, ourselves, made, my *Mondspiel* (*Moon Play*). With these works, to be sure, we went beyond the immediate task of the Bauhaus.[6]

Schreyer has no more to say about this performance of his *Mondspiel*, the only theatrical work he was able to execute during his more than two years at the Bauhaus. His summary treatment of this might lead us to suspect that the play was not a success; and in a letter of March 30, 1923, to Meyer-Amden, Schlemmer commented laconically:

The Bauhaus theater, directed heretofore by Lothar Schreyer, failed completely with a trial performance, rejected by the majority of masters and students alike. In consequence of this, Schreyer will leave the Bauhaus. The result is that they come running to me as the next candidate who, as they say, has proven himself more than once, to get me to do this and that of a theatrical nature for the exhibition this summer.[7]

Lothar Schreyer, Costume for *Man*

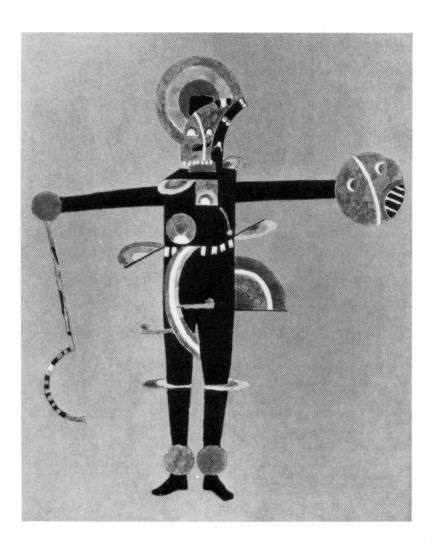

The Bauhaus theater. Unidentified girl on horseback

A combination of causes led to Schreyer's resignation from the Bauhaus. It seems clear that the immediate one was the rejection, by the masters and students generally, of his approach to the theater. The Bauhaus community was not prepared to accept a cult theater, a theater with an underlying religious motivation. And Schreyer himself was so steeped in his mystic ideology that he was unwilling, and probably unable, to change his approach. He leaned strongly, even then, toward Roman Catholicism; he says in his book, "... my conversion, which took place ten years later, was being prepared for at the Bauhaus."[8]

For Schreyer, art was not an end in itself; it had to serve a higher cause, namely religion. In this he differed from Klee, Feininger, and Schlemmer who, however much they sought to incorporate "inner" spiritual values in their art, never associated these with the supernatural, much less with any specific religious dogma. Schreyer made the only possible sound decision in leaving the Bauhaus before it moved to Dessau. As long as the school continued to be the "citadel of expressionism," as he called it, he was in his proper element. When, in Dessau, it became—as I knew it— the "citadel of atheism," he would never have been able to adjust to it.

Schlemmer was not reluctant to take over Schreyer's theater workshop. Some years later, in a lecture held at the Bauhaus in Dessau, Schlemmer, with characteristic generosity, pointed out that the failure of Schreyer's theater in Weimar was due, not to his inadequacy, but rather to the state of mind which prevailed at that time in the school:

It was possible for the attempt made by Lothar Schreyer in 1922 to create a Bauhaus stage to fail only because of an intense skepticism, since almost no taste for philosophical viewpoints, especially when clothed in the sacral garb of expressionism, existed. There was, on the other hand, a pronounced feeling for satire and parody. It was, doubtless, an inheritance from Dadaism to ridicule, above all, everything which reeked of pathos and ethics. So the grotesque flourished. It lived from travestying, from mocking the outmoded forms of the existing theater; but it was basically negative. Its positive aspect was the recognition of the origin of all theatrical play, of its requirements, its laws. The dance continued to live![9]

The students, in any case, were fitted temperamentally for creative work in the theater:

There was theater at the Bauhaus from the first day of its existence, because the impulse to play was present from the first day. The play impulse, which Schiller in his still wonderful "Briefe uber die ästhetische Erziehung des Menschen" ("Letters Concerning the Aesthetic Education of the Individual") designates as the power out of which the truly creative values of the human being flow, is that unreflecting, naïve desire to produce and create, without asking about value or the lack of value, sense or nonsense, good or bad. This desire to create was especially strong in the beginning, not to say the infancy, of the Bauhaus in Weimar, and it expressed itself in exuberant parties, rapid improvisations, in the making of fantastic masks and costumes. This naïve condition, out of which the play impulse grows, is replaced, in the course of development, by reflection, doubt, and criticism, which can develop so far as to destroy the original condition, unless a second kind of skeptical naïveté, so to speak, resolves the dangerous crisis. We have become, today, much more conscious; laws have detached themselves from the unconscious and the chaotic and concepts like norm, type, synthesis indicate the way which is to lead to the idea of creation.[10]

I had no personal contact with the theater workshop in Dessau and although I used to see Schlemmer about the school, unfortunately I never became acquainted with him.[11] I did attend the performances, however, and I encountered something new when I saw Schlemmer's players on the stage. From one to three persons participated. No word was spoken, no story suggested by sign or gesture, no human emotion communicated to the audience. It was unrelated to any drama I had enjoyed in New York City. The performances consisted solely of bodily movements synchronized with music, a form of the dance. The movements were abrupt, staccato, angular—more like mobile geometry than fluid arabesques. The performers appeared only remotely human, as did the mannequins

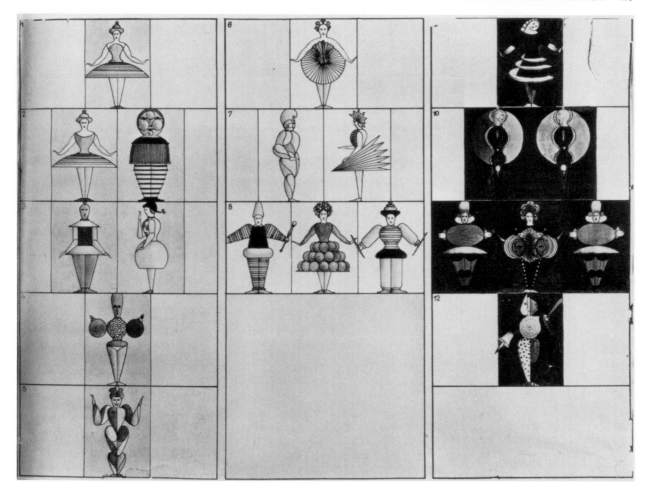

Oskar Schlemmer, plan of figures for the *Triadic Ballet*, 1920

in Schlemmer's paintings, divested of their human identity and wholly of their individuality by being encased in costumes which converted them into assemblages of geometric shapes, such as cylinders, cones, spheres, or disks. Schlemmer did not believe in total abstraction, the elimination of all reference to the human being. His continuing objective was to "place the human figure in space," to create compositions, whether moving or static, or half-human, half-geometrized forms put in just relation to each other and to the real or imagined space in which they existed or seemed to exist. The person must remain the central subject in art, shaped for this role by generalization and sublimation.

Though Schlemmer occasionally designed the sets for works by others than himself (Kokoschka, Andreyev, Schönberg, Stravinsky), his major theatrical achievement resides in his own abstract stage. By far the most significant was his *Triadic Ballet*. The first performance of the complete work took place in Stuttgart on September 20, 1922, with Gropius and more than twenty Bauhaus students in attendance. It was a big hit. It was performed in the National Theater in Weimar during the Bauhaus Week in the summer of 1923 and, following this, in Dresden. In 1926 Schlemmer was invited to take the ballet to the music festival in Donaueschingen, and for this performance his friend Paul Hindemith composed the music. It was later performed in Frankfurt and Berlin and finally, in 1932, in Paris. This was the last of the original performances of the *Triadic Ballet*, for thereafter Schlemmer's theatrical activities were banned by the National Socialists.

Oskar Schlemmer, sketches of figures for the *Triadic Ballet*, ca. 1920

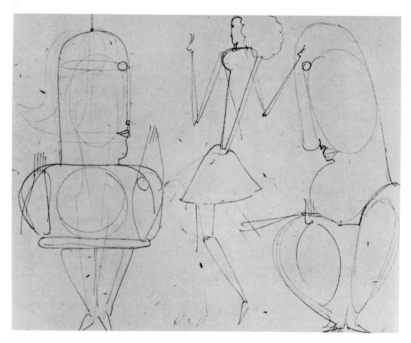

A journalist, "A. Ho," attending the Bauhaus Week in Weimar, saw a performance of the ballet in the National Theater:

The ballet consisted of three parts, in the case of the first of which the stage was hung with lemon-yellow draperies and the dance of this part was comic-burlesque. The second part was carried out in a festival manner on a rose-colored stage. The third part, mystic-fantastic in nature, was danced before a background of black hangings. The twelve dances were danced in eighteen different costumes alternately by three persons, two male dancers and one female. One of the dancers was Oskar Schlemmer himself.[12]

Schlemmer's wife, Tut, wrote a brief outline of the ballet as it was staged in Stuttgart for the catalog of the Schlemmer theater exhibition held in Zurich nearly forty years later (1961):

Standing under the Goethe-Schiller monument, we asked each other anxiously, "Do you know what a *Triadic Ballet* is?" And the critic of

Oskar Schlemmer. Costumed figures from the
Triadic Ballet, 1920

a newspaper with a worldwide circulation inquired cautiously how long the fun could be expected to last and whether it would be possible to slip out of the theater during the performance. His train was to leave at 9-something. . . .

But at 10-something he still sat on his little seat clapping his hands, and the Berlin train, long since departed, was forgotten.

When this happens to the green wood of criticism, how will the dry wood of the uncritically oriented be affected?

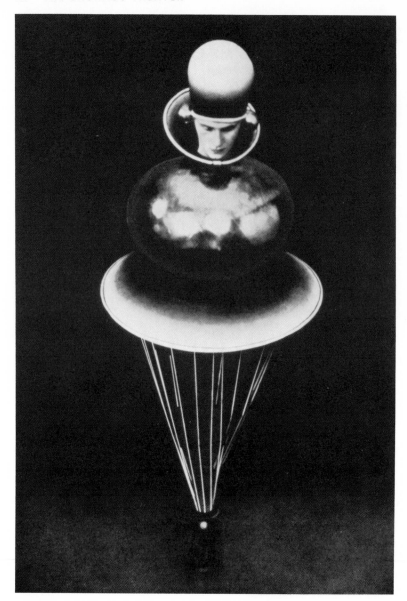

Oskar Schlemmer, detail from illustration, page 175

Oskar Schlemmer, detail from illustration, page 177

In any case, we were all delighted and happy, the critical and the uncritical. Probably because the brain was completely switched off and only the eye remained in operation. Brain activity is work, is torture; but pure seeing is gladness, peace, and gaiety. The purest pleasure is the pleasure of the eyes.[13]

In 1929 Schlemmer took his Bauhaus (Dessau) stage, then at the peak of its achievement, on a several months' tour, in the course of which it performed in five cities—Berlin, Breslau, Frankfurt-am-Main, Stuttgart, and Basel—and eleven short pieces, varying in content, were presented. A report on the Basel performance, written by "dt" for the *National-Zeitung* of that city, concludes:

He who seeks "something" behind all this finds nothing, because there is nothing *behind* it. Everything is in what one perceives with

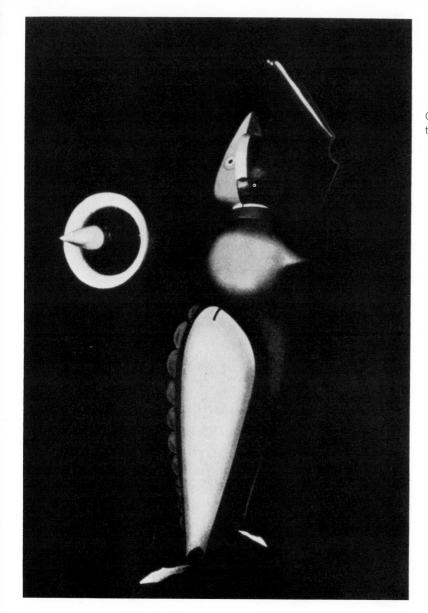

Oskar Schlemmer, *The Abstract One*, figure from the *Triadic Ballet*, 1922

his senses! No feelings are "expressed" but, rather, feelings are aroused. . . . The whole thing is play, emancipated and emancipating play . . . pure, absolute form, just as in music.[14]

Schlemmer's was the largest contribution to the development of the stage at the Bauhaus. He not only laid a theoretical foundation for his work in his thinking and writing but also, over a period of years, executed his ideas with conviction and consistency. In 1925 Schlemmer's book *Die Bühne im Bauhaus* was published, in which his article "Mensch und Kunstfigur" ("Man and the Art Figure") is devoted to an analysis of the basic elements of the theater. The "man" of the title is Man the Dancer, and Schlemmer explains his relationship to the space in which he moves and his transformation by means of costume and mask. The treatment of the art figure, which is to say the artificial or mechanical figure, is relatively short. One wonders why Schlemmer should have wanted to stress this subject in the first place in an article which was intended to be the core of the book.

Schlemmer also tried to continue the tradition of using puppets and marionettes. In October 1923 he wrote to Meyer-Amden:

Stage: I proposed that a marionette theater finally be set up. This is taking place now following a story out of *The Thousand and One Nights*, freely adapted. I wanted to do a Thuringian folk legend, *The Smith from Apolda*. One could have played it for the farmer in return for produce. The students don't want this because it is so tiresome, too moral—but especially because it comes from one of the masters. They wish to do it themselves. They are in it heart and soul and it will also succeed. The first principle is that the students must have the feeling that the thing stems from them.[15]

Schlemmer says no more about the success or failure of the marionette theater. Pictures of some of the figures have survived, however, such as those made by workshop students Kurt Schmidt and Toni Hergt for what was evidently an original playlet, *The Adventures of the Little Hunchback*. Marionettes made by Hilde Rantzsch are also pictured on the last page of *bauhaus* 3, but there is no mention of any piece in which they appeared. Like Schlemmer's live performers, these marionettes are more or less geometrized, though there is never any doubt that they represent human beings.

The step from marionettes, activated by strings, to figures, semi-realistic or abstract, made to move by mechanical means, is not a large one. Schlemmer believed there were great possibilities in an artificial figure, although he and his students never carried very far the exploitation of what he considered to be its high potentialities. It may be that he began to harbor doubts about a stage whose actors were inanimate objects. As he wrote in his diary on September 7, 1931:

I have never done a "mechanical ballet," as fascinating as it could be to devise figures which were made to move automatically ·by machine. The relatively slight gain in the possibilities of spatial movement would not justify the high costs of the apparatus. Even the mechanics of the marionette are limited, since it is, after all, no automaton like E. Th. A. Hoffmann's Olympia but, rather, is set in motion by the keyboard of the human hand. The flat figures of my *Figural Cabinet* are carried and moved by disguised dancers. The fluid human being, therefore, is always a part of the play.[16]

Schlemmer's most memorable experiment in the use of artificial figures was the *Figural Cabinet*, to which he refers above. It was

Oskar Schlemmer. *Company of Figures* for the *Figural Cabinet*, 1923

presented only twice, once in the spring of 1922 and again during the Bauhaus Week in 1923. The second performance was a modified version of the first. Schlemmer, commenting in his diary on the role his sculpture, painting, and theater are to play in the coming Bauhaus exhibition says, "the *Figural Cabinet* will show the comic side."

The dozen-and-a-half forms in the *Figural Cabinet* were indeed comic: all of them had the general, upright shape of human beings and what purported to be bodies, and each had a head, the features of which, however geometrized, exaggerated, or otherwise removed from the natural, were recognizably human. Composed of incongruous parts—a fiddle body with head and feet; a human head perched on a torso of geometric shapes, with a volute instead of legs; a very military-looking configuration, bearing upon its breast a great heart, like any knight-errant of old; sinuous, zigzag, scallop-fringed, square, circular, or vase-shaped bodies—they somehow appear funny. Set in motion and made to perform in singular ways, they were probably hilarious. And considering that these strange creatures were also painted in vivid colors, their performance, however brief, must have been one of exceptional gaiety.

The 1923 exhibition also featured a performance of the *Mechanical Ballet*, with pasteboard figures constructed by three other Bauhaus students, Georg Teltscher, F. W. Bogler, and Kurt Schmidt. Composed entirely of flat, geometric shapes, it was an attempt to create a constantly changing composition of mobile abstract forms. Osborn reported on the performance:

... But the main feature followed: the *Mechanical Ballet*.

I don't know whether the raw young artists Georg Teltscher and Kurt Schmidt, who devised this play, know anything about the ballet experiments which Natalie Gontcharova and her Russian countryman Larionov, carried out years ago in Paris. Perhaps they do, but it is also possible that these productions only appear to be similar. In any case, Teltscher and Schmidt also constructed jagged color planes with movable members, behind which they hid from sight and, accompanied by original music with rumbling beats of the kettledrum, they carried out rhythmic steps, dance movements—how should I describe them? The sight of the shifting, bowing, saluting, pursuing, retreating of these colored objects which, though impersonal, were nonetheless directed by a will, was strangely realistic-visionary, not only bewildering but also a visual display of never-before-seen fantasy.[17]

An actual mechanical stage was beyond the resources of the Bauhaus in Weimar, which had no stage at all; its theatrical productions had to be presented in the German National Theater in Weimar or the Municipal Theater, remodeled by Gropius, in Jena.* Gropius did, however, provide a stage in his new building in Dessau, a stage which could be opened in two directions, toward the auditorium and toward the cafeteria. Though the technical equipment of this stage fell lamentably short of the facilities possessed by the big theaters in Berlin and other large cities, the stage seemed a luxury to Schlemmer, who was accustomed to making do with very little. But his chances of testing the possibilities of the mechanically operated art figure remained slim.

The only works of this sort known to me are two models of mechanical stage sets made by the Weimar-Dessau student, Heinz Loew.[18] The photographs give no clue to the scale of the models, but it is easy to conceive of them enlarged to the size of a normal stage. The shapes in both models are geometric—disks, spheres, cylinders, rectangular planes. Once the apparatus was set in motion it would have produced changing compositions of moving geometric shapes. But, as Schlemmer said in his lecture to the Circle of Friends of the Bauhaus in 1927, "... it is a question of ... how long the rotating, oscillating, whirring contrivance, combined with all sorts of variations of forms, colors, and lights, can hold the spectator's interest."[19] The same thing would also doubt-

*In 1922, Gropius with Adolf Meyer, was commissioned by the city of Jena to renovate an existing entertainment hall. The structure was quite unfinished, raw, with exposed rafters. While Gropius was not able to achieve anything approaching his Total Theatre project (1927), "the creation of a great and flexible instrument" as he termed it, he was able to begin to breakdown the barrier a proscenium creates between audience and stage, achieving, at Jena, something approaching a unified space in which stage and audience become one.

Kurt Schmidt, F. W. Bogler, and Georg Teltscher, figures for the *Mechanical Ballet,* 1923

less hold for Moholy-Nagy's "Light-Space Modulator," now in the Busch-Reisinger Museum. This is a construction of metal and glass forms which can be set in motion so that the elements change their positions and form different compositions. It is called "Kinetic Sculpture," but it is of the same order as Heinz Loew's mechanical stage models. Both are art machines rather than art works, and both are unmistakable offspring of the industrial age. Near the beginning of "Man and the Art Figure," Schlemmer, echoing the thoughts in his diary, wrote:

> [One of the emblems] of our time is mechanization, the inexorable process which now lays claim to every sphere of life and art. Everything which can be mechanized *is* mechanized. The result: our recognition of that which cannot be mechanized.[20]

the reflected light plays

Originated by Hirschfeld-Mack and Kurt Schwertfeger, students at the Weimar Bauhaus in 1922, *Reflektorische Lichtspiele* grew out of a chance discovery made during a simple shadow play entertainment. They consisted of projections on a translucent linen screen of spotlighted geometric planes which were moved up, down, and sideways behind it. What the public saw, standing out from a black background, was a sequence of yellow, red, green, and blue shapes, constantly moving and regrouping themselves into new abstract patterns. The appeal of these plays, once the novelty of the technique had worn off, would have depended upon the quality of the changing light compositions produced by the behind-the-scenes operators who manipulated the colored forms. To judge by examples of these compositions plucked by the still camera from several of the shifting sequences, the operators must have worked with both dexterity and sensitivity.

The reflected light plays may be compared with the pioneering work of Viking Eggeling, who started his *Diagonalsymphonie*, an abstract film made by a multiple drawing method, in 1917, and the work of Hans Richter, Eggeling's follower, who made abstract films both as animated cartoons and by the photography of moving objects. Richter's film *Rhythmus*, produced in 1921, with its geometric forms moving against a black background, bears certain affinities to the reflected light plays.

Hirschfeld-Mack and Schwertfeger each formed a group of operators and presented his version of the light plays in a number of different cities. Hirschfeld-Mack and his group, for example, appeared, among other places, in Berlin and Vienna. Hirschfeld-Mack was gifted musically and composed an instrumental accompaniment for his performances. It was he, also, who presented two light plays during the Bauhaus Week in 1923.

And now came truly strange presentations. First, "reflected plays," colored light pictures in movement, abstract form elements—circles, crescents, rectangles, bars, curves, all in the most finely conceived tones, which touched, penetrated, displaced each other and shone forth in a shimmering profusion of pictorial harmonies. One recognized the endless possibilities of this decorative magic and also its sensuous attraction, which is so frequently underestimated.[21]

Kurt Schwertfeger, *Reflected Light Ray*, ca. 1923

moholy-nagy, kandinsky and the bauhaus theater

Moholy-Nagy's contribution to reforming the theater, at least during his Bauhaus period, remained wholly theoretical. An article called "Theater, Circus, Variety," was inserted (without Schlemmer's knowledge) into Schlemmer's book *The Theater of the Bauhaus*,[22] which enlarged upon the idea of a "mechanized eccentric,"

a synthesis of space, form, motion, sound, and light, "a concentration of stage action in its purest form," that is, without literary encumbrances, and included in the article a specimen score for such a mechanized eccentric.

Moholy envisioned "total stage action" as a "great dynamic-rhythmic creative process which can compress the greatest clashing masses or accumulations of media ... into compact elemental form," and recommended the use of new technical devices to produce novel effects of light, sound, form, and movement. A new kind of theater building was required for this new kind of performance, equipped with suspended bridges, drawbridges, movable space constructions, disklike areas, variations of level, wire frames, antennae, mirrors, and other optical devices. Moholy was far from

Wassily Kandinsky, two designs for stage sets for *Pictures at an Exhibition*, 1928 *see overleaf*

being alone, at this time, in stressing the limitations of the proscenium ("peep-show") theater and calling for a new type which would bring the audience closer, into the midst of the action.

The situation in the Europe of the 1920s was no more conducive to an acceptance of new departures in the arts than it is now. Looking back at the contrasting art movements which followed each other in quick succession at that time, we are inclined to think that these were rewarding days for the artist. What we should remember is that while pioneering advances were made in the arts, these were summarily rejected by the general public. It is not surprising, therefore, that Kandinsky, for instance, whose discoveries revolutionized painting, was able to put theatrical principles to the test only once. It is to the enduring credit of the erstwhile stage manager, Hartmann, of the Friedrich Theater in Dessau, that he invited Kandinsky to do this in the spring of 1928.

The vehicle which Kandinsky chose to use for the unique demonstration of his stage synthesis was Modest Mussorgsky's *Pictures at an Exhibition*. The musical work consists of sixteen "pictures" or parts which express the impressions made upon the composer by an exhibition of paintings. Though, as Kandinsky says, these pictures were naturalistic, the orchestral composition was in no sense program music but went far beyond the "content" of the painted works to take on pure musical form. Whereas Mussorgsky had been inspired by the pictures to create "absolute music," Kandinsky was inspired by the music to create absolute pictures, mobile abstract visual compositions which synchronized with the music. So the pictorial-musical progression came full circle, so to speak—pictures to music to pictures—but the character of the pictures changed radically in the process.

This synthetic theatrical work, a kind of posthumous collaboration by Mussorgsky with his fellow countryman Kandinsky, was staged on April 4, 1928. Kandinsky designed all of the visual features of the presentation—stage sets, lighting—and directed the performance himself. I arrived in Dessau several months too late, unfortunately, to see this, but Kandinsky later wrote of it as follows:

> With the exception of two pictures—*Samuel Goldenbury and Schmuyle* and *The Market Place in Limoges*—(in which I had two dancers take part) all of the stage settings were "abstract." Here and there I also used forms which were remotely "objective." I, too, did not proceed "programmatically" but, rather, employed forms which hovered before me as I listened to the music.[23]

This once, Kandinsky had a free hand in carrying out his conception of a union of the arts in the theater.

15 the metal workshop

It is uncertain who was form master of the metal workshop during the first two or three years of the Weimar Bauhaus, but serious and substantial work in the shop started when Christian Dell was appointed technical master in 1922, with Moholy-Nagy as form master from 1923 to 1928. Dell, like Josef Hartwig of the sculpture workshop, was a creative person as well as an experienced craftsman and surely deserves more credit than his title of "technical master" would seem to warrant. The distinction in rank between the "form master" and the "technical master" of a workshop did an injustice to some of the outstanding people who served at the Bauhaus in this capacity.

Dell's work, for example a silver tea service with teapot, creamer, sugar bowl, and tray, made between 1923 and 1924, is handsome, and free of the formalism that characterized most of the other Bauhaus metal objects of that period. He was highly respected by his colleagues and, when the Bauhaus closed in Weimar late in 1924 and he left to direct the metalworking class of the Frankfurt Art School, he was given a written accolade which ran something like this: "He has caused the workshop to blossom from small beginnings."

Original pieces from the metal workshop are rare today and only a few institutions such as the Busch-Reisinger Museum (Harvard), the Schloss Museum (Weimar) and the Bauhaus Archive (Berlin), have them in any quantity.[1] Certain of the earlier metal objects created at the Weimar Bauhaus, such as a door handle and escutcheon of nickel-plated iron, together with a fragment of the door and door frame to which they are attached, represent an attempt

Christian Dell, tea service, 1923–24

Nickel-plated iron door handle and escutcheon
made in the metal workshop, Bauhaus, Weimar

Otto Lindig, cocoa pot, 1923

Otto Lindig, beer jug without lid

to make a constructivist composition out of everyday objects. The ensemble, of unknown authorship, resembles the wood carvings made by Schmidt at about the same time (1922) for the stairhall of Gropius's Sommerfeld House in Berlin. However, the Weimar metal-workers looked upon themselves principally as artists; though they consented to make objects of use, they made those only which, by proper treatment, could be turned into minor works of art. Even the metals with which they chiefly worked, bronze and silver, show that their intent was to produce *objets de vertu*. Due to the lack of money, the silver which they used was *Neusilber* (German silver), an alloy of copper, zinc, and nickel; they also used a certain amount of brass, tombac (an alloy of copper and zinc), and just plain copper. In Dessau, the shift from the making of quasi art objects to the production of models for mass production was accompanied by the extensive use of aluminum, especially for lamp shades and other lighting accessories, and, of course, steel, lacquered and nickel- and chromium-plated, for tubular furniture. It is possible to trace the path of the Bauhaus toward modern methods of pro-

Marianne Brandt, bronze teapot, inside silver-plated, made in the metal workshop, Bauhaus, Weimar

duction by the changes in materials employed by the metalworkers: the metals used in Weimar were those preferred by craftsmen; the metals used in Dessau were those for contemporary manufacture.

Almost all the vessels made in Weimar were based upon pure geometric forms—the cylinder, the sphere, the hemisphere, and the cone. They deviate from these forms enough only to satisfy functional requirements. The metalworkers never used the cube— indeed they made no flat-sided receptacles whatever. The strong geometry of this form severely limited the variety of objects that could be made. In this the metal workshop resembled the furniture and the textile workshops, where the products have only the barest pretence of serving any other use than that of art.

The work from the pottery, on the other hand, was much freer in form, although it always drew on the primitive. The difference, between the metal and pottery workshops at least, can be traced to the teaching of the form masters of the respective workshops, Moholy-Nagy and Marcks. Marcks, apparently, gave his students free rein in their search for satisfying form, whereas Moholy drew heavily on constructivism.

The most prolific, and probably the most talented, student metalworkers in Weimar were Marianne Brandt, who accompanied the Bauhaus to Dessau and became one of the leaders there in the design of metal objects for mass production, and Wilhelm Wagenfeld, who executed a number of fine table-pieces and became

Fire-resistant tea service, designed by Wilhelm Wagenfeld and made by the Jena Glassworks, 1922

one of the foremost designers of fine metal and glass objects in Germany.

The metal workshop in Dessau underwent the same change in orientation as did the weaving studio and the furniture workshop. Gropius's slogan "Art and Technology, a New Unity" became the watchword. The metalworkers transferred their energies from the creation of unique handcrafted objects to the making of models for mass production. Though certain table objects continued to be made (Brandt even executed a very handsome piece of kitchenware, a pot for cooking eggs) the emphasis was shifted to the creation of lighting fixtures. Practically all of these Dessau lighting fixtures were designed by Brandt, who dominated the metal workshop in Dessau as Stölzl and Berger dominated the weaving studio and Breuer the furniture workshop.

Brandt made all kinds of lighting fixtures—suspended lamps with hemispherical aluminum shades; hanging lamps with frosted glass globes and with globes whose bottom half was of opal glass and upper half of mat, to provide a combination of indirect and muted direct lighting; cylindrical and domical frosted glass fixtures at-

Marianne Brandt, pot for cooking eggs. Aluminum with handle of ebony.

tached directly to the ceiling, an innovation at that time; ceiling fixtures of concentric frosted glass cylinders, the ancestors of our present-day indirect lighting devices composed of concentric metal rings or louvers; extensible wall fixtures for indirect lighting, and various desk and table lamps. Of the latter, her adjustable table lamp (ca. 1927) seems as simple, neat, and flawless today as it must have appeared to the many people who, in the late 1920s and early 1930s, purchased it under the trade name of Kandem Night Table Lamp. This lamp and many other lighting fixtures of Bauhaus design (mostly Brandt's) were mass-produced by the firm of Körting and Mathiesen in Leipzig, which sold over 50,000 of them between 1928 and 1932, when the Bauhaus ceased functioning in Dessau. With the production of machine-made objects of this char-

K. J. Jucker, extensible wall lamp of nickel-plated brass and iron, ca. 1923, Bauhaus, Weimar

Marianne Brandt, night table lamp, nickel-plated and lacquered, made in the metal workshop, Bauhaus, Dessau

Left Wilhelm Wagenfeld and K. J. Jucker, table lamp, made in the metal workshop, Bauhaus, Weimar, 1923–1924.

Right Ceiling light designed in the metal workshop, Bauhaus, Dessau. The metal parts are aluminum and the globe is partly opal glass and partly mat glass.

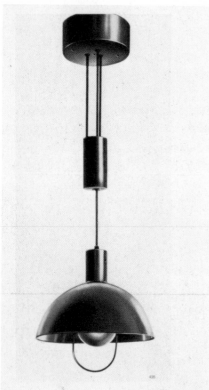

Marianne Brandt and Hans Przyrembel, extensible hanging lamp of aluminum, Bauhaus, Dessau

acter, the Bauhaus severed its tie with handicrafts and entered the realm of "industrial design."

Another outstanding metalworker in Dessau was Breuer, his invention of the tubular steel chair virtually revolutionizing the furniture industry. The Breuer of those days, however, was known as a furniture designer rather than metalworker, and the question immediately arises as to how to classify his work. The fact is that everyday objects are generally made of a combination of materials, just as Brandt's lighting fixtures were part metal and part glass. One would hardly call her a glassblower, any more than one would claim Breuer to be a weaver merely because he used textiles for the seats and back rests of his metal chairs.

We have reached the point, in our discussion of the objects of use created at the Bauhaus, where it is difficult to determine in what category or under which workshop to place a particular article. With the invention of the tubular steel chair, the boundary between the metal workshop and the furniture workshop ceased to exist; and when Moholy-Nagy left the Bauhaus in 1928, the metal shop was incorporated into the furniture workshop. To complete the story of the integration of the workshops, during the Bauhaus directorship of Mies van der Rohe all the shops were amalgamated into a single *Ausbau*, or interior design workshop. This step confirmed the intimate interrelationship of all the arts of design, as well as their contributing role within the totality, architecture.

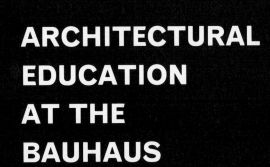

ARCHITECTURAL EDUCATION AT THE BAUHAUS

16

the teaching
of architecture
under
walter gropius

The third, and supposedly most important, part of the Bauhaus
curriculum was training in architecture, which was offered only to
the more gifted students after they had obtained their journeyman's
certificate. Here is the way Gropius explains this culminating phase
of the curriculum in "Idee und AufBau":

Only the graduate journeyman, thanks to his craft and form training,
is emotionally and manually mature enough to participate in building.
He brings with him to the work the preparation required by the new
architectural spirit.

The most important, final stage of the instruction at the Bauhaus is
the training in architecture with its objective of work in and for building, both at the experiment stage and on the building site. No apprentices are admitted to the experiment stage but only the most
talented journeymen, those who, by virtue of their own creative abilities, are capable of testing and developing manual and formal problems. They have access to the design atelier connected with the
experiment plot, as well as to all of the Bauhaus workshops, in order
that they may acquire proficiency in other handicrafts. Insofar as
existing commissions permit, they are drawn into formal and manual
collaboration in actual building projects so that, through practical
experience, they may become acquainted with the cooperation, in
architecture, of all of the building trades and, furthermore, have the
opportunity of earning a living. To the extent that the Bauhaus does
not offer supplementary courses in the technical engineering sci-
ences it is desirable that students especially gifted in architecture,
after consultation with their masters, complete these studies at tech-

nical universities and polytechnic institutes. A basic requirement for trained journeymen is that they should also work in outside craft and industrial plants in order to enlarge their understanding and to stimulate each other.[1]

Walter Gropius and Adolf Meyer, machinery hall of Fagus factory, 1919

One of the most striking aspects of Gropius's program was that a student was required to work for three and a half years before he became eligible to begin his architectural studies, and even then had to show a special aptitude to be admitted to the architecture atelier. Thus, for three and a half years after the opening of the Bauhaus in 1919, there could have been no bona fide architecture students because of Gropius's regulations governing admission to architectural study. In fact, neither an architectural department nor a place for the testing of building materials was ever established in Weimar.

I have already quoted Schlemmer on this subject. But I will quote him again. His remarks are contained in a letter written in March 1922, to his friend Otto Meyer:

What disturbs me and robs me of my peace of mind is the Bauhaus. Just imagine that thing, almost without a point of rest, with a thousand clashing ideas. The fact is, and people coming from the outside confirm it, that the name Bauhaus calls up images, justifiably enough, of construction and building, and what we actually have is a modern art school. . . . The class or workshop for construction and architecture, which should be the heart of the Bauhaus, does not officially exist, but instead of it the private office of Gropius. These commissions, factories, individual houses, more or less well solved, consequently constitute the thing about which everything else is supposed to revolve. It is an architecture business, contrasting with the scholastic function of a workshop. Whatever good things issue from the latter are made use of, skillfully or unskillfully, by the architectural office. This sore and shady point at the Bauhaus is and always has been a matter of anxiety to me.[2]

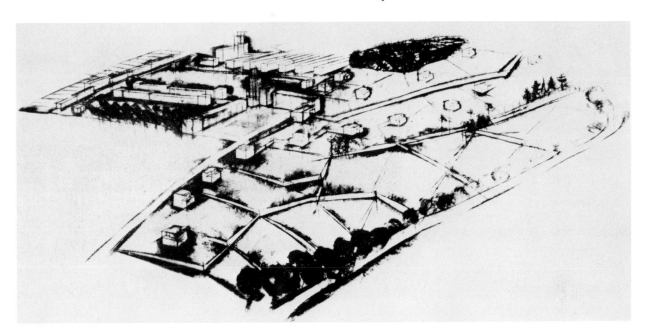

Walter Gropius, Fred Forbat and others, design for housing development for Weimar, 1923. Drawing by Farkas Molnár

This is more than a criticism of Gropius for failing to carry out the stated major objective of his program; it also shows that he used the students' talents to further his private architectural ends.

If one were to have asked Gropius why he failed to set up an architecture workshop, he could not have said that he had no money for it. It does take money to establish a metal workshop, a furniture workshop, a weaving studio, or a pottery shop, because expensive equipment is needed in these. But in an architecture department, all a student needs, basically, is a T-square, a couple of triangles, a drafting board, some tracing paper, and three or four grades of drafting pencils; and this equipment he customarily provides for himself. Thus an architecture workshop could have been inaugurated on the very day the Bauhaus opened since space for this was available. Gropius's refusal to do this has to be looked upon as a peculiar inconsistency in his thinking and a major shortcoming in his program as it was carried out in Weimar.

The failure to establish an architecture workshop or department occasioned much controversy at the Bauhaus in Weimar. In a diary entry of March 18, 1924, Schlemmer again comments on this. The situation in respect to architectural teaching at the Bauhaus had not improved, it seems, since he had complained about it to Otto Meyer two years before:

The Bauhaus has its March Revolution: ideal and practical recommendations of the Bauhaus journeymen for our Bauhaus which is

Farkas Molnár, design for a half-timbered house, 1922

continually in process of building. March had to come around before the experiences of last summer—a reference to the Bauhaus exhibition—could be summarized and interpreted. The declaration was so firm and so convincing that one is bound to reply to it.

It is always a happy occasion for the Bauhaus when the banner of architecture is held aloft and the allegiance to building is proclaimed. Inasmuch as the numbers of those who are seriously intent upon devoting themselves intensively and exclusively to building are on the increase, since, in other words, a young architecture guard exists, it is not to be wondered at that they struggle to acquire a basis for the realization of their aims. It seems to me that they are seeking to establish for themselves a kind of workshop which, similar in its basic assumptions, rights, and duties to the other Bauhaus workshops, will guarantee to them the pursuit of their ideal and practical objectives. It has always been a riddle to me why such a fundamental workshop never existed at the Bauhaus. I have for a long time stressed the need for a strong architecture workshop and I believe, in spite of all objections, that it must be established. I think that the danger of "drawing-board architecture," now that its terrors have been gruesomely depicted, no longer exists. Furthermore, things have changed; the time of wild stylistic eclecticism during which the drawing board architects flourished, is today opposed by an eagerness to investigate materials and come to grips with them, which will create new prerequisites.

Once this workshop is established at the Bauhaus, problems such as that of the questionable experimental stage and others will be solved more readily and of themselves.

I am uncertain whether or not the clamor for this workshop has been brought about by the perils of the Bauhaus, which is to say, its successes. Two workshops, pottery and weaving, are well on the way to becoming representative of the Bauhaus, if they are not already this. If, therefore, we find ourselves labeled as a good arts and crafts school, we ought not to be surprised.[3]

It was the students, as we noted, who urged that the intention of the Bauhaus to create architecture be realized in a model house, to be included in the 1923 exhibition, with the famous "House on the Horn" as the result. This was to have been the first unit of a Bauhaus housing development planned, under Gropius's direction, for a vacant site bordering on the Weimar park. Though a company was actually formed to carry out this *Siedlung*, it was destined to remain drawing-board architecture. It is probably just as well that it did, if the dwellings comprising it were to have been patterned after the House on the Horn with its "blind" living room.

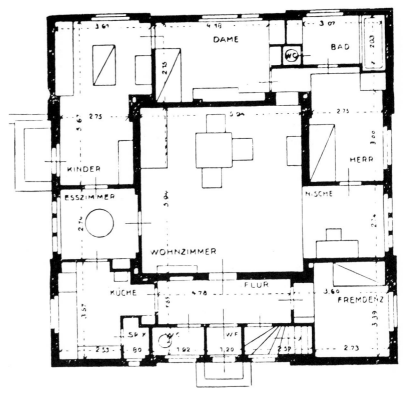

Georg Muche, plan of House on the Horn, Weimar, 1923

In spite of this, the students continued to press their demands for legitimate architectural study, so that in the spring of 1924 the director and council of masters, reluctantly, no doubt, gave them permission to form an architectural coöperative or association, the objective of which was to investigate problems of housing. This might have formed the basis of an architecture department if it and the Bauhaus in Weimar had been allowed to continue their work.

Despite the absence of architectural instruction in Weimar, a

Georg Muche, drawing of apartment building (not executed), 1924

few creditable architectural projects were turned out there, such as the apartment house designs by two of the moving spirits of the architectural association, Breuer and Muche. Other projects of interest, made as early as 1922, were two house designs and a "U-theater" by Farkas Molnár, and a multistory atelier-dormitory by Fred Forbat. The latter had an ingenious typical floor plan. Forbat later became an architect and planner of distinction. It is evident that talent for architecture existed at the Bauhaus in Weimar and that all it needed was encouragement.

When the Bauhaus moved to Dessau, the Mayor persuaded the Dessau legislature to spend a million marks to erect Gropius's first Bauhaus building[4] and the masters' houses (three two-family dwellings for the older professors and a one-family house for the director, Gropius. The new Bauhaus building was dedicated with a fitting ceremony in December 1926. Gropius never believed in halfway measures. When an exhibition was to be held or a building by him dedicated, he saw to it that all the instruments in the orchestra, and some that theretofore had never been included in it were called upon to celebrate the occasion.

The structures erected by Gropius in Dessau, considering the time, place, and the speed with which they were built, were, if by no means earth-shattering achievements tolerably good. I lived and worked for four years in and about the Bauhaus in Dessau, and I must say that I was not overwhelmed by the beauty of its architecture. For one, I was disturbed that in the exterior treatment of the canteen-auditorium (*Aula*), Gropius attempted to simulate a continuous band of windows by painting the columns between the openings black. Wright, who made such bands of windows long before Gropius, never stooped to so rudimentary a subterfuge. Gropius was never overly scrupulous in his functionalism; to his dying day, he loved to hang balconies on his buildings. He did this on the *Prellerhaus* of the Dessau Bauhaus. This was the atelier-dormitory wing of the building and it derived its name from the corresponding atelier building in Weimar. The balconies of the *Prellerhaus* were useless appendages. Gropius likewise hung balconies on his otherwise sober and restrained project for the Chicago Tribune Tower merely to enhance the design. These features always looked tacked on as an afterthought, whereas, when Le

Marcel Breuer, model of apartment building (not executed), 1924

Walter Gropius, houses for the Bauhaus Masters, erected in Dessau, 1928

Walter Gropius and Adolf Meyer, Chicago Tribune
Tower competition entry, 1922

Corbusier employed extrusions, protrusions, or projections in his
buildings, these became integral parts of an organic whole, a plastic, sculptural design wholly mastered and always unified.

17 the teaching of architecture under hannes meyer

In Dessau, Gropius finally took the long overdue step of establishing an architecture department at the Bauhaus. In 1927 he called in the Swiss architect Hannes Meyer to teach there. Suddenly, on February 4, 1928, Gropius tendered Mayor Hesse his resignation, and surrendered his office on April 1. Moholy-Nagy, Bayer, and Breuer left with him. His official reason for taking this step was that his long preoccupation with the affairs of the Bauhaus had forced him to neglect his architectural practice in Berlin. He maintained, furthermore, that the school was now in a prosperous posture and no longer needed his guiding hand. Privately, years later, he reiterated these reasons for his departure, in a conversation we had.

When Gropius resigned as director of the Bauhaus, he recommended Mies van der Rohe for the job; Mies turned it down. His second choice was Meyer, who was glad to accept. As director of the Bauhaus, Meyer was to prove to be nobody's puppet. He strongly modified the orientation of the school, turning it toward the sociological, the material, the functional, and, as he claimed, the psychological. Under his aegis, science flourished; art was harried. I recorded this transformation down almost fifty years ago in an article called "Sounder Aims and Methods in Teaching at Bauhaus," which was printed in the September 1930 issue of the *German-American Commerce Bulletin*; it was one of the earliest articles about the Bauhaus published in the United States:

> The removal of the Bauhaus to Dessau, where the present modern structure was built for it by Walter Gropius, may be said to mark the opening of the second and sounder phase in the history of the school.

This phase is characterized by a broader viewpoint of architecture, by the ideal of an architecture built for human beings and based upon a study of human psychological and physiological requirements. Architecture ceases to be the plaything of artists prepared to compromise human convenience, comfort, and health in the interest of a plastic ideal. The problem is no longer one of fitting ground plans to preconceived facades. It is further no longer one of forcing human beings into preconceived ground plans. The individual and his needs are studied and buildings are designed to meet these needs.

Walter Gropius, Törten housing development, Dessau

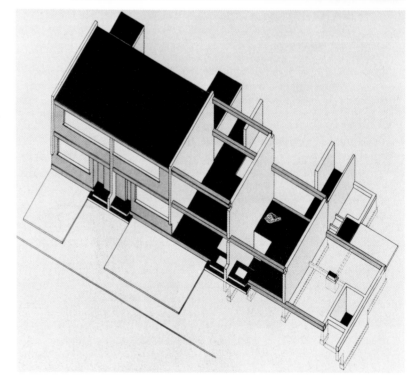

Walter Gropius, isometric diagram showing prefabricated concrete construction of Törten row houses, Dessau

To the question of the place of aesthetics in this architecture of practical needs, we answer that the beauty of this type of building, a beauty more deeply satisfying than that of pleasing exterior proportions or rich ornament, lies in the simplicity and logic of its construction, the orderliness of its planning, and its genuine adaptation to the life unfolding within it.

This article was written under Hannes Meyer's influence, but my interpretation of his principles scarcely conveys the flavor of his polemical position. There is a brashness in this which is wholly lacking in my tame recital and as it will give the reader a clue to his character, I will quote a part of his best known article, "bauen," which is all set in lowercase in accordance with the Bauhaus usage of that day:

all things in this world are a product of the formula:
(function × economics)
so none of these things are works of art:
all art is composition and consequently opposed to function
all life is function and therefore inartistic.
the idea of the "composition of a seaport" is enough to make one double up with laughter!
yet, how does the design of a city plan come about? or of a house plan? composition or function? art or life???? *building is a biological process. building is not an aesthetic process.* basically the new dwelling is not only a machine for living but also a biological apparatus serving the needs of body and spirit—the present day provides new building materials for the new way of building houses [Meyer lists here some 30 of these new materials]. we organize these building

Hannes Meyer, ca. 1928

elements, in accordance with economic principles, into a constructive whole. thus the individual form, the body of the building, the color of the material and the texture of the surface arise spontaneously, determined by life itself. (coziness and display are no leitmotifs in house building.) (the first is a matter of the human heart and not of the wall of a room. . . .)
(the second depends on the attitude of the host and not on his persian rug!)

architecture as an "emotional achievement of the artist" is unjustified.

building means the considered organization of living processes.
building viewed as a technical operation is therefore only a partial operation. the functional diagram and the economic program are the determining guidelines for a building ambition.
building is no longer the individual plaything of an architect's ambition.
building is a cooperative enterprise of workers and inventors. only he who, as master in the working community of others, masters the living process itself . . . is a master builder.
building therefore, instead of being the private affair of individuals (promoted by unemployment and lack of housing), becomes the collective concern of fellow citizens.

building is only organization: social, technical, economic, psychological organization.[1]

Mies van der Rohe once expressed to me his opinion that Meyer was a weak and immature person, unfit to direct a school like the Bauhaus. Gropius, in a letter to Tomás Maldonado, an admirer of Meyer's and director, at the time, of the *Hochschule für Gestaltung* in Ulm, also had some uncomplimentary things to say about his Bauhaus successor; and Arthur Niggli, publisher of Claude Schnaidt's monograph on Meyer, appended the letter at the back of the book. Among other things, Gropius says of Meyer:

I erred in my judgment of his character and am to blame that he became my successor—for I did not recognize the mask over his face. . . . Meyer's reputation as an architect with strong public interests had attracted me, and during the first period of his work with the Bauhaus, I never doubted his qualifications. I liked his work for the Trade Union School at Bernau which he had done with the modest and gifted Hans Wittwer. Nevertheless I never made true personal contact with him for he was taciturn and—as it turned out later—purposely concealed his personal views and intentions. . . . I should like to say in conclusion that after dispassionate reflection I value his contribution to architecture, as I have always done. But I cannot allot to him the importance with which you credit him during the years of the Bauhaus. His strategy and tactics were too petty; he was a radical petit bourgeois. His philosophy culminates in the assertion that "life is oxygen plus sugar plus starch plus protein," to which Mies promptly retorted: "Try stirring all that together; it stinks."[2]

Unlike Gropius, I doubt that Meyer was a knowing conniver, concealing his dark intentions until the opportunity of carrying them out presented itself. I am inclined to agree with Mies that he was an immature individual who endeavored to compensate for his feelings of insecurity by obstreperousness in his speech and rashness in his actions. Only this can explain the fact that, having been relieved of his position as director of the Bauhaus, he sought out Mies in his atelier in Berlin and wept as he pleaded his cause.

Meyer was always deferential to me, possibly because I was an American, who, along with my friend Fischer, who also entered the Bauhaus in 1928, enabled him to add the New World to the conquests of his school. He was outgoing and approachable and he associated on familiar terms with the students, something which one could hardly say of Mies. This is a reason, no doubt, why such a furor was raised when he was fired in 1930.

Reception at the Bauhaus for visiting South African students

Meyer brought a kind of order into the Bauhaus curriculum which had not existed under Gropius. He placed the emphasis in the teaching on architecture and introduced into the curriculum the courses which would give the students a well-rounded architectural education—those technical courses which Gropius, in his "Idee und Aufbau," had recommended, so lamely, that a student take at another institution. It now became possible for the Bauhaus to offer a *bona fide* architectural diploma. The students sought this certification of their achievement because it proved to be a genuine aid in landing a job. The Bauhaus diploma was unique in this category of scholastic documents. Mine, number 76, consists of five legal-size sheets of paper which, following a title page carrying the signatures of Mies van der Rohe and Hilberseimer and Schlemmer's Bauhaus seal, lists, semester for semester, the courses I took with the names of the instructors who taught them. A final page describes the projects I completed at the Bauhaus.

I don't remember attending any seminars with Meyer although I often talked with him in the Bauhaus canteen and elsewhere. During my first year at the Bauhaus a group of South African students, shepherded by a rather stuffy professor, paid the school a visit and Meyer asked me to conduct them about. It was on this occasion that I nearly had my picture taken in illustrious company—with Mayor Hesse, Dr. Hugo Junkers, head of the great Junkers airplane works, Kandinsky, Meyer, the stuffy professor, and his student protégés. While I was visiting the men's room, the photographer lined them all up in the stairhall of the Bauhaus and, upon my return, the photo had been taken.

I recall vividly the occasion when Meyer deliberately brought in a speaker to provide sport for the *Bauhäusler*. The man was the expressionist architect Hermann Finsterlin. The lecture took place in the *Aula* and Finsterlin showed slides of his projects, none of which, to be sure, had ever been executed. His building designs, like those of a number of German expressionist architects, were based upon the shapes of seashells, snail shells, and other natural objects. When he showed an irregular house plan, divided by partitions into irregular cells, a student in the audience asked him the purpose of the various rooms. Finsterlin replied that he had not assigned functions to the rooms, but that people living in the house would discover an appropriate use for each of them. More questions ensued and unabashed hilarity prevailed among the students. Meyer sat in the audience with a grin on his face, enjoying the spectacle. He had intended to throw Finsterlin to the wolves. His petty scheme had worked like clockwork, and he was pleased.

After the lecture I walked home with Finsterlin, trying, with kindness, to make up for some of the ill treatment he had received; I was ashamed of the Bauhaus, its students, and its director. We headed for the masters' houses, in one of which, I suppose, he was staying, possibly with Meyer. Years later I read some pronouncements written by Finsterlin in *Ja! Stimmen des Arbeitsrat für Kunst in Berlin*. Whatever one may think of his architecture, he was a cultivated man of the highest intelligence, a fact which opens an unbridgeable gap between him and Meyer.

One of my Bauhaus teachers, Dr. Karlfried Graf (Count) von Dürckheim of Leipzig, was a man of superior intelligence and a person of the utmost refinement. It is to Meyer's credit that he brought him to the Bauhaus. Dürckheim lectured on psychology. The students respected him, in spite of his aristocratic provenience, and he never lost control of his audience, even though, on occasion, someone asked him a crude question. I took careful notes in his course and Wingler has printed an abstract of these in his book.

Hannes Meyer also engaged Hilberseimer to set up a department of city planning at the Bauhaus. Hilbs had a distinguished background as a critic of art, architecture, and planning and had long been a correspondent of the *Sozialistische Monatshefte*,[3] *Das Kunstblatt*[4] and other influential periodicals. He had published a number of books on architecture and was to write many more on that subject and on planning. I purchased one of these, *Internationale Neue Baukunst* while traveling in the Rhineland, before I knew anything about Hilberseimer or the Bauhaus. His judgment was unerring and the book still constitutes the most reliable guide to the architecture of the twenties.

I always boasted to Hilbs, as we called him and as he insisted on being called, that I was an older *Bauhäusler* than he. I actually did reach the Bauhaus before he did. I once shared a compartment of a train bound for Berlin with Hilbs and Meyer, and I listened while they argued over the salary Hilbs was to receive for teaching

Hilberseimer, *Das Rheinlandhaus*, Berlin

at the Bauhaus; they settled on something like 2000 marks a year. I stood in the corridor with Meyer as we approached Berlin, looking at the grim suburban apartment houses we were passing. I was amazed when he averred that these were good architecture because they truly reflected the spirit of their period.

Hilbs was also a practicing architect and some of his early projects, minutely detailed and traditional in character, were published in the July 1919 issue of the magazine *Deutsche Kunst und Dekoration* (*German Art and Decoration*),[5] an issue which he succeeded in suppressing during his lifetime.*

A characteristic example of Hilbs's large building projects was his design for the Chicago Tribune Tower, which he made for the famous competition of 1922 but never sent in. This was reproduced in the catalog of the exhibition, *50 Years Bauhaus*, and in his book, *Contemporary Architecture—Its Roots and Trends*. However sound a solution this may have represented, the drawing, like his others, looked bald and poverty-stricken, almost amateurish. Hilbs was altogether lacking in facility as a draftsman, unlike his colleague, Mies van der Rohe, who was a supremely talented architectural delineator. Hilbs was apparently aware of this deficiency. I gather that it didn't disturb him very much. He once told me that architect friends in Germany used to accuse him of putting in the windows of his architectural drawings with a rubber stamp.

Hilbs built a number of substantial, if not inspiring, houses, one of them in the *Weissenhofsiedlung* in Stuttgart at Mies's invitation. The Stuttgart *Siedlung* and Hilbs's house were badly damaged by bombing in World War Two. Hilbs also erected a combined restaurant and office building on a corner in Berlin (1927), called the Rheinlandhaus. The very year he returned to that city to receive his second doctorate, after an absence of a quarter century, the municipal authorities, with seemingly calculated malevolence, demolished this, his only major building. Hilbs received the news with a resigned shrug of the shoulders. He had found his métier in planning and no longer set too much store by his accomplishments as an architect.

Hilbs was a notoriously formidable character who could strike terror in the hearts of grown men. I fell into disfavor with him early on. Actually, I gave him ample reason to think ill of me, because I did next to nothing for him in his city planning course. It was not that I disliked Hilbs and the material he taught but, rather, that I

Hilberseimer, Chicago Tribune Tower competition entry

*Call it vanity or attribute it to embarrassment, like many other architects whose early works are seldom representative of their later, mature designs, Hilberseimer did not want his traditional, highly detailed early works known, so he told no one of this publication. Dearstyne's use of the term "suppressing" might be misleading. It should be taken to mean that Hilberseimer was able to keep from public knowledge the publication of his early work. According to the Brookhaven Press of La Cross, Wisconsin, the microfiche they made of *Deutsche Kunst und Dekoration*'s entire production includes Hilberseimer's work on pages 208–216, the publications pagination being uninterrupted.

esteemed Kandinsky and his subject more. I did research under the latter in the elements of pictorial design and delivered several lectures on painting in his class. I devoted so much time to these activities that I had little left over for Hilbs. He was determined to kick me out of the Bauhaus but Kandinsky intervened. I am proud to have been retrieved from the brink of banishment by so distinguished an individual.

Hilbs once examined the scribbled notebook I used in his and other courses and rebuked me for my sloppiness. I was so stung by his criticism that I turned over a new (notebook) leaf and thereafter kept exemplary notes, transcribing them carefully at the end of each day. These notes, or most of them, in longhand German, are now in the Bauhaus collection of the Busch-Reisinger Museum at Harvard.

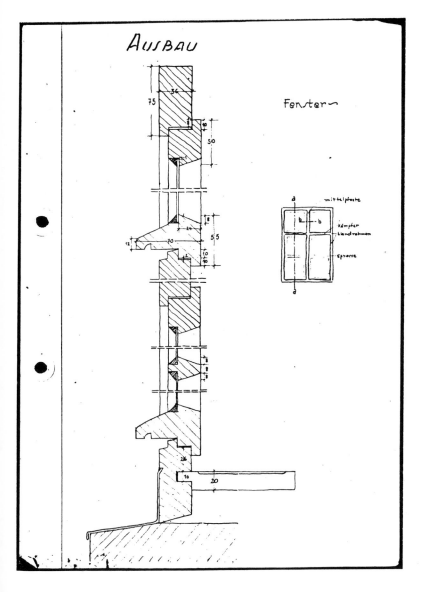

Two exerted pages from a notebook of Howard Dearstyne containing his Bauhaus course notes
see overleaf

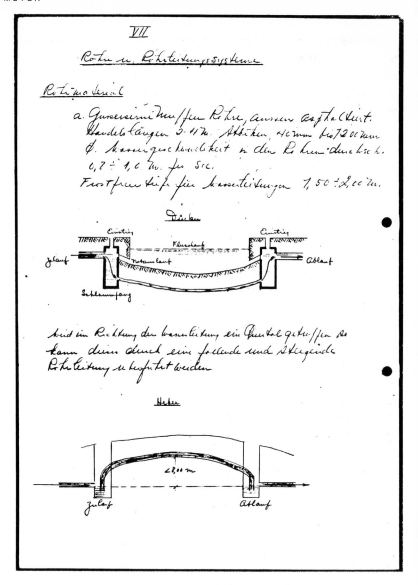

At Dessau, Hilbs adhered faithfully to Hannes Meyer's doctrines. I recall the time he ridiculed an architecture student for shifting the windows in a house design in order to attain a more pleasing facade. He accused the young man of the crime of formalism, an anathema in Meyer's hard-line functionalist era. Under the influence of Mies van der Rohe Hilbs moderated his views—he had met his master, and he listened to his voice. Hilbs proved to be a useful counterbalance for Mies later, in that he stressed the functional aspects of architecture and planning, which the latter was prone to neglect. He insisted, for example, that buildings be so oriented as to receive optimum sunlight. Mies agreed with him in the matter of houses but neglected orientation altogether in his apartment buildings. Hilbs once asked him if he thought that the truth changed with the number of stories. He never reported Mies's answer.

Whatever I failed to learn from Hilbs at the Bauhaus I caught up on when I came to teach at the Illinois Institute of Technology, for his instruction there was a continuation and extension of his teaching in Dessau. His principles were simple enough but, because of the political and economic structure of American society, difficult to execute. As I mentioned, he believed in situating buildings in such a way as to obtain for them the most desirable sun penetration during the various seasons of the year. He believed that housing developments should have a combination of high- and low-rise structures to allow people the choice of living in apartments, row-houses or detached single-family dwellings. He believed that workers should live near their work in order to reduce their traveling time and curtail the volume of automobile traffic; he placed factories in close proximity to housing developments but in such a position that prevailing winds would carry most of their smoke away from the dwellings. He believed that children should be able to walk to school without crossing busy thoroughfares, so he dead-ended the access streets in his developments and placed schools in parks between them. These are among the main points he stressed in his teaching, and he saw to it that his students observed them in their planning projects. He also had them make plans for the stage-by-stage transformation of deteriorated existing cities and introduced them to the problems involved in the long-term development of entire regions. He furnished them the tools with which to create healthier and happier living conditions and many of them, doubtless, have already made contributions to these goals. Hilbs was one of the world's outstanding city planners, and his teachings provided useful guidelines for the future shaping of our environment. I always revered the man, whose

Hilberseimer, house in Weissenhof settlement, Stuttgart, 1927

virtues outweighed his shortcomings a hundredfold.

Among Meyer's other appointees was Peterhans, photographer, philosopher, pedagogue, and perfectionist. Meyer brought Peterhans to the Bauhaus to establish a photographic department which, however much photography had been propagated at the school in Weimar and Dessau by Moholy-Nagy and embraced by the students, had never existed before as such. His job also included taking photographs for publication of objects produced in the workshops. Some of the finest photos made, at the time, of Bauhaus textiles and other objects were his work. He also taught higher mathematics to those who were interested.

Peterhans's major achievement was his exquisite photographic compositions. He carefully arranged his compositions of various objects, bits and pieces of inconsequential things—a slice of lemon, a scrap of yarn, a twist of wire, a fragment of a veil, a scarified board, almost anything—and then recorded them with the camera. The black and white prints he created are rich and satisfying combinations of forms, tones, and textures. When he came to the United States, World War Two was approaching and the government confiscated his photographic equipment on the ground that he was a potential enemy alien and might use it for espionage purposes. Peterhans was so incensed by this that he gave up photography altogether, concerning himself with other things. Only in his latter years did he begin to toy with the camera again, trying his hand at color, in a sort of tentative way.

He and I became friends in Dessau and remained so until his death in 1960. Our amicable relations became temporarily strained on one occasion, however, when Hubert Döllner, a fellow student, and I locked ourselves in the only Bauhaus darkroom (it was Döllner's bright idea), in order to get some work done undisturbed. We didn't exactly endear ourselves to Peterhans, who knocked furiously on the door, demanding that we open it. We opened it.

Peterhans was a strange and difficult man. He was embittered by his experiences in World War One in which, it was said, he was shell-shocked. And he was lonely. I remember he called one afternoon at my apartment in Berlin-Steglitz, where my wife and I moved after the closing of the Bauhaus in Dessau, insisting that he could remain only a short time. He stayed and stayed until my wife and I invited him to supper, which he accepted. Following this, he sat for so long that we felt it necessary to ask him to spend the night. He spent the night, had breakfast with us and eventually departed.

Hilberseimer joined Mies in the United States by prearrangement. Not so Peterhans. Mies, who prior to settling down in Chicago sojourned twice for several weeks in New York City, ran into Peterhans one day on Fifth Avenue and invited him to teach at the Illinois Institute of Technology. Together they devised the course

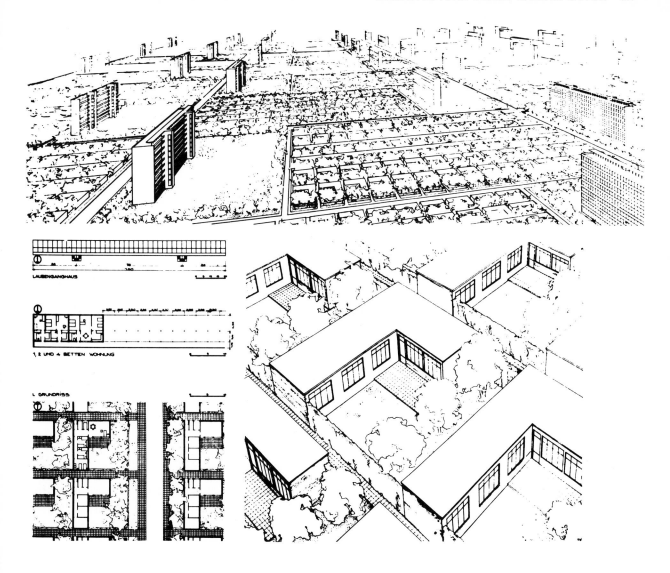

LAUBENGANGHAUS

1, 2 UND 4 BETTEN WOHNUNG

L. GRUNDRISS

which Peterhans subsequently taught for over twenty years. This course, called Visual Training, was Mies's substitute for the *Vorkurs* taught by Albers at the Bauhaus. He had not been overly content with Albers's course, since he considered it too *spielerisch*, serving inadequately as a foundation for architecture. The visual training course was a course in abstract design, purporting to develop in the students a feeling for proportions, space relationships, and the harmonious juxtaposition of forms, colors, and textures. It was a much more rigorously controlled basic course than anything Albers had ever taught and could serve as fundamental training for artists as well as architects. Peterhans taught the course with the utmost sensitivity, though he left many students in the dark as to the utility of the exercises which he gave them.

Plan for housing combining high-rise apartments and single-family dwellings, by an unidentified student of Hilberseimer

the dismissal
of hannes
meyer

Dissension within the Bauhaus and attacks from without led to Meyer's dismissal by the Mayor of Dessau, without notice, on August 1, 1930. Though there were a number of active communists at the Bauhaus and differences of opinion existed, I was not aware of any serious discord in the school. It is true that Klee and Kandinsky had consistently resisted Meyer's rigorous functionalism and it was no secret that the latter supported Mayor Hesse's move to replace Meyer. The step was actually taken in an effort to placate the rising political opposition to the Bauhaus in the Dessau legislature, where conservative nationalists (*Deutschvölkischen*) and National Socialists were gaining in power and were clamoring for an end to the "Judeo-Syrian desert architecture"* of the "inartistic high-toned Bolsheviks (*Edelbolshewisten*) of the Bauhaus." Hesse had instructed Meyer to eliminate the communist cell at the Bauhaus; the latter had procrastinated. When, in addition to this, the Nazi legislators denounced Meyer for contributing money in the name of the Bauhaus to aid striking Mansfeld miners and demanded his dismissal, Hesse yielded to their pressure.[6]

Many people have assumed that Meyer was a communist, chiefly because, following his dismissal from the Bauhaus, he went to Russia to work as an architect and planner. He remained in Moscow until 1936 and held there a number of teaching and planning positions which sound impressive but which, apparently, resulted in nothing tangible. I suspect that his work was a disappointment either to him or to the Russians, since he left their country so soon.[†] He went back to his native Switzerland where he resided in Geneva until 1939. While there he built a children's home at Mumliswil. He also, according to Schnaidt, "returned to a study of painting and its laws of composition." This was the man who, in his article "bauen," had sneered at artists and artistic composition and had harassed the painters at the Bauhaus. I recall reading a letter (now lost) written by him from Mexico to Dr. Charles Kuhn, then curator of the Busch-Reisinger Museum, in which he

---

*The National Socialists coined the term "Judeo-Syrian desert architecture" to describe any buildings (usually those by members of the Modern Movement) that did not meet their criteria as *völkisch*, national or pure German. The reference to Judea and Syria is pejorative but has little to do with either the religion of the architect in question or the location of his buildings since, for example, the term was also used by the National Socialists to catagorize the buildings at the *Weissenhofsiedlung*, Stuttgart (1927).

[†] Meyer seems to have been frustrated in his attempts to realize projects undertaken during his years in the Soviet Union for two reasons: He was basically impatient with bureaucracy; and, more important, he was unsympathetic to the prescribed nature of Stalinist architecture.

claimed Klee and Kandinsky as ornaments of his Bauhaus directorship as though he had championed them. Meyer, it seems, after
his over-zealous functionalist spree, finally came to his senses.

In 1938 he traveled to the United States and Mexico and, in the
latter country, attended three congresses. On June 1, 1939, he was
invited to work in Mexico by the government of the enlightened
President Lázaro Cárdenas. He remained there until 1949, teaching
planning and making planning studies for various towns and dis-
tricts in Mexico. He once more returned to his homeland, settling
near Lugano, where he devoted himself to architectural writing.
This work was interrupted by illness and he died on July 19, 1954.

18

**the teaching
of architecture
under
mies van der rohe**

When Hannes Meyer was dismissed, Mayor Hesse again asked Gropius to recommend a candidate for the directorship; Gropius once more proposed Mies van der Rohe. This time, surprisingly enough, Mies accepted and took over the Bauhaus in Dessau in August, 1930.*

Gropius couldn't have found a more solid citizen than Mies. He had first met Mies in Peter Behrens's office, where they and (for a brief time) Le Corbusier had worked together. Since that time, Mies had designed the Barcelona Pavilion, one of the outstanding architectural works of this century; directed the building of the *Weissenhofsiedlung*, the most notable experimental housing development ever undertaken; and made revolutionary designs for skyscrapers, department stores, and houses. He was one of the most highly respected architects in Germany both because of his accomplishments and because of his well-established integrity.

When Mies arrived at the school, his reception was scarcely wholehearted. A large number of students, egged on by a handful

*Mies disliked administrative responsibilities. However, the case can be made that when the first offer of the Bauhaus directorship was made (in 1928), his private practice made it difficult (if not impossible) to consider accepting the position: he was at work on two houses in Krefeld, Germany, one for Dr. Jurgen Esters (1928), the other for Hermann Lange (1928); in addition, he was responsible (with Lilly Reich) for the design of the exhibits in the German section of the International Exposition, Barcelona, as well as the design of a reception pavilion for the German government, the Barcelona Pavilion, (1928–1929). Further, he had received the commission to design a residence for the Tugendhat family in Brno, Czechoslovakia (1928–1930). By 1930 these works were completed; and, perhaps, the directorship represented (albeit short-lived) financial security. Considering the generally worsening world-wide economic condition, Mies's decision to accept a contractually agreed upon annual salary was not an unreasonable decision.

Mies van der Rohe in Crown Hall, 1965 with bust of Mies by Hugo Weber in background. Photo: Dirk Lohan

Le Corbusier (left) and Mies van der Rohe walking together, at the Weissenhof settlement, Stuttgart, 1927

of militant communists, gathered in the canteen and demanded that he exhibit his work, to enable them to decide whether or not he was qualified to direct the Bauhaus. Mies was incensed and called in the Dessau police to restore order. I was not among the students who gathered in the canteen to voice their protest against Meyer's firing and the hiring of Mies. Actually, I was not heart-broken when Meyer left. I had become weary of his exaggerated functionalism; I had even considered leaving the Bauhaus to study elsewhere. So my mind was open in respect to the new director, about whom, however, I knew next to nothing. I had never even heard of the Barcelona Pavilion, though I was in Europe in 1929 at the time it was erected. I have regretted ever since that I failed to see it. I shall not forget how Behrens reacted to the pavilion when he saw it. "Mein Herz ging auf" ("My heart leaped up"), he said later, describing the experience. It was Mies who, gratified that he had won the praise of his master, told us of this.

Mies van der Rohe teaching at the Bauhaus, Dessau. *Left to right* Annemarie Wilke, Newmann, Mies, Dr. Hermann Klumpp

The internal disorder at the Bauhaus caused the closing of the school for some six weeks. By the time the Bauhaus reopened in the summer of 1930, Mies had expelled the main troublemakers and tranquility reigned. Taking no chances, he interviewed each remaining student individually in his office on the bridge (the two-story building element which spanned the street between the Bauhaus and the Trades School, which was a separate institution). When my turn came, I entered the new director's office with some trepidation. He sat there in silence and, out of sheer embarrassment, I opened the conversation. Said I, "What do you think of our American architect, Frank Lloyd Wright?" Mies replied, without hesitation, "Er ist ein ganz grosser Architekt" ("He is a very great architect"). Then, warming to his subject, he told me how, when Gropius, Le Corbusier, and he were working together in Behrens's office, the latter had shown them the first drawings of buildings by Wright, which they had never seen (presumably plates from the Wasmuth portfolio). "Es war für uns wie eine Offenbarung" ("it was like a revelation to us"), he added. I asked him another question, one inspired by my long subjection to Meyer's materialistic doctrines. I said to Mies, "Is it no longer right to seek beauty in architecture?" He quickly assured me that one might still strive for beauty in architecture. I came presently to realize that the search for architectural excellence had been a lifelong preoccupation of Mies's and, indeed, he soon dispatched us students in quest of it.

The Bauhaus architecture department occupied a fairly large L-shaped space on the second floor of the bridge. A smaller rear room communicated with this, where Alcar Rudelt and Friedrich Engemann conducted their classes in the technical aspects of architecture. Mies lectured mostly in the bigger space, as befitted his stature.

When Mies arrived at the Bauhaus, I had completed the courses required for admission to the architecture department and so became one of his students. There were six or seven of us in the class. This was the first course that Mies taught at the Bauhaus and, for that matter, anywhere else. If I take a certain pride in the fact that I was among his first students, I think that this is pardonable. I landed at the Bauhaus partly by accident; once there, I had the good sense to stay.

The students whom I remember distinctly from Mies's first class were Eduard Ludwig, Hermann Blomeier, Willy Heyerhoff, and Hubert Döllner. I came to the class with nothing to show from my two years of architectural study at Columbia. It was lucky for me that I had left at home my design plates, somewhat misguided attempts at a new architecture—Mies couldn't cast his sharply critical eye over them. But Blomeier and Heyerhoff were not so fortunate as I. They had the temerity to bring their previous work with them. Both fresh from a period of study with Paul Klopfer, a reputable architect and teacher who conducted a building trades school in Holzminden, they were steeped in their own achievements. They showed Mies some prints of buildings designed by them under Klopfer. Mies ran roughshod over them, marking them up with a soft pencil to indicate how they should have been done. Blomeier and Heyerhoff were so hurt by Mies's ruthlessness that they stayed away from class for a full month. In time they recovered, becoming Mies's devoted students. When Mies died in August 1969, Hermann wrote me a touching letter in which he said, among other things,

> If you are able to attend his funeral, dear Howard, please cast a red rose in his grave for me.
>
> We have just lost the greatest master builder of this century and one of the noblest persons. How thankful must we be that we were privileged to be his students.

The first problem which Mies gave us was a single-bedroom "court house,"* a house, that is, facing a walled-in garden. Actually, the project involved the design of a series of such houses and gardens, joined together to form a settlement. This problem

*Through the 1930s, Mies seemed drawn to (or preoccupied with) the problem of a walled house with courtyards. These court houses, rich in their variety, clearly demonstrate the ingenuity and the originality Mies brought to his work. That he should have given this as a problem for his students to investigate seems reasonable considering his own interest in it.

Howard Dearstyne, sketch for one-bedroom
house, 1931. Corrections and freehand perspective by Mies van der Rohe

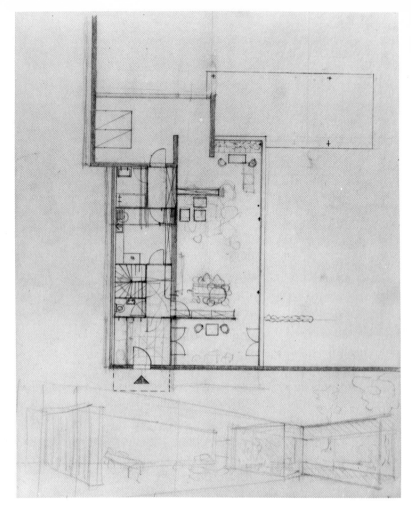

Mies van der Rohe, sketch of entrance hall of
Howard Dearstyne's one-bedroom house, incorporating Mies's changes

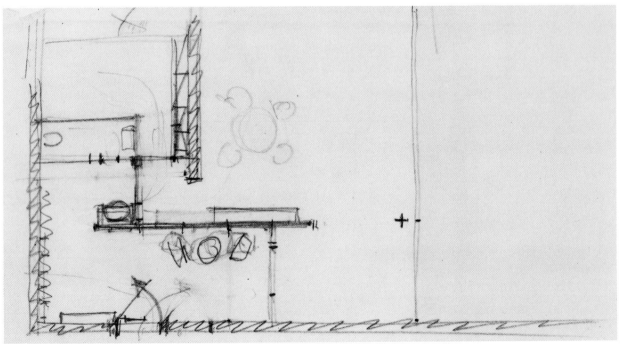

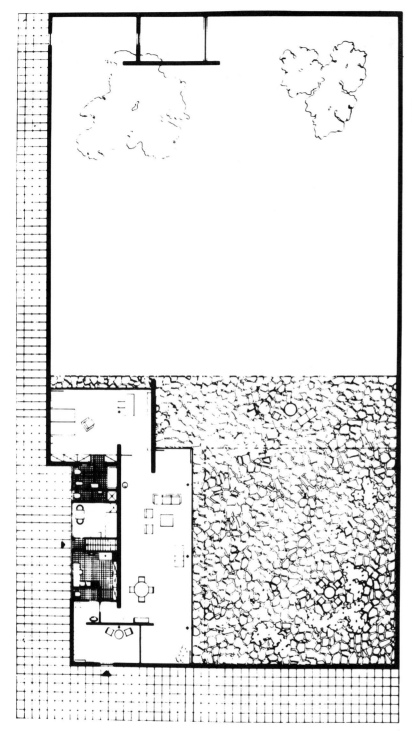

Howard Dearstyne, final drawing of one-bedroom house, 1931

gave us our first introduction to Mies's open planning. The houses that we did, guided by the hand of the master, were very much alike. They consisted of an elongated rectangle enclosed on three sides by brick walls and on the fourth, the long side facing the garden, by floor-to-ceiling glass. There was a bedroom and bath at one end and a kitchen and utility room at the other. The living-dining room, separated from the sleeping area by only a cabinet wall, occupied the central space between these. A garage and open service court adjoined the rear wall of the house. Mies could hardly have made the problem simpler, yet this house was eminently livable.

Mies's court houses amounted to a revival, in modified form, of an ancient architectural usage; in light of the prevalence today of the exposed, free-standing house, it was an important innovation. Mies was to make many ingenious variations of this simple court house, and his students, including me, were also to experiment with it.

Mies was designing houses in those days and he set us to designing houses too, one after another. He was an exacting teacher. Time and again, when I presented him sketch plans which I thought had merit, he would say laconically, "Versuchen Sie es wieder" ("Try it again"). We respected his judgment too much to argue with him. Little by little, we began to catch on, to develop a feeling for this new kind of architecture.

The teaching of architecture, or of any other art, for that matter, involves the tediously slow awakening in the student of aesthetic insight; it has relatively little to do with the training of the intellect, however important this may be. It is concerned with the development of wisdom rather than with the accumulation of knowledge. Mies van der Rohe had this profound understanding and he attempted, with some measure of success, to impart this to us.

After making many sketches for him (Mies insisted that one should do at least a hundred!), I finally produced a house plan he liked. This was a one-story court house, with an elongated living-dining room and a single bedroom which communicated with it. Two external sides of the house were continuous with the walls of the court, while the living room and bedroom, facing the garden, were enclosed in floor-to-ceiling glass. A porch roof, supported by a centrally placed row of free-standing columns, connected the house with the court wall opposite.

I shall not forget the trouble we had smoothing out the rough spots in the plan. At one point we were about to abandon the scheme because we could find no place in the kitchen for the garbage pail! The entrance also posed a difficult problem. In my original plan, the connection of the foyer with the living room was too abrupt. After sketching over my layout for hours, Mies finally hit upon a solution which provided an indirect transition from the entrance hall to the living room and, at the same time, an indirect route from the kitchen to the dining area. This kind of circuitous passage from one space to the next was a characteristic feature of Mies's spatial architecture.

Mies used to remark that if one could design a house well, he could design anything. I am so firmly convinced of the truth of this that I have repeated it to my students for years to impress upon them the necessity of mastering the fundamentals of architecture as these are encountered in the simpler problems.

Early in 1932, Mies brought Lilly Reich to the Bauhaus in Dessau to assist him. She was accomplished in interior design and had worked with Mies in this capacity on a number of his projects. She was an astute woman who, I have always believed, had learned most of what she knew about architecture, interior and exterior, from Mies. How they became associated is something which no one of my acquaintance knows and into which no one inquired. We simply accepted Reich as Mies's right-hand-"man."*

Lilly Reich teaching at the Bauhaus, Dessau. *From left* Dr. Hermann Klumpp, Emanuel Lindner, Frau Reich and Annemarie Wilke. Author, barely visible, at right

Reich designed a house for the Berlin Building Exposition of 1931. It was connected by a free-standing wall with Mies's house in that same show. Though Mies doubtless helped her with it, it was hardly up to his standard. This was, I believe, the only house or, for that matter, the only building she ever created, for she had been, primarily, a textile designer. It was for this reason, doubtless, that Mies put her in charge of the weaving workshop when she came to the Bauhaus. He also made her head of interior design (one never spoke of "interior decoration" in those days and Mies and Hilberseimer subsequently banned even the term "design"). In any event, Reich instructed us in the appropriate uses of furniture and textile materials in the houses and other buildings we did, and even brought to class samples of upholstery, drapery, and floor-covering materials to aid us in selecting the furnishings for our buildings.

*Dearstyne treads too carefully in order to protect Mies's and Reich's reputations. Shortly after his separation from his wife (late 1925 or early 1926), Mies began a long personal and professional relationship with Reich which lasted until he immigrated to the United States (1938).

The story has been told, though never in print, of how Hudnut was rebuffed by Reich. Professor Hudnut, my teacher of the history of architecture at Columbia, and an architect, had become head of the School of Architecture there and then head of architecture at Harvard. He came to Europe in 1936 to find a likely person to direct that institution's Graduate Department of Architecture and first contacted Mies. I understand that Reich presumed to speak for the always reticent and indecisive Mies and stated "his" conditions in so aggressive a manner that the sensitive, scholarly, and somewhat stuffy Hudnut was offended and turned, instead, to Gropius, whom he hired. Whether, if this story is true, Reich did Mies a disservice is a question. Had he gone to Cambridge, his opportunities there would doubtless not have been so great as those which awaited him in Chicago.

One of my letters home, dated December 20, 1931, runs, in part, as follows:

I'm using the few days until Christmas to put the finishing touches on the house design I've been working on since I arrived (from a trip to the United States). The house is a small one with living room, one bedroom, and the necessary utility rooms such as bath, kitchen, etc. The house is of the same character as the two designs I had with me in America. Mies van der Rohe continues to hold us to the small problems. But that he is right in doing this is indicated by the fact that it takes weeks or months to do a small house of this nature in a decent way. The very simplicity of these houses is their chief difficulty. It's much easier to do a complicated affair than something clear and simple.

We're learning a tremendous lot from Mies van der Rohe. If he doesn't make good architects of us, he'll at least teach us to judge what good architecture is. One of the uncomfortable sides of associating with an architect of the first rank is that he ruins your taste for about all but one-half of one percent of all the architecture that's being done the world over. Mies van der Rohe not only comes down hard on the American architects (for which he has, without the shadow of a doubt, the most perfect justification) but holds that one doesn't need the fingers of one hand to count the German architects who are doing good work.

He sets a very high standard, which is a fact that should only cause us to rejoice. It's much easier to work under less critical men and content yourself with middle-rate work. That's what I was doing at Columbia and what most of the students in America (and here) are doing. But I thank my stars that I landed where I did.

Mies had moved into one of the masters' houses and he spent three days each week in Dessau. If I am not mistaken, he had

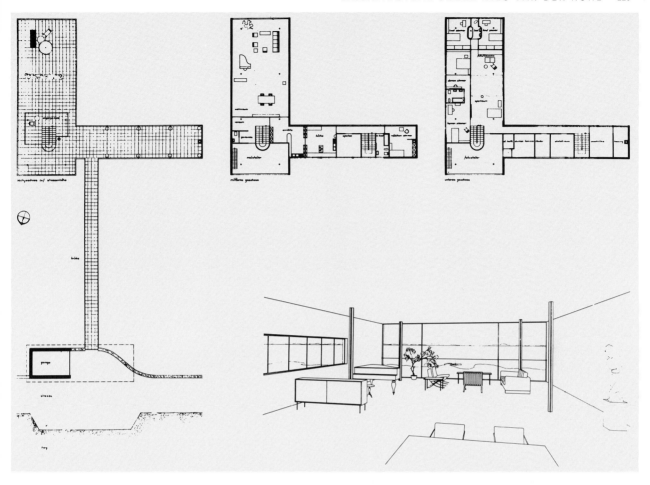

Pius Pahl, house on a lake shore, plans and interior view, 1931. Project done under Mies van der Rohe

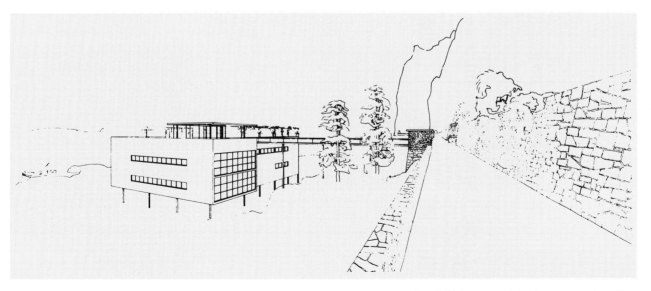

Pius Pahl, house on a lake shore, perspective of house as viewed from road approaching it, 1931. Project done under Mies van der Rohe

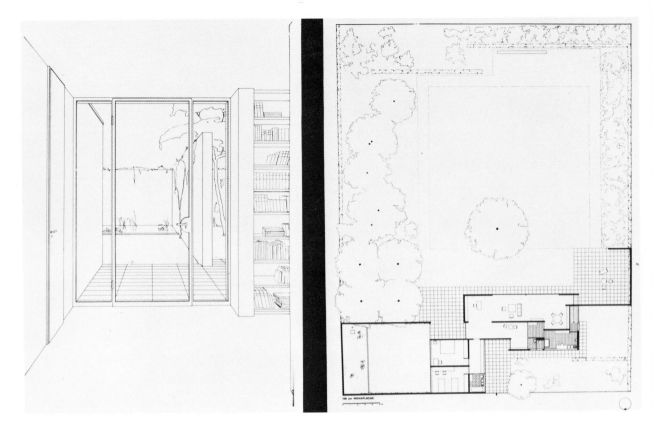

Herman Blomeier, two-bedroom house designed in Mies van der Rohe's architecture class at the Bauhaus, Dessau, 1931

equipped it with his own furniture. He invited some of us students in to talk, one evening, and served us aquavit. It is strange how one frequently forgets big things and remembers only little ones. The only thing I can remember about it, other than drinking aquavit for the first time, is Mies's rising suddenly from his easy chair to adjust the full-length window curtain which was somewhat disarranged. This had doubtless disturbed him for some time and his mounting uneasiness about it finally spurred him to action. I'm sure that Mies told us important things that evening but this simple act is all that I recall. It evidently said something about order which impressed me; and after all, order in architecture was a subject upon which Mies frequently discoursed.

My classmate, Hertel, took it upon himself, with the acquiescence of the director, of course, to arrange a series of exhibitions of modern art at the Bauhaus—works of Klee, Kandinsky, and Feininger, paintings by Bauhaus students and also of outside artists. He got little encouragement from Mies, who was intent on promoting architecture. One of the exhibitions which Hertel arranged consisted of oil paintings by a one-armed Berlin artist named Werner Scholz. The paintings were good (Hertel would otherwise not have hung them) but the subject of one canvas was abortion, and it bore, as a title, the number of the article in the German statutes of that day which forbade that practice. When Mies, who

Eduard Ludwig, redesign of old department store in Dessau, 1932. Project of architecture class under Mies van der Rohe. The two pictures show building before and after its renovation

had not seen the paintings beforehand, viewed the exhibition and came upon that one, he was beside himself and forthwith had the offending work removed. There ensued a furious battle of words between him and Hertel, who was rather excitable. Mies claimed, no doubt rightly, that the picture would draw down upon the Bauhaus the wrath of the townspeople who saw the exhibit and who, for the most part, were ill-disposed toward the school. Hertel, also rightly enough, defended the artist's right to freedom of expression. Naturally, his arguments were unavailing; I believe this was the last of his exhibitions.

Mies apparently felt guilty about his action because he asked me what I thought about Hertel's exhibitions. I was bold enough to tell him that if he didn't care for art he should not allow them to continue. This was a cutting remark because, though he owned some paintings, Mies, at that time, was more or less indifferent to the fine arts. (Later he became an enthusiast and assembled a fine collection of paintings.)

Mies and Hilberseimer had worked out an arrangement whereby they commuted between Berlin and Dessau alternately so that one of them was at the Bauhaus while the other was in the capital. When the last semester arrived, our class was reduced to four people. Eduard Ludwig and Edgar Hecht were two of these and I am fairly certain that Döllner was the third man who, with me, completed the quartet. We moved from the architecture department on the "bridge" connecting the two wings of the school to a ground-floor atelier in the workshop wing of the Bauhaus. We were assured of privacy because the room, to which we each had a key, was kept locked. Here we worked on our final projects, our "diploma problems" (*Diplomarbeiten*). I elected to do a combined restaurant and bathing pavilion for the Kühnau Lake on the outskirts of Dessau. Mies and I walked out to see the site.

Howard Dearstyne, model of one of four-bedroom row houses designed under Mies van der Rohe Bauhaus, Berlin, 1932–1933

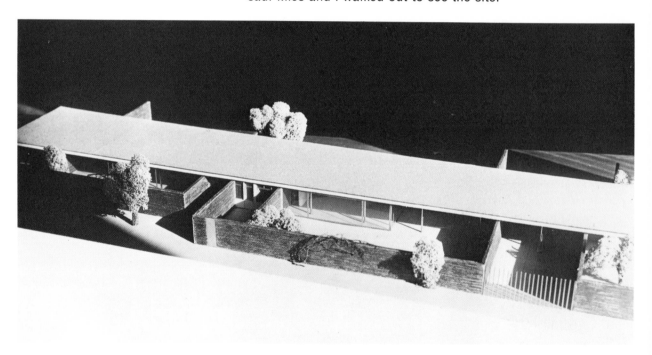

In our last semester, we four students had enviable opportunities to talk to Mies. Isolated from the rest of the school, we had him to ourselves for hours at a time. I wrote my parents about this on June 12, 1932:

We saw a lot of Mies van der Rohe last week. He came on three different days to our atelier. Wednesday he spent over three hours with us and ordered coffee for us from the canteen. Thursday he came for about an hour. Friday he came twice and spent about 5 hours with us, all told. We had coffee again. We [the 4 of us] have gotten well acquainted with him and he seems to enjoy talking with us more than with the lower semesters.

We discuss everything, architecture, art, philosophy, politics, etc. These discussions don't, therefore, always have a direct bearing upon our work but are tremendously interesting and valuable because Mies van der Rohe is a man of profundity and richness of experience. It would be worth my while being here just for these discussions if I did no designing whatsoever. My hope is that the Bauhaus doesn't break up and that I can return [from a planned trip to America.]

All four of us received our coveted Bauhaus diplomas in July 1932, although Hecht almost failed to make it, chiefly because he put such atrocious-looking trees in a rendering of his project. He and his wife were much upset when they learned that Mies had threatened to flunk him, and they asked me to use my good offices with the director in an effort to rescue him. I did so, and Mies reluctantly relented and let him pass. I have heard nothing from or about Hecht in the intervening years. Blomeier has reminded me that he and Heyerhoff likewise received their diplomas in July 1932, having been permitted to do their diploma projects away from the school.

We "upperclassmen" just managed to get in under the wire with our Bauhaus diplomas. The Nazis, who had persistently threatened to close the school and, for that matter, to raze the building, at last gained control of the Dessau legislature. Fully intending to extirpate the hated Bauhaus, they nevertheless saw fit to give their contemplated action some appearance of legality by arranging a *pro forma* trial of the school. They required the director to make an exhibition of Bauhaus work, on the basis of which, they claimed, they would decide whether the school deserved to continue or should be closed. They appointed as judge Schultze-Naumburg, an ultraconservative architect who despised the Bauhaus and who, in turn, was despised by it.

Mies who, despite his misgivings, had no alternative, assembled the best of the student work for the fruitless exhibition. I recall that one joker insinuated a thick slice of ham into the exhibition and placed it, under glass, on one of the display tables. Mies, whom the critical situation had made more than usually exacting, expelled the girl and her ham forthwith from the Bauhaus. Most of us students took the challenge seriously however, and strove to turn out our very best work. Before the inevitable blow fell, my wife and I had left for a vacation in the United States. When we returned to Dessau in October 1932, Schultze-Naumburg had passed judgment on the school, and the Bauhaus was closed. Mies, a number of the instructors, and many of the students had departed for Berlin, where Mies established a new Bauhaus on a private basis. My wife and I gave up our apartment in Dessau and followed them.

Bauhaus diploma of Howard Dearstyne

bauhaus dessau hochschule für gestaltung

durch beschluss der konferenz vom   5. juli 1932   ist

dem studierenden   h o w a r d   d e a r s t y n e

geboren 2.8.1903   zu   albany/ u.s.a.

als beleg für das mit erfolg abgeschlossene studium

in der   b a u / a u s b a u   –   abteilung

dieses   **b a u h a u s - d i p l o m**
nr.76

zuerkannt worden.

dessau, den 11. juli 1932

die direktion:

professor mies van der rohe

die abteilungsleitung:

architekt l.hilberseimer.

mies's unknown project

Nobody has ever said or written anything about it. As far as I know, no one has ever heard of it; and I am the only person who has pictures of it. It may be the only architectural work of Mies's that has been built but never published. I refer to a project called *Das Loch in der Klagemauer* (1930). The story of Das Loch hinges on the fact that the grounds of Gropius's master houses in Dessau were partially enclosed by a white stuccoed brick wall, over head-height. At the intersection of three streets, the wall described a kind of hyperbolic curve. The Dessau city fathers, to whom matters of the first importance, such as this, were entrusted, concluded that this was a promising location for a refreshment stand and commissioned Mies to design it. He accepted the job and worked over it with as much care as if he were designing a new statehouse.

At the junction of the three streets, he cut a rectangular hole in the wall extending from a point about waist-high to the top, provided this with a counter, erected a shelter behind it to accommodate the refreshments and the refreshment man, and covered the whole thing with a projecting flat-slab roof. The result was sim-

Mies van der Rohe, refreshment booth in Dessau, dubbed "The Hole in the Wailing Wall"

ple, clean-cut, and "Miesian": we students hailed it as another architectural triumph of the master. It turned out to be a financial flop because not enough thirsty people passed by it. A rabidly anti-Bauhaus weekly magazine, the *Anhalter Woche*, a yellow periodical with a yellow cover, seized upon this unsuccessful commercial venture and castigated Mies, accusing him of squandering wantonly the municipal substance; the magazine scornfully designated his architectural gem as "the Hole in the Wailing Wall."

GOODBYE
BAUHAUS

19

bauhaus berlin— bauhaus finis

Mies decided to go it alone with his new Bauhaus in Berlin. The school became, for the first time, a private institution without government subsidy. An agreement was reached, however, between the mayor of Dessau and Mies which, considering the fact that the Nazis had gained control of the legislature and had closed the Bauhaus, was very favorable to Mies. Though the teachers' contracts had been canceled as of October 1, 1932, the arrangement guaranteed the full payment of Mies's salary until March 31, 1933, and the payment of half of his salary from April 1, 1933, until March 31, 1935, when, presumably, his contract with the city of Dessau expired. Similar agreements were reached with the other instructors; all of these were later rescinded by the city of Dessau, which terminated the salary payments on May 1, 1933.

The contract made by Mayor Hesse beween Mies and the city also stipulated that the city would surrender to Mies its claim to the royalties from all Bauhaus patents, as well as those paid by the manufacturer of the Bauhaus wallpapers. Furthermore, the dossiers of all the students and instructors who intended to continue with the Bauhaus were to be turned over to Mies. The contract stipulated, in respect to the use by the new institution of Bauhaus equipment, that further negotiations would be undertaken. Eventually, the city of Dessau lent to the Berlin Bauhaus the looms and other appliances needed to continue the weaving department there. In return for these concessions, Mies agreed to relinquish all further claims against the city of Dessau.

The contract between the city of Dessau and Mies was a remarkable document; it showed that legal procedures in the state of Anhalt had not yet been wholly corrupted; it revealed, too, that Hesse continued to support Mies totally, trying to preserve whatever he could from the political debacle, before the breakdown of law and order took place. This courageous and enlightened man was later persecuted for various "crimes"; to the best of my knowledge, he survived the Nazis.

Above Sign directing public to Bauhaus, Berlin

Above, right Lila Ulrich, an American student, painting an interior wall of the Bauhaus, Berlin

The transfer to Mies of Bauhaus patent rights and, especially, of the royalties from the sale of Bauhaus wallpapers, promised him a kind of financial security as he undertook to reestablish the Bauhaus in Berlin. The Bauhaus wallpapers continued to be sold throughout the subsequent political convulsion and the global war which this induced. The Nazis, alert to every trace of "Jewish-Marxian" influence, could find nothing subversive in them.

Above Bauhaus, Berlin, formerly a telephone factory, 1932

Left Two students of the Bauhaus, Berlin. 1932

Another significant clause in the contract between the city of Dessau and Mies was that which granted to him the rights to the name "Bauhaus." Although Gropius had originated this, the city had apparently acquired title to it by virtue of having footed the bill for the erection of the Bauhaus building and having underwritten the expenses of the school. The now-famous two-syllable word was thus returned to the school's last director.

The Bauhaus in Dessau was formally closed on October 1, 1932. Mies, surprisingly enough, was able to open his brand-new Bauhaus in Berlin less than three weeks later on October 18. As a new home for the school, he rented a vacant former telephone factory in Steglitz, a southern suburb of the sprawling city of Berlin, far from the center of town. The building, a two-story elongated brick structure with large areas of glass, was no architectural showpiece, but it served the purposes of the school. Under Mies's direction (he was, after all, a trained mason), the students erected concrete block partition walls to divide the open interior spaces into the necessary classrooms and thereby got some of the practical building experience so much emphasized by Gropius and Hannes Meyer. A new program for the school was promulgated, and classes began on January 3, 1933.

The Dessau faculty, with the exception of Arndt and Schmidt, had followed the Bauhaus to Berlin. Mies and Hilberseimer continued to teach architecture and planning, respectively. Reich headed the interior design department and the weaving studio. Rudelt and Engemann carried on their instruction in the technical branches of the architecture curriculum. Scheper directed the wall-painting workshop, his domain in Dessau. Albers, as might be expected, was in charge of the beginning courses. Kandinsky delivered his lectures on aesthetic theory and held his free-painting class, as usual. Peterhans, director of the photo workshop, added the advertising department to his responsibilities. Wingler writes that Ernst Walther, the engineer who assisted Mies on the Barcelona Pavilion, was engaged to take over Rudelt's courses when the latter left in the spring of 1933. This seems questionable to me, because Rudelt was still at the Bauhaus when the Nazis closed the school on April 11, 1933. Mies may have contemplated appointing Walther but he never had the chance to install him as an instructor.

I remember meeting my good friend and fellow student, Paul Naeff on my way to the Bauhaus on the morning after the Reichstag fire in February, 1933. Naeff was at least as old as Mies. He had practiced architecture for many years in Argentina, and then felt the need to return to Europe to inform himself on more recent developments in that field. We shook hands, and immediately began discussing the destruction of the Reichstag. Practically with one voice, we expressed our verdict: "The Nazis done it!" It was

Mies van der Rohe rubbing his hands after showing a student how to lay concrete block, Bauhaus, Berlin, 1932

Hinnerk Scheper teaching at Bauhaus, Berlin, 1932

all so transparent that we needed no trial to determine where the guilt lay. The fire enabled the Nazis to seize absolute power and destroy representative government in Germany. They could also have burned the Berlin Bauhaus to suppress freedom of artistic expression. However, they followed an equally effective, if less dramatic course. On April 11, 1933, about six weeks after the Reichstag affair, they sent some one hundred Berlin policemen and storm troopers to "investigate" the school. These well-armed agents of the state surrounded the building and required everyone they found in it to show identification. Those who had no credentials with them were loaded into a police van and carted off to the main police station in the center of Berlin for further questioning. One of the persons thus apprehended and transported was our mathematics and technics teacher, Rudelt. Despite the gravity of the situation, some of us snickered a little at this, since Rudelt was suspected of having Nazi leanings.

Another person who was quizzed on the spot was our Italian painter-architect-journalist friend, Ivo Pannaggi, who had enrolled in the Bauhaus chiefly in order to report on the school to newspapers and magazines in his homeland. According to Pannaggi, his interrogators were flabbergasted when he produced an invitation signed by Joseph Goebbels to some Nazi soirée or other.

I was in the center of Berlin at the time of the *Haussuchung* (building search); but the police had confiscated the student enrollment list, so that everyone not present at the school on that day was subjected to his own private examination. Two *Schupos* (*Schutzpolizei*) turned up at our apartment a few evenings later to question me. They were courteous and made no attempt to enter our dwelling. When they found that I was an American citizen with a valid Berlin police pass, they terminated their investigation.

The Nazis trumped up the charge that communist literature had been discovered and seized, and padlocked the Bauhaus. That, to all intents and purposes, signaled the end of the school. Mies,

after an interview with Alfred Rosenberg, Nazi minister of culture,
received permission from the Gestapo to reopen the Bauhaus. The
stipulated conditions were so humiliating (Kandinsky and Hilberseimer were to be fired and the curriculum was to be revised) that
on July 20, 1933 he and the faculty decided to dissolve the institution.

In 1953 Mies recounted the story of the closing of the Bauhaus
for some students. It is worth repeating here:

One morning, I had to come from Berlin in the streetcar and walk a
little, and I had to pass over the bridge from which you would see
our building, I nearly died. It was so wrong. Our wonderful building
was surrounded by Gestapo—black uniforms, with bayonets. It was
really surrounded. I ran to be there. And a sentry said, "Stop here."
I said, "What? This is my factory. I rented it. I have a right to see it."

"You are the owner? Come in." He knew I never would come out if
they didn't want me to. Then I went and talked to the officer. I said,
"I am the director of this school," and he said, "Oh, come in," and
we talked some more and he said, "You know there was an affair
against the mayor of Dessau and we are just investigating the documents of the founding of the Bauhaus." I said, "Come in." I called
all the people and said, "Open everything for inspection, open everything." I was certain there was nothing there that could be
misinterpreted.

The investigation took hours. In the end the Gestapo became so tired
and hungry that they called their headquarters and said, "What should
we do? Should we work here forever? We are hungry," and so on.
And they were told, "Lock it and forget it."

Then I called up Alfred Rosenberg. He was the party philosopher of
the Nazis's culture, and he was the head of the government. It was

Rear, from left Ludwig Hilberseimer, Lilly Reich,
and Ivo Pannaggi meeting with students outside
the Bauhaus, Berlin, on the morning it was
closed

called *Bund Deutsche Kultur*. I called him up and said, "I want to talk with you." He said, "I am very busy."

"I understand that, but even so, at any time you tell me I will be there."

"Could you be here at eleven o'clock tonight?"

"Certainly."

My friends Hilberseimer and Lilly Reich and some other people said, "You will not be so stupid as to go there at eleven o'clock?" They were afraid, you know, that they would just kill me or do something. "I am not afraid. I have nothing. I'd like to talk with this man."

So I went that night and we really talked, you know, for an hour. And my friends Hilberseimer and Lilly Reich were sitting across the street in a cafe window so they could see when I came out, if alone, or under guards, or what.

I told Rosenberg the Gestapo had closed the Bauhaus and I wanted to have it open again. I said, "You know, the Bauhaus has a certain idea and I think that it is important. It has nothing to do with politics or anything. It has something to do with technology." And then for the first time he told me about himself. He said, "I am a trained architect from the Baltic states, from Riga." He had a diploma as an architect from Riga. I said, "Then we certainly will understand each other." And he said, "Never! What do you expect me to do? You know the Bauhaus is supported by forces that are fighting our forces. It is one army against another, only in the spiritual field." And I said, "No, I really don't think it is like that." And he said, "Why didn't you change the name, for heaven's sake, when you moved the Bauhaus from Dessau to Berlin?" I said, "Don't you think the Bauhaus is a wonderful name? You cannot find a better one." He said, "I don't like what the Bauhaus is doing. I know you can suspend, you can cantilever something, but my feeling demands a support." I said, "Even if it is cantilevered?" And he said, "Yes." He wanted to know, "What is it you want to do at the Bauhaus?" I said, "Listen, you are sitting here in an important position. And look at your writing table, this shabby writing table. Do you like it? I would throw it out of the window. That is what we want to do. We want to have good objects that we have not to throw out of the window." And he said, "I will see what I can do for you." I said, "Don't wait too long."

Then from there on I went every second day for three months to the headquarters of the Gestapo. I had the feeling that I had the right. That was my school. It was a private school. I signed the contract.

It was 27,000 marks—a lot of money. And when they closed it I said, "I will not give up that thing." And it took me three months, exactly three months, to get to the head of the Gestapo. He must have had a back door somewhere, you know. And he had a bench in the waiting room not wider than four inches, to make you tired so that you would go home again. But one day I got him. He was young, very young . . . and he said, "Come in. What do you want?" I said, "I would like to talk to you about the Bauhaus. What is going on? You have closed the Bauhaus. It is my private property, and I want to know for what reason. We didn't steal anything. We didn't make a revolution. I'd like to know how can that be."

"Oh," he said, "I know you perfectly, and I am very interested in the movement, the Bauhaus movement, and so on, but we don't know what is with Kandinsky." I said, "I make all the guarantees about Kandinsky." He said, "You have to, but be careful. We don't know anything about him, but if you want to have him it is O.K. with us. But if something happens, we pick up you." He was very clear about that. I said, "That is all right. Do that." And then he said, "I will talk with Goering, because I am really interested in this school." And I really believe he was.

Finally I got a letter saying we could open the Bauhaus again. When I got this letter I called Lilly Reich. I said, "I got a letter. We can open the school again. Order champagne." She said, "What for? We don't have money." I said, "Order champagne." I called the faculty together: Albers, Kandinsky . . . they were still around us, you know, and some other people: Hilberseimer, Peterhans, and I said, "Here is the letter from the Gestapo that we open that Bauhaus again." They said, "That is wonderful." I said, "Now, I went there for three months every second day just to get this letter. I was anxious to get this letter. I wanted to have permission to go ahead. And now I make a proposition, and I hope you will agree with me. I will write them a letter back: 'Thank you very much for the permission to open the school again, but the faculty has decided to close it!' "

I had worked on it for this moment. It was the reason I ordered champagne. Everybody accepted it, and was delighted. Then we stopped.[1]

While Mies's negotiations with the Nazis were in progress, many of the students remained in Berlin, confident that the school would be reopened. During this interlude, Mies, Reich, and Hilberseimer took us on boat trips to the environs of Berlin, which is crisscrossed by branches of the Spree River and by various canals, one of which, the Teltow Canal, skirted Steglitz. One such trip carried us southwest to Potsdam where, in the neighboring royal park, we saw a number of small, informal, loosely articulated retreat structures built for the German princes by Karl Friedrich Schinkel, one of Mies's great heros. Another such nautical outing carried us to Wannsee on the Havel River near Potsdam, where we picnicked in the garden of a restaurant. Mies always sought to combine profit with pleasure, so we went to see, on this trip, another Schinkel building, Babelsberg Castle, at a place called New Babelsberg. Mies's daughter Georgia accompanied us on this excursion.

During our enforced waiting period, I did some voluntary work for Gropius whose office was then located in Erich Mendelsohn's Columbushaus on Potsdamer Platz. He had been asked to make an analysis of the plan of the city of Berlin for the fourth C.I.A.M. (International Congress for Modern Architecture) meeting, which was to be held in Athens during October and November 1933, and he needed draftsmen. So I did menial work for him for several weeks. I also searched out every Schinkel building I could find in Berlin and spent weeks, day after day, roaming through the city's rich museum collections, spending hours on end examining the paintings and sculpture. So the time between the closing of the Bauhaus by the Nazis and the dissolution of the school by Mies was by no means ill spent.

My wife and I remained in Berlin for a full year after Mies and his colleagues terminated the Bauhaus in July of 1933. Despite Mies's valiant but doomed attempt to perpetuate the school the Bauhaus—established, as was the German Republic, in Weimar in 1919—died with the German Republic in Berlin in 1933. Hitler assumed absolute power and began to prepare for foreign conquest.

Soon after the demise of the Bauhaus, I learned that certain of my architecture friends were studying privately with Mies at his atelier home in the center of Berlin at Am Karlsbad 24. I wanted to continue my studies, so I also arranged to see him. We all

Mies van der Rohe, front elevation of competition design for an extension to Reichsbank in Berlin, 1933

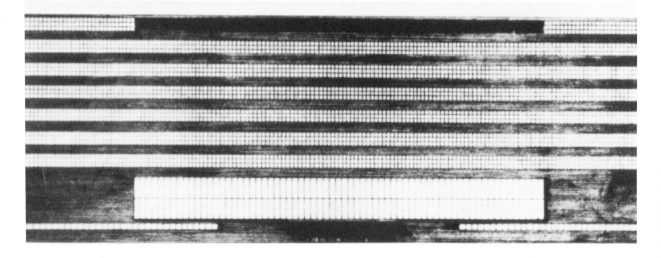

worked at home and carried our plans to him for his criticism about once a week. We paid him, of course, for his assistance, because, thanks to the Bauhaus fiasco, he was financially insecure. I also continued designing houses for him and, working in this way, learned as much from him as if I had been attending the Bauhaus.

It was at this time that Mies, along with twenty-nine other architects, was invited to enter a competition for the design of an extension to the Reichsbank, a competition which had been arranged before Hitler's accession to power. Mies was one of six prize winners, but neither his nor any of the other premiated designs was ever executed because, by this time, Hitler, who had his own ideas about architecture, had seized the reins of government. After Mies finished the Reichsbank competition drawings and turned them in, he decided, in September 1933, to go to Lugano in the province of Ticino in south Switzerland for a change and a rest. He proposed taking some of us students along on a paying basis, both because he was still hard up for cash and because he knew we were anxious to continue our architecture studies. We were to pay him the equivalent of one semester's tuition at the Bauhaus, approximately two hundred marks, I believe. So he and Reich went down ahead of us and rented a cottage on the terrace of a hillside vineyard a few miles outside Lugano. There were five of us students and two student wives. I was one of the married students; the other was Jack Rodgers, who had applied for admission to the Berlin Bauhaus just as it was closing. Not knowing that Mies was going to take students in his atelier, Rodgers had gone to Paris to study with André Lurçat. When he learned that we were heading for Lugano to work with Mies, Rogers and his recent bride joined us there. They and my wife and I rented rooms in a one-story house in the valley, near Lake Lugano, and we lived and worked there for several weeks. Another of Mies's Ticino stu-

Boat trip to Wannsee, 1933. *From left* Ludwig Hilberseimer, Annemarie Wilke, Georgia van der Rohe (one of Mies's daughters), and others not identified.

Mies van der Rohe and students sitting on a terrace near his cottage in Lugano, 1933. *Left to right* Mies, Jack Rodgers, Paul Naeff, Howard Dearstyne, and, with back to camera, E. Burzi.

Heinrich Hartwig, Vico di Morcote, 1933. Visited by Mies van der Rohe and his students on a boat trip on Lake Lugano

Mies van der Rohe *right* and Ludwig Hilberseimer in the garden of the Wannsee Restaurant, 1933

Mies van der Rohe "at work" near Lugano, 1933

dents was Paul Naeff. Another Bauhaus student, Fritz Schreiber, the only German in the quintet, also joined us in Lugano, as did E. Burzi.

This trip to Lugano was no mere pleasure excursion. We each selected a site in the area and designed a house for it. We brought

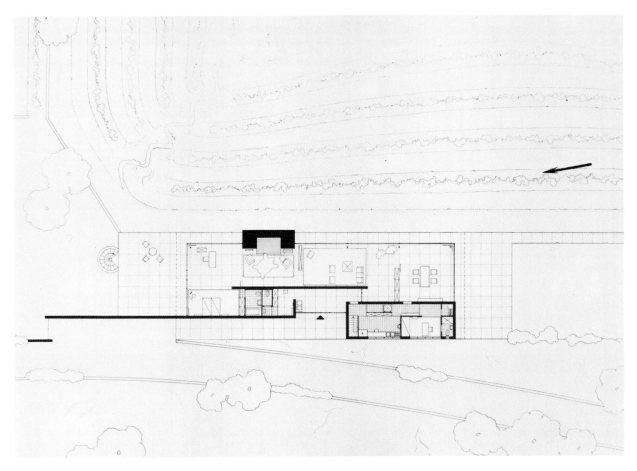

Howard Dearstyne, plan of house for plateau site near Lugano

Plateau in vinyard near Lugano chosen by Howard Dearstyne as the site for his house project

our projects to Mies every few days for his criticism. With Mies's help, I chose a rather unusual plot. It was a long, narrow plateau overlooking a vineyard, commanding a magnificent view of Lake Lugano. An existing road gave easy access to it. I designed for this a one-bedroom house which met Mies's exacting standards, and built a rather modest model of it (we had few materials to work with at the time). I have forgotten what the other students did, except for Rodgers. He designed a three-bedroom house, and since I was well acquainted with Mies's form language and Rodgers wasn't, I helped him with it.

We didn't work all the time during the six weeks or more we spent in the environs of Lugano. The countryside was magnificent. We took boat rides with Mies and Reich on Lake Lugano and long walks with them among the hills. Mies was delighted with the small mountain villages which nestled so naturally in the landscape that they seemed to have grown there.

The city of Milan was so close to Lugano that one could go there by trolley and return the same day. Mies proposed that we make the trip to see the Triennale, the big exhibition of art and architecture. We were not much impressed by it. Following this, we gravitated to the huge square before the Milan Cathedral and sat down for some refreshments at a sidewalk cafe. I suggested to Mies that we cross the plaza and see the inside of the fantastic structure (with which I was well acquainted). He refused to budge. Though he was a profound admirer of the Gothic, he would have no truck with this mongrel example of it. Then I risked another proposal: that we pay a visit to Bramante's church, Santa Maria della Grazie, the refectory of which houses Leonardo's *Last Supper*. This time Mies agreed, and we went to see it.

We were resting from our exertions at another sidewalk cafe when Mies suddenly exclaimed, "Da latscht der Pahl!" ("There goes old Pahl shuffling along!") And, sure enough, it was Pius Pahl, one of our Bauhaus students, pushing a bicycle loaded with his luggage. He had pedaled from Berlin through South Germany and had crossed the Alps into Italy. Pahl was astonished to see Mies and his student friends in Milan and he joyfully joined us for a drink. Pahl, following World War Two, continued his southward march and ended up in South Africa where, for a number of years, he practiced architecture successfully.

We all returned to Germany some time early in November 1933. I was still not ready to give up my studies with Mies, so my wife and I remained in Berlin until the summer of 1934. I remember taking my leave of Mies at a sidewalk cafe near his atelier where we had gone for a goodbye drink. Maria and I packed most of our belongings in two great shipping boxes and sent them home. We then went our separate ways (she to bid farewell to relatives and I to do some last-minute sightseeing), agreeing to meet in Aachen

(Aix-la-Chapelle) on July 11. On this last German sightseeing tour of mine, armed with a new Leica, I visited Braunschweig, Hildesheim, Hameln, Osnabrück and Soest and then headed west to Krefeld to see Mies's Lange and Esters houses. My wife and I met on the appointed day and left for Paris. The last city I saw in Germany, Aachen, was Mies's birthplace, and I have always considered this appropriate. And the last friend I met in Europe was Kandinsky, for my wife and I visited him and Madame Kandinsky in Neuilly-sur-Seine, Paris, just before boarding ship for America.

I was to see Mies again before the decade ended. The first time was in 1938 when, by prior arrangement, Mies and Hilbs met in New York City, where I was living. Mies had resettled in the United States that year. In 1939 Reich came for a visit. She too met Mies in New York. At the time I was working for the architect Wallace Harrison, who had designed several buildings for the World's Fair. During their stay, I showed them around the fair. But I doubt that they were much impressed by what they saw. Reich continued on to Chicago with Mies. To my surprise, considering their close relationship, she returned to Germany. She died of cancer in 1947.

I do not wish my account of my rich experiences at the Bauhaus to end on a somber note. Just as Mies closed the school with the celebration of a victory (of sorts) and champagne, I will close my narrative with a brief account of the Bauhaus *Feste*, especially the last two.

The Bauhaus had had a long and illustrious tradition of balls and parties from the kite and Japanese lantern festivals in Weimar

Mies van der Rohe *right* and Ludwig Hilberseimer in front of their hotel in New York City, 1938

Mies van der Rohe seated next to Frank Lloyd Wright, Taliesin, Wisconsin, 1937

Hinnerk Scheper dressed for a costume party held in his home, 1930

Joost Schmidt dressed as a sea captain at a costume party held in the home of Hinnerk Schepper, 1930

to the "White Festival" of 1926, the "Beard-Nose-Heart Festival" of 1928, and the "Metal Festival" of 1929 in Dessau. These took place during February and March, *Fasching*, or carnival time, in Germany. As one might expect, the Bauhaus band and the Bauhaus theater played important roles in these big events. The only one of them which occurred during my time in Dessau was the Metal Festival; my wife and I naturally participated. We also went to private parties such as one given by Albers, for which he printed his invitations on million-mark (inflation) notes.*

In light of the success of previous Bauhaus festivals, it is not surprising that Mies van der Rohe decided to hold one at the Bauhaus in Berlin in February 1933. This was not primarily for hilarity's sake but, rather, to raise money for the school. A friend and fellow-student of mine, Annemarie Wilke, gives an interesting account of the ball in a letter of February 21, 1933, to Julia Feininger[2]. She lays great stress on the *Tombola* (lottery), to which a number of famous artists, sympathetic with the Bauhaus, contributed either paintings or sculpture. It is rather amusing, in view of today's prices, that she considered the price of the lottery tickets (three marks) expensive.

The decorations of the several festival rooms were designed by the various instructors and executed by the students. Mies took over a large L-shaped room on the first floor. I proposed that we hang some large colored disks from the ceiling, and Mies and Reich, after giving respectful consideration to my idea, decided to stand them upright on one of the end walls. As main motif, however, Mies finally decided on an S-shaped wall placed in the middle of the space. He covered this with colored metal foil and I spent hours mending rents or bare spots in this and thereby elicited Mies's commendation for my interest and industry. This was, after all, the main ballroom for the event and deserved to be treated with loving care.

Wilke speaks of various bands which provided music in the different rooms. I know that at either the first or second ball (for the *Feste* was repeated a week later), an organ grinder with a monkey supplied the dance music in Mies's room.

The building was filled nearly to capacity at the first ball—Wilke speaks of some seven hundred guests. I recall seeing one of Mies's daughters, Marianne, dancing in his room. Mendelsohn was also there, wearing an embroidered jacket of Chinese silk and acting like the great panjandrum that he was.

*As Dearstyne indicates, there was a long-standing tradition of costume balls at the Bauhaus. They served at least two other functions beyond entertainment and fund raising: they provided a much-deserved relief from the classes, and they were an important creative outlet. The costumes and decorations were as original and creative as the studio work, and the balls' themes were selected to provoke the most creative responses from students and faculty.

There is a description of the *Feste* signed by "Sch—" and entitled "Bauhaus Festival in Steglitz" which is worth including here:

With the transfer of the Bauhaus from Dessau to Berlin, as was demonstrated on Saturday, the series of great artist balls was increased in number by an affair which had a very special flavor. I accepted the invitation with some misgivings. After all, what could the students of this institution, which was in the midst of being reestablished on a private basis, have made so quickly out of the empty rooms of the former telephone factory in the Birkbusch Street of Steglitz? Would the nocturnal expedition to the banks of the Teltow Canal be worthwhile?

A few steps' distance from the last stop of the 44 [trolley], on a wooden fence, is a shining yellow circular signboard—the entrance. One goes across an empty snow-covered courtyard, through an unpretentious door in the old boxlike factory—and is suddenly in a strange world. Bauhaus students, dressed completely in white, pilot the stranger into rooms which remind one of fantasies of the interior architecture of the year 2000. It must have taken a tremendous amount of work and cost a considerable amount of money to create these festival rooms out of the form world of the Bauhaus style. Some of the workrooms are divided up, new walls and ceilings have been installed, everything is hung with creosoted white or black material. All around the walls, black cushions serve as seats. In one corner, stacked-up sheets of parquetry form a dance platform. Half-high walls of transparent chickenwire subdivide the rooms once more and confuse one's space conception. Glowing spheres hover somewhere in

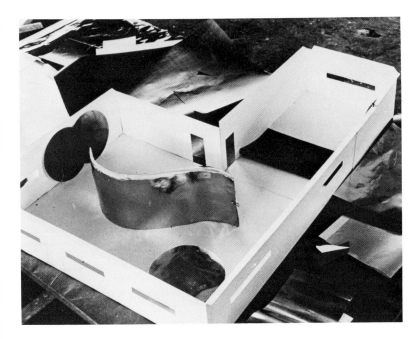

Mies van der Rohe, study model of his treatment of main room for Bauhaus party, 1933. The slots in model walls were to look through, in order to see the effect of the interior

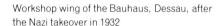
Workshop wing of the Bauhaus, Dessau, after the Nazi takeover in 1932

the air and send out diffuse light. Shadowless reflectors bathe part of a white wall in glittering light so that people in front of it appear as silhouettes. Strange phosphorescent green and blue moon disks in darker room areas. The white walls of the staircase to the second floor are livened up with drawings made of insulation tape. Upstairs is a room at whose ends steplike constructions have been erected, upon which one can squat if he wishes to sit. . . .

At first, all this strikes one as cold and constructed. But he soon adjusts himself to this new world. He constantly discovers new, bewildering effects and finally falls completely under the spell of the magic realism of the rooms swarming with fantastically dressed people. Right through until morning continues the happy confusion, which frees even the poorest artist for a few hours from all earthly cares. What remained for one to do but to wait until the first streetcar was running again? Those who became exhausted by the party excitement hopped upon a drawing cabinet and, as at an academy ball, fell blissfully asleep. And then, as the last guests stamped home through the snow, they agreed that this well-attended but, fortunately, not overcrowded first Bauhaus ball which, despite all the merriment, was unmarred by excesses and which, by the way, will be repeated next Saturday, should be ranked among the most remarkable events of the winter ball season.*

The second Bauhaus *Feste* was held a week later, as Herr Sch— promised; and thanks to the favorable publicity given the first one by him and other commentators (the Berlin newspapers had not yet been *gleichgeschaltet*—regimented), the attendance, though not so great as at the first affair, was very gratifying.

*During Dearstyne's preparation of the manuscript, a suitcase containing Bauhaus-related materials was stolen (and not recovered). It is possible that the source for this description of the *Feste* was lost at that time.

January 17, 1986

Dearstyne's narrative ends here. The legacy of the Bauhaus does not.

In retrospect one can see that the Bauhaus was part of a larger historical tradition rooted in the Industrial Revolution itself. As an idea, the Bauhaus represents more than Gropius's valiant, albeit ill-fated, attempt to achieve a synthesis of art and technology, because it forever changed our view of the role design plays for, with, and in society.

The ultimate legacy of this all-too-human institution lies in the teachings and work of its faculty, the world-wide impact of its students, and the continued questioning of the relationship between society and technology which Dearstyne's work prompts.

Workshop wing of the Bauhaus, Dessau, 1959

notes

1

[1]The occasion was an all-day visit of Frank Lloyd Wright to Lawrence College in Appleton, Wisconsin—a visit which had been arranged by Wallace Baldinger and me. Wright, Mr. Ralph Watts, acting president of the college, and I were on our way to lunch when we passed a group of new fraternity houses built in a mixture of styles. Mr. Watts had the temerity to ask Mr. Wright what he thought of them. Wright glanced at the buildings and said, "Do you mean these old buildings built recently?"

[2]Dearstyne later married Fraulein Godde. When he left Germany after the Berlin Bauhaus closed, she did not accompany him to the United States and they were subsequently divorced.

[3]Howard Dearstyne, extract from a letter written to his mother on October 11, 1928.

[4]Howard Dearstyne, extract from a letter written to his mother in 1928.

2

[1]Hans Curjel, Introduction, *Zum neuen Stil* (Munich: R. Piper & Co. Verlag, 1955).

[2]Karl Ernst Osthaus, *Henry van de Velde: Leben und Schaffen des Künstlers* (Hagen: Folkwang Verlag, 1920), pp. 47–48. This is Volume 1 of the monograph series: *Die neue Baukunst* (*The New Architecture*).

[3]Henry van de Velde, "Die Rolle der Ingenieure in der Architektur," in *Zum neuen Stil*, pp. 112–113. This essay was first published in *Die Renaissance in modernen Kunstgewerbe*.

[4] Henry van de Velde, "Ein Kapitel über Entwurf und Bau moderner Möbel," in *Zum neuen Stil*, pp. 64–65. This essay was first published in 1897 in the magazine *Pan*.

[5] Henry van de Velde, "Was ich will," ("What I Seek"), in *Zum neuen Stil*, pp. 83–84. This essay was first published in the magazine *Die Zeit* (Vienna, March 1901).

[6] Walter Gropius, excerpt from letter, in *Henry van de Velde: Persönlichkeit und Werk*, p. 31.

[7] August Endell (1871–1925), a German Art Nouveau architect whose most notable work was the façade of the Elvira Studio in Munich. (See Pevsner, *Pioneers of Modern Design*, p. 120.)

[8] Hermann Obrist (1863–1927), German Art Nouveau architect who influenced Endell. (See Pevsner, *Pioneers of Modern Design*, p. 118.)

[9] van de Velde, letter written to Walter Gropius on July 8, 1915. Bauhaus file of Walter Gropius.

3

[1] It is not strictly correct to apply the word "verbatim" to this version since it is translated from the German, and a word-for-word rendition of it would tax the reader's patience. However, it is much closer to the original than the authorized version of the pronouncement which appears in the Bayer and Gropius book, *Bauhaus 1919–1928*, (hereafter referred to as *Bauhaus 1919–1928*) published originally by the Museum of Modern Art, New York. The latter has also been retrospectively modified by the authors.

[2] The original German version of the proclamation and the accompanying program may be found in the German edition of *Bauhaus 1919–1928* and in Wingler, *Das Bauhaus*.

[3] It was not an accident that the cover of the first Bauhaus manifesto, a woodcut by Lyonel Feininger, depicted a cathedral, or at least a church.

[4] See note 2 above.

[5] Mies van der Rohe told this bit of information to me in Chicago on August 5, 1957.

[6] Copied from the official minutes of the meeting of the legislature of Thuringia, Weimar, July 9, 1919.

[7] Ibid.

[8] Lyonel Feininger, excerpt from a letter of May 19, 1919, to his wife, Julia, (presumably still in Berlin). It is taken from a typed compilation of fragments of letters written by Feininger to his wife between 1919 and 1926. This collection, entitled *Sidelights*, is signed by Julia and Lyonel Feininger and dated May 1947. The original typescript is in the Bauhaus collection of the Busch-Reisinger Museum at Harvard University.

[9] Ibid.

[10] Ibid.

[11] *Der Austausch*, Bauhaus file of Walter Gropius.

[12]E. Schrammen, *Der Austausch*, May 1919.

[13]Johannes (?) Auerbach, *Der Austausch*, May 1919.

[14]Käthe Brachmann, *Der Austausch*, May 1919.

[15]Ibid.

[16]Heinrich Linzen, *Der Austausch*, May 1919.

[17]Lothar Schreyer, *Erinnerungen an Sturm und Bauhaus*. p. 185.

[18]Brachmann, *Der Austausch*, May 1919.

[19]Schrammen, *Der Austausch*, July 1919.

[20]Feininger, *Sidelights*.

[21]Bauhaus file of Walter Gropius. This is an undated typescript with many handwritten interlineations. My photocopy is four pages long and incomplete, although apparently little is missing, since Gropius has already stated that he is about to complete his speech.

[22]No works of any of these students appear in the sumptuous *Staatliches Bauhaus Weimar* in 1923. Could this mean that they didn't fulfill the promise that Gropius found in them?

[23]Bauhaus file of Walter Gropius.

[24]Feininger, *Sidelights*.

[25]Ibid., letter of July 8, 1919.

[26]Ibid., letter of June 14, 1919.

4

[1]M.O., "Entscheidungskampf in Weimar" ("Critical Struggle in Weimar"), Berlin, *Vossische Zeitung*, July 9, 1922.

[2]Source cited Chapter 3, note 22.

[3]Schlemmer, letter of December 21, 1920, *Briefe und Tagebücher*, p. 103.

[4]Georg Muche, *Blickpunkt*, p. 167.

[5]Schlemmer, *Briefe und Tagebücher*, pp. 106–108

[6]Ibid., p. 106.

[7]Statement by Gropius, translated from the German by P. Morton Shand (Boston, Massachusetts: Charles T. Branford Company, n.d.) pp. 52–54.

[8]*The Journal of Architectural Education* was formerly an independent magazine published quarterly by the Association of Collegiate Schools of Architecture. To reduce the cost of publication it was placed at the back of the *A.I.A. Journal* but still bore its distinguishing title. The Post Office Department, however, looked on this combination as two magazines which were being mailed for the cost of one. So the *A.I.A. Journal* continued to publish the supplement but without its independent title. I will henceforth refer to these combined magazines as the *A.I.A. Journal* (*A.I.A.J.*).

[9]Dearstyne, letter to the editor, *A.I.A.J.*, vol 39, No 6, June 1963, p 122.

[10]Gropius, letter to the editor, *A.I.A.J.*, vol 40, No 3, September 1963, p 106.

[11]Copied from the official minutes of the meeting of the legislature of Thuringia in Weimar, July 9, 1920.

[12]Schlemmer, *Briefe und Tagebücher*, pp 110–111.

[13]Feininger, *Sidelights*.

[14]Gropius, *A.I.A.J.*, September 1963, p. 106.

[15]Werner Graeff, "Mit der Avantgarde," in the unpaged catalog of an exhibition of his paintings held from November 9 to December 9, 1962, in the Düsseldorf Kunsthalle by the Kunstverein für die Rheinlande und Westfalen.

[16]Wingler, *Das Bauhaus*, second edition, p. 15.

[17]Graeff, "Mit der Avantgarde."

[18]Wingler, *Das Bauhaus*, second edition, pp. 62, 63.

[19]Feininger, letter from the private collection of Julia Feininger. Cited by Wingler, *Das Bauhaus*, second edition, p. 83.

5

[1]Source cited Chapter 3, p. 45

[2]An excellent example of this is in the article "What We Intend To Do" by the Baroness Mathilde von Freytag-Loringhoven, published in the *Weimarische Landeszeitung "Deutschland,"* January 1, 1920, as follows:

The field of criticism is a very broad one, its range of vision embraces a very great deal, otherwise it would forfeit the right to call itself criticism. The more one circumscribes it, the more it becomes the megaphone of party interests, from which every art interest which deserves to be taken seriously should hold itself aloof. Partisanship in matters of art is always a proof of insufficient general education. The criticism of the *Weimarische Landeszeitung "Deutschland"* has always attempted to steer clear of such avowed art-political partisanship. It has always been accessible to the new, to the extent that it has been valuable and good; and for this there is in creative art a standard, which lies within the art work itself. This speaks so irrefutably for itself or against itself that no glorification can enhance it, no tearing down can injure it. . . . In the case of genuine art there is no today and tomorrow, no new and old, only good and bad. The task which we, not misled by art trends, have striven to fulfill has been to keep this good and bad always in sight. He who calls this bias in favor of old art, would thereby, in fact, present to the new the melancholy testimonial that it was unable to bring forth anything good. And yet this is not the case. We have always, and have at times been the first to do this, recognized the good and newest things which have been produced here. . . . There are no old and young artists. There are only those who have outlived their time, and vital ones. Old artists long forgotten can be vital, and the most modern young ones can carry within them the seeds of early death. This is determined by the nature of genuine and spurious art. No confused

twisting of words can talk itself around this and no attacks and vili-
fication can silence the advocates of this viewpoint. For if they did
not see fit to express this, the time alone would speak for itself.
Everything political or artistic which is imposed upon a people, especially in a time such as this when they wish to be free, arouses
opposition and, as a reaction, a longing for that epoch in which artistic
viewpoints, at least, were still free. He who in Weimar tries to set
himself up as a dictator of taste calls forth the deepest bitterness,
nothing further. . . . "Wait and see," demands the newest so-called
art. Well and good—we have now waited for years to see what is
going to come out of the experiments in the new German art, and
things get worse instead of better. It has become disastrous for the
new young art life of Weimar, since an art dictatorship resembling
the old army regimen has been exercised in our art school. . . . We
demand that our good indigenous art be respected, that it, as was
hitherto the case, be fostered and valued, along with the new. . . .
True to our custom our motto has always been, openly and without
subterfuge, "To support good art, whether old or new," and so it
remains today. But we guard ourselves against things which pose
as "art" and which would like to assume authority over the taste of
Weimar, under the pretext of presenting the very latest revelations.

[3]"Eine offene Erklärung der Kunstlerschaft Weimars" ("A Public
Declaration of the Artists of Weimar") in the *Weimarische Landeszeitung "Deutschlande"*, January 29, 1920. Some forty artists,
professors of art, and friends of art signed the article, with Professor Max Thedy first.

As is apparent from its letter to our Ministry of State, the "German
Werkbund" seems to assume that we, out of "philistinism, pedantry,
and hostile politics" are fighting in blind fury against the Bauhaus
idea of Mr. Gropius.

We declare positively that we have never closed our minds to the
Bauhaus idea as such, that we have cultivated for years, through
Henry van de Velde, the closest association of art with handwork and
industry, and that we strive for a more painstaking training in art
techniques and handwork for painters, following the example of the
old master schools. But we will not permit our old Art Academy,
whose reputation has spread far beyond the boundaries of Germany
and whose space, even before the war, was insufficient for the painters and sculptors, to be further drastically reduced in size through
the installation of workshops and to be transformed more and more
into a school for handworkers.

(We declare) that we take exception to the one-sided and intolerant
rule in the Bauhaus of the extremist expressionism and demand the
restoration on its old premises of the Art Academy in which every art
trend can develop freely. . . .

If our small band has courageously taken up the fight against the excesses of that extremist expressionism and against new spirit of impiety, intolerance and destruction which seeks to entrench itself right in our dear city, we have done this with the knowledge that we are united not only with all true friends of Weimar and its hallowed cultural sites but also with those who have recognized the decadent effect which this morbid and intolerant art trend is exercising especially upon our youth and which they, along with us, wish to combat vigorously, consciously and openly. . . . (Here follow the signatures.)

[4] Speech of Delegate Lehmann, as recorded in the official stenographic notes of a debate over the Bauhaus budget held in the Weimar legislature on July 17, 1920. Bauhaus file of Walter Gropius.

[5] See Wingler, *Das Bauhaus*, second edition, pp. 48–52.

[6] A craftsman gives his opinion of the Bauhaus in the *Weimarische Landeszeitung "Deutschland,"* January 7, 1920.

[7] Brenner, *Die Kunstpolitik des Nazionalsozialismus*, p. 24. The handwork and the technical masters were the same persons; Miss Brenner confuses the technical masters with the form masters, who were definitely not in collusion with the craftsmen in the town.

[8] Dr. Emil Herfurth, in Wingler, *Das Bauhaus*, second edition, p. 47.

[9] Augusta de Wit, review of Bauhaus exhibition in *Nieuwe Rotterdamsche Courant*, August 27, 1923. A German translation of Miss de Wit's account of the Bauhaus Week, which was written, of course, in Dutch, was found by the writer in the Bauhaus file of Walter Gropius. I have excerpted and translated into English those parts of the article which seemed to be of most importance here.

[10] Ibid., discussion of *Mechanical Ballet*, as performed in Jena City Theater.

[11] Ibid., review of Bauhaus exhibition; report on concert of works by Busoni and Hindemith.

[12] Walther Scheidig, *Bauhaus Weimar, 1919–1924: Werkstatt Arbeiten*, p. 35.

[13] See chapter 14.

[14] de Wit, *Nieuwe Rotterdamsche Courant*. Report on lantern parade, the reflected light plays of Hirschfeld-Mack, and dance in the Armbrust.

[15] Mies van der Rohe was being questioned by his grandson, Dirk Lohan, about his impressions of the Bauhaus exhibition of 1923. The conversation took place a little more than three weeks before Mies's death on August 17, 1969. Lohan had the foresight to record it on tape.

[16] Bauhaus file of Walter Gropius.

6

[1] Gropius. Introduction to *Staatliches Bauhaus Weimar*. I quote here only the part dealing with the preliminary course.

[2] Helmut von Erffa, "Bauhaus: First Phase," in *The Architectural Review*, August 1957, p. 104.

[3] Ibid., pp. 104, 105.

[4] Schlemmer, *Briefe und Tagebücher*, p. 112.

[5] Ibid., p. 121.

[6] Ibid., p. 131.

[7] Josef Albers, "Werklicher Formunterricht," *bauhaus* 2, No. 3 (1928): 3–7.

7

[1] Gropius, *A.I.A.J.*, June 1963, p. 121.

[2] Marcel Breuer, *Bauhaus 1919–1928*, (German edition), p. 126.

[3] Ibid.

8

[1] Feininger, *Sidelights*.

[2] Feininger, extract from a letter in T. Lux Feininger, "The Bauhaus: Evolution of an Idea," *Criticism* 2, no. 3 (1960): 264.

[3] Feininger, "Sidelights," letter of June 18, 1920.

[4] Schlemmer, *Briefe und Tagebücher*, p. 103.

[5] Feininger, remarks quoted in the catalog of his exhibition in the Curt Valentin Gallery, New York, 1952.

[6] Laszlo Moholy-Nagy, "Ismus oder Kunst" ("Isms or Art"), *Vivos Voco* 5, nos. 8, 9 (1926). The article is also reproduced in Wingler, *Das Bauhaus*, second edition, pp. 124, 125.

[7] In a special Bauhaus number of *Offset, Buch und Werbekunst* (*Offset Book and Advertising Art*), no. 7 (1926): 376.

[8] Ibid., pp. 384, 385.

[9] The book was translated by Howard Dearstyne and published in Chicago by Paul Theobald & Co., 1959.

[10] Ibid., p. 88.   An example of the ideas is this:

Both the Church and industry tried to monopolize those artistic abilities which, being creative, were constantly finding expression, in order to provide effective bait for their products (for the ideal-material as well as the purely material). In this way, as the saying goes, "the pill of utility is sugar coated."

[11] Ibid., pp. 76, 77.

9

[1] Muche, *Blickpunkt*, p. 128.

[2] Osborn, *Vossische Zeitung*, 1923.

[3] Schreyer, *Erinnerungen an Sturm und Bauhaus*, pp. 189, 190.

[4] Muche, *Blickpunkt*, p. 164.

10

[1] Muche went from Dessau to Berlin where he taught at the art school Itten had established there. He was called to a professorship at the Bresslau Academy in 1931 and remained there until he was forced out by the Nazis in 1933. He returned to Berlin where he devoted himself to a study of fresco technique. From 1939 until his retirement in 1959 he directed the master class in textile art at the Krefeld Textile Engineering School.

[2] Muche, *Blickpunkt*, p. 168.

[3] Osborn, "Eindrücke von der Weimarer Ausstellung," *Vossische Zeitung*, September 20, 1923.

[4] Muche, *Bauhaus*, no. 1 (1926).

[5] Schlemmer, *Briefe und Tagebücher*, p. 198.

[6] Ibid., p. 200.

[7] Schreyer, *Erinnerungen an Sturm und Bauhaus*, pp. 271, 272.

[8] Gunta Stölzl, *bauhaus* (July 1931).

[9] "Communications of the German Werkbund," *Die Form* (November 1925).

11

[1] Klee, "Exakte Versuche im Bereich der Kunst" ("Exact Experiments in the Realm of Art"), *bauhaus* 2, no. 2–3 (1928).

[2] Klee delivered a now-famous lecture in Jena in 1924, the notes for which have been published in English (translation by Douglas Cooper) by Faber and Faber. Herbert Read, in his introduction to this thin volume, says:

He [Klee] had already been teaching for four years at the famous school of design the Bauhaus established under the direction of Walter Gropius at Weimar, and these notes are the product of his deep meditation upon the problems of art which the task of teaching had brought to a head. In my own opinion they constitute the most profound and illuminating statement of the aesthetic basis of the modern movement in art ever made by a practicing artist. . . .

Nevertheless, the reader must be prepared for difficulties. These are partly due to the cryptic, aphoristic nature of the writing; partly to the structure of the German language, which is more abstract or conceptual than English, and therefore cannot always be exactly translated; but chiefly to the inherent difficulty of the subject. . . .

[3] One of the finest books on Klee, and one of the earliest, was brought out by Will Grohmann, a distinguished German art critic and a long-time friend of Klee's.

[4] Gerhard Kadow, "Paul Klee und Dessau in 1929." The introduction to the catalog of an exhibition of Klee's work held in Düsseldorf

in November and December 1948. Translated into English by Lazlo Hetenyi and published in the Autumn 1949 issue of the *College Art Journal*.

[5]Christof Hertel, "Genesis der Formen—Über die Formentheorie von Klee" ("Genesis of Forms—Concerning the Form Theory of Klee"), *bauhaus*, December 1931.

12

[1]Kandinsky, catalog of "Musikraum, Deutsche Bau Austellung, Berlin 1931," ("Music Room, German Building Exhibition, Berlin 1931"), (Berlin: Bauwelt Verlag): pp. 170–171.

[2]Kandinsky, "Die Arbeit in der Wandmalerei des Staatlichen Bauhauses" ("The Work in the Wall-Painting Workshop of the State Bauhaus"), Wingler, *Das Bauhaus*, second edition, pp. 93–94.

[3]Anyone desiring more precise information about the painting materials and techniques taught by Scheper in the wall-painting workshop may consult *Bauhaus 1919–1928* (German edition), p. 159.

[4]Kandinsky in *bauhaus* 2, no. 2–3 (1928).

[5]See Chapter 11, note 2.

[6] Schreyer, *Erinnerungen an Sturm und Bauhaus*, p. 235.

[7]From the first edition of *Rückblick* (Berlin: Verlag Der Sturm, 1913), pp. XXIV–XXVI. The article occurs at the back of a catalog of his work and is entitled *Rückblicke* rather than *Rückblick*.

[8]Ibid., p. XXVII.

[9]Ibid., p. XXIX.

[10]Dearstyne, unpublished essay on Kandinsky, written in 1946.

13

[1]Schlemmer, *Briefe und Tagebücher*, p. 139.

14

[1]Schlemmer, *Briefe und Tagebücher*, p. 112.

[2]Ibid., p. 113.

[3]Ibid., p. 122.

[4]Schreyer, *Erinnerungen an Sturm und Bauhaus*, pp. 21, 22.

[5]Ibid., p. 92.

[6]Ibid., p. 190.

[7]Schlemmer, *Briefe und Tagebücher*, p. 144.

[8]Schreyer, *Erinnerungen an Sturm und Bauhaus*, p. 197.

[9]Schlemmer, excerpt from a lecture delivered to the Circle of Friends of the Bauhaus on March 16, 1927. See *bauhaus* 3 (1927).

[10]Ibid.

[11]Things were different for my friend Ed Fischer (the other American at the Bauhaus in 1928–29). Fischer was so taken with Schlemmer's theater that he entered the stage class and performed in some of its productions. I studied all the photographs I could find of the Bauhaus stage in Dessau, hoping to identify him in

one or other of them, but as the actors were almost always masked my search was unsuccessful.

[12]Tut Schlemmer, description of *Triadic Ballet*, p. 15, catalog of the Schlemmer exhibition held in Zurich. Jean Paul was the sobriquet of Jean Paul Friedrich Richter, a German romantic poet and novelist, 1763–1825.

[13]"A. Ho," review in the Erfurt *Allgemeiner Anzeiger in Stadt und Land*, August 18, 1923.

[14]"dt," review in the Basel *National-Zeitung*, April 20, 1929. File of Walter Gropius.

[15]Schlemmer, *Briefe und Tagebücher*, p. 152.

[16]Ibid., p. 284.

[17]Osborn, in *Vossische Zeitung*, Berlin, September 20, 1923; reprinted in *Pressestimmen fur das Staatliche Bauhaus, Weimar*, a bound collection of articles written by friends of the Bauhaus with the hope of influencing the Weimar government to preserve the school (Weimar 1924).

[18]A photograph of one of the models is reproduced in *bauhaus* no. 3, (1927): 2. The other one is shown in *Bauhaus 1919–1928* (German edition), p. 164.

[19]See note 9.

[20]Schlemmer, "Mensch und Kunstfigur," in *bauhaus* 4, *Die Bühne im Bauhaus*. The passage has been taken from the facsimile edition of the book printed by Florian Kupferberg (Mainz and Berlin, 1965), pp. 18, 19. It has been translated by the author and differs from the corresponding passage of Arthur Wesinger's translation (*The Theater of the Bauhaus*, Middletown, Connecticut: Wesleyan University Press, 1961) in *Die Bühne im Bauhaus*.

[21]Osborn, *Vossische Zeitung*, September 20, 1923, reprinted in *Pressestimmen*. See note 17.

[22]Tut Schlemmer told me, in a letter of April 2, 1963, that the contribution of Moholy-Nagy to *bauhaus* 4 came as a complete surprise to her and her husband. No one, she says, knew that he was working on the subject of the theater. Moholy never had anything to do with the Bauhaus theater, and his article was theoretical.

[23]Kandinsky discusses his visual interpretation of Mussorgsky's *Pictures at an Exhibition* in *Das Kunstblatt*, August 1930.

15

[1]The best illustrations are to be found in Scheidig, *Bauhaus Weimar 1919–1924.*

16

[1]Gropius, "Idee und Aufbau des Staatlichen Bauhaus," in *Staatliches Bauhaus Weimar 1919–1923*, p. 15.

[2]Schlemmer, letter of March 1922, *Briefe und Tagebücher*, pp. 124–125 (my translation).

[3]Schlemmer, diary entry of March 18, 1924, *Briefe und Tagebücher*, pp. 159–160.

[4]The Bauhaus Archive in Berlin was the second Bauhaus building by Gropius.

17

[1]Hannes Meyer, "bauen," in *bauhaus* 2, no. 4, 1928. The magazine was founded by Meyer.

[2]Gropius, excerpt from letter written to Tomas Maldonado, published in Claude Schnaidt, *Hannes Meyer—Buildings, Projects and Writings*, pp. 121, 123.

[3]*Sozialistische Monatshefte*. This magazine had three periods of publication which ran, with interruptions, from 1897 to 1933. It was published in Berlin by the Verlag of the Sozialistische Monatshefte under the editorship of Josef Block.

[4]*Das Kunstblatt*, published by Paul Westheim, M. Spaeth Verlag, Berlin.

[5]Hilberseimer, *Deutsche Kunst und Dekoration* (Darmstadt: Verlag Alexander Koch, July 1919), no. 10.

[6]Meyer's subsequent career is best recorded in Schnaidt, *Hannes Meyer*.

19

[1]Ludwig Mies van der Rohe, "The End of the Bauhaus," *North Carolina University State College of Agriculture and Engineering, School of Design Student Publication* 3, no. 3 (Spring, 1953): 16–18.

[2]Annemarie Wilke, "Carnival Party at the Bauhaus, Berlin." Letter to Julia Feininger in Wingler, *Bauhaus*, p. 186.

**select
bibliography**

Abel, Adolf. "Köln's Rechtes Rheinufer." *Moderne Bauformen*
27 (October 1928): 377–397.
———. "Kölner Ausstellungsbauten." *Wasmuths Monatshefte
für Baukunst* 12 (1928): 381–391.
Akademie der Künste. Die Mitglieder und ihr Werk. Catalog.
Akademie der Künste, Berlin, 1960.
Banham, Reyner. *Die Revolution der Architektur.* Hamburg:
Rowolt Taschenbuch Verlag, 1964.
Barr, Alfred H., Jr. *Cubism and Abstract Art.* New York:
Museum of Modern Art, 1936.
———. "Die Wirkung der Deutschen Ausstellung in New
York." *Museum der Gegenwart* 2 (1931): 58–75.
Bartning, Otto. "Die Baukunst als Deuterin der Zeit." *Die
Form* 1 (1922): 13–14.
———. "Das evangelische Kirchbauprogramm." *Die Form* 1
(1922): 26–27.
Bauen in Berlin. Catalog. Akademie der Künste, Berlin,
October 4 to November 8, 1964.
*Bau und Wohnung, Die Bauten der Weissenhofsiedlung in
Stuttgart.* Published by the German Werkbund and printed
by the Akademie Verlag Dr. Fr. Wedekind & Co., Stuttgart,
1927.
Bayer, Herbert, Gropius, Walter, and Gropius, Ise, eds.
Bauhaus 1919–1928. New York: Museum of Modern Art,
1938; Boston: Charles T. Branford Co., 1952; and Stuttgart:
Verlag Gerd Hatje, 1955 (German edition).
Behne, Adolf. "Viking Eggeling." *Kunst der Zeit* 3 (1928): 32.

Behne, Adolf, Hilberseimer, Ludwig, and Friedlander-Mynona, S. *Erwerbungen 1922–23*. Gabrielson Collection, Göteborg, 1923.

Behrens, Peter. "Stil?" *Die Form* 1 (1922): 5–8.

Bense, Max, Brock, Bazon, and Thiele, Joachim. *Kranz 69—Reihen und Konstellationen*. Hamburg: Hans Christians Verlag, 1969.

Bild und Bühne—Bühnenbilder der Gegenwart und Retrospektive: "Bühnenelemente" von Oskar Schlemmer. Catalog. Staatliche Kunsthalle, Baden-Baden, January 30 to May 9, 1965.

Bill, Max. *Ludwig Mies van der Rohe*. Milan: Il Balcone, 1955.

———. *Wiederaufbau*. Erlenbach—Zürich: Verlag für Architektur, 1945.

Blaser, Werner. *Mies van der Rohe: The Art of Structure*. Zurich and Stuttgart: Architectural Publishers, 1965.

———. *Objective Architecture, Example, Skin and Skeleton*. Krefeld: Scherpe Verlag, 1970.

Bredt, E.W. "Böcklin Handzeichnungen." *Die Kunst* 23 (December 1921): 90–100.

Carter, Peter. "Mies van der Rohe." *Architectural Design* 31 (March 1961): 95–121.

cimaise, present day art and architecture. Special Bauhaus number, 16 (April, May, June, July 1969): 11–79.

Citroen, Paul. *Introvertissimento*. The Hague: L.J.C. Boucher, 1956.

Concepts of the Bauhaus: The Busch-Reisinger Collection. Catalog. Busch-Reisinger Museum, Cambridge, Massachusetts, April 30 to September 3, 1971.

Cooper, Douglas. *Paul Klee*. London: Penguin Books, 1950.

Crevel, René. *Paul Klee*. Paris: Librarie Gallimard, 1930.

Dearstyne, Howard. "Sounder Aims and Methods of Teaching at Bauhaus." *German-American Commerce Bulletin* 5 (September 1930): 13–15.

———. "Basic Teaching of Architecture." *Liturgical Arts* 12 (May 1944): 56–60.

———. "The Bauhaus Revisited." *Journal of Architectural Education (AIA Journal)* 17 (October 1962): 13–16.

———. "The Bauhaus: Crafts or Industry?" *AIA Journal* 39 (December 1963): 104–106.

———. Review of *Hannes Meyer: Buildings, Projects and Writings*. *AIA Journal* 44 (December 1965): 70.

De Fries, H. *Frank Lloyd Wright—Aus dem Lebenswerk eines Architekten*. Berlin: Verlag Ernst Pollak, 1926.

Deutsche Bauausstellung Berlin, 1931. Complete catalog and guide. Berlin: Bauwelt Verlag, 1931.

Doesburg, Theo van. *Grundbegriffe der neuen gestaltenden Kunst*. Mainz and Berlin: Florian Kupferberg, 1966.

Dormay, Marie. "Neue Bauten von A. und G. Perret, Paris." *Wasmuths Monatshefte für Baukunst* 13 (May 1929): 190–197.

Dorner, Alexander. *the way beyond 'art'—the work of herbert bayer*. New York: Wittenborn, Schultz Inc., 1949.

Drexler, Arthur. *Ludwig Mies van der Rohe*. New York: George Braziller, 1960.

Die Durchgeistigung der deutschen Arbeit. Wege und Ziele in Zusammenhang von Industrie, Handwork und Kunst. Yearbook of the Werkbund. Jena, 1912.

Eckstein, Hans. "Hermann Blomeier. The Biological Institute of Tübingen." *Bauen und Wohnen* 24 (March 1969): 111–116.

"Emil Fahrenkamp und der Sieg der Rheinländer im Schauseiten-Wettbewerb der D.A.Z." *Wasmuths Monatshefte für Baukunst* 9 (1925): 1–20.

Feininger, Julia, and Feininger, Lyonel. "Wassily Kandinsky." *Magazine of Art* 38 (May 1945): 174–175.

Fischer, Grete. "Zukunftsmusik." *Kunst der Zeit* 3 (1928): 62–63.

Fischli, Hans, and Rutzler, Willy. *Henry van de Velde 1863–1957. Restbuildibbert und Werk*. Catalog. Kunstgewerbmuseum, Zurich, June 6 to August 3, 1958.

Form Givers at Mid-Century. Catalog. Organized and sponsored by *Time Magazine* for the American Federation of Arts, 1959.

Franciscono, Marcel. *Walter Gropius and the Creation of the Bauhaus in Weimar: The Ideals and Artistic Theories of Its Founding Years*. Chicago: University of Illinois Press, 1971.

"Frank Lloyd Wright." Monograph in *Les Maîtres de l'Architecture Contemporaine*, edited by Christian Zervos. Paris: Éditions "Cahiers d'Art," 1928.

Glaser, Curt. "Die Geschichte der Berliner Sezession, Part I." *Kunst und Künstler* 26 (October 1927): 14–20.

Gombrich, E.H. *The Story of Art*. London and New York: Phaidon, 1967.

Goodrich, Lloyd. *The Decade of the Armory Show—New Directions in American Art 1910–1920*. Catalog. New York, St. Louis, Cleveland, Philadelphia, and Chicago, 1963; Buffalo, 1964.

Graeff, Werner. "Bemerkungen eines Bauhäuslers." Catalog. Städische Kunstgalerie, Bochum, March 3–31, 1963.

―――. "Concerning the So-Called *G* Group." *The Art Journal* 23 (Summer 1964): 280–282.

―――. "Mit der Avantgarde." Catalog. Kunsthalle, Düsseldorf, November 9 to December 9, 1962.

―――. "Zur Form der Automobile." *Die Form* 6 (November 15, 1931): 419–426.

Grohmann, Wil. *The Drawings of Paul Klee*. New York: Curt Valentin, 1944.

―――. *Kandinsky*. Paris: Éditions "Cahiers d' Art," 1930.

―――. *Oskar Schlemmer: Handzeichnungen*. Privately published, 1961.

―――. *Paul Klee*. Paris: Éditions "Cahiers d'Art," 1929.

―――. *Paul Klee (1879–1940)*. New York: Harry N. Abrams, 1956.

―――. *Paul Klee*. New York: Harry N. Abrams, n.d.

―――. *Wassily Kandinsky*. Leipzig: Verlag von Klinkhardt & Biermann, 1924.

―――. *Wassily Kandinsky*. Privately printed: Kandinsky Society.

―――. "Zehn Jahre Novembergruppe." *Kunst der Zeit* 3 (1928): 1–9.

Grohmann, Wil, Morlion, E., and Marlier, Georges. *Wassily Kandinsky*. Antwerp: Éditions Sélection, 1933.

Gropius, Walter. "Another Visit to the Bauhaus." *AIA Journal* (January 1963): 10–12. Reprinted in *AIA Journal* (June 1963): 120–121.

―――. *Apollo in der Demokratie*. Mainz and Berlin: Florian Kupferberg, 1967.

―――. "The Architect and our Visual Environment." *Arts and Architecture* 14 (March 1954): 34–36.

―――. "The Bauhaus, Crafts or Industry?" Letter to the editor. *AIA Journal* (September 1963): 105–106.

―――. *Bauhaus. Idee-Form-Zweck-Zeit. Dokumente und Äusserunjen*. Catalog. Göppinger Galerie, Frankfurt-am-Main, February 1 to March 28, 1964.

―――. *The New Architecture and the Bauhaus*. Translated by P. Morton Shand. Boston: Charles T. Branford Co., n.d.

―――. *Scope of Total Architecture*. London: George Allen & Unwin, 1956.

Gropius, Walter, and Meyer, Adolf. "Schufabrik, Alfeld." *Wasmuths Monatshefte für Baukunst* 7 (1923): 48–50.

―――. "Ausgeführte Bauten und Entwürfe." *Wasmuths Monatshefte für Baukunst* 7 (1923): 323–354.

Grote, Ludwig. "Lyonel Feininger zum 60. Geburtstag."
   Museum der Gegenwart 2 (1931): 41–49.

————. Introduction to catalog of exhibition, *Die Maler am
   Bauhaus*. Munich: Prestel Verlag, 1950.

Grünthal, Ernst. "Abstrakte Kunst." *Kunst der Zeit* 3 (1928):
   49–51.

Gutheim, Frederick. *One Hundred Years of Architecture in
   America*. New York: Reinhold Publishing Corp., 1957.

Haesler, Otto, and Völker, Karl-Celle. "Fortschritt zur
   Synthese." *Innen-Dekoration* 42 (July 1931): 269–272.

Haftmann, Werner. "Oskar Schlemmer." *Suites* (April-May
   1964): 6.

————. *Paul Klee—Wege Bildnerischen Denkens*. Munich:
   Prestel Verlag, 1950.

Hamlin, Talbot. "The Development of Russian Architecture,
   II." *Magazine of Art* 38 (May 1945): 180–185.

Hartlaub, G.F. "L'art graphique moderne." *Documents, Revue
   mensuelle des questions Allemandes* (1951): 59–69.

Hartwig, Heinrich. "Tessiner Landkirchen und ihre
   Umgebung." *Wasmuths Monatshefte für Baukunst* 13 (May
   1929): 201–217.

Haseloff, Arthur. "Die Kieler Kunsthalle." *Museum der
   Gegenwart* 1 (Third quarter 1930): 62–70.

Hausmann, R. "Die Kunst und die Zeit." *Kunst der Zeit* 3
   (1928): 76–81.

Hayter, Stanley William. "The Language of Kandinsky."
   Magazine of Art 38 (May 1945): 176–179.

Hegemann, Werner. "Ausstellungsbauten in Düsseldorf und
   Köln." *Wasmuths Monatshefte für Baukunst* 12 (1928): 392–
   395.

————. "Hans Herkommers neue Kirchen." *Wasmuths
   Monatshefte für Baukunst* 13 (May 1929): 177–186.

Hegemann, Werner, and Adler, Leo. "Warnung vor
   'Akademismus' und 'Klassizismus.' " *Wasmuths
   Monatshefte für Baukunst* 11 (1927): 1–11.

Helms, Dietrich. *Kurt Kranz. Picture Sequences and
   Assemblages with Movable Parts*. Hamburg: Hans
   Christians Verlag, 1970.

Herbert, Robert, ed. *Modern Artists on Art: Ten Unabridged
   Essays*. Englewood Cliffs, N.J.: Prentice-Hall, 1964.

The Heritage of Edward Weston. Catalog. The Museum of Art,
   University of Oregon, January 12 to February 7, 1965.

Herrmann, Wolfgang. "Bruno Paul: Entwurf für ein Hochhaus
   am Kleistpark in Berlin." *Kunst und Künstler* 27 (March
   1929): 239–241.

Heuss, Theodor, former Bundes president, sponsor of *Rat für Formgebung* ("Dem Gute zum Siege zu verhelfen"), Darmstadt, 1951.

———. "Stil und Gegenwart." *Die Form* 1 (1922): 14–16.

Hilberseimer, Ludwig. *Contemporary Architecture: Its Roots and Trends*. Chicago: Paul Theobald and Co., 1964.

———. "Eisenbeton-Architektur." *Das Kunstblatt* 12 (November 1928): 337–341.

———. *Internationale neue Baukunst*. 2nd edition, enlarged. Stuttgart: Verlag Julius Hoffmann, 1928.

———. *Mies van der Rohe*. Chicago: Paul Theobald and Co., 1956.

———. "Reflections on a Greek Journey." *Inland Architect* 10 (February 1967): 7–14.

———. "Tugendhat, Grete and Tugendhat, Fritz. Die Bewohner des Hauses Tugendhat äussernsich." *Die Form* 6 (November 15, 1931): 437–439.

———. "Die Umformung einer Großtadt." *Medizin und Städtebau*, edited by Dr. Paul Vogler and Erich Kühn. Munich, Berlin, and Vienna: Urban & Schwarzenberk, 1957.

———. "Vorschlag zur City-Bebauung." *Das Kunstblatt* 13 (March 1929): 93–95.

Hildebrandt, Hans. *Oskar Schlemmer, Leben und Werk*. Munich: Prestel Verlag, 1952.

Hirsch, Karl Jakob. "Novembergedanken." *Kunst der Zeit* 3 (1928): 18–19.

Hitchcock, Henry-Russell. "*Frank Lloyd Wright.*" Introduction to *Les Maîtres de L'Architecture Contemporaine*, edited by Christian Zervos. Paris: Édition "Cahiers d'Art," 1928.

———. *In the Nature of Materials. The Buildings of Frank Lloyd Wright, 1887–1941*. New York: Sloan and Pearce, 1942.

———. *Painting Toward Architecture*. New York: Duell, Sloan and Pearce, 1948.

Hobhouse, Christopher. *1851 and the Crystal Palace*. London: John Murray, 1950.

Hoff, Dr. August. "Aufgaben heutiger kirchlicher Kunst." *Die Form* 1 (1922): 12–18.

Hudson, Kenneth E. *Werner Drewes—retrospective exhibition, 1935–1965*. Catalog. Washington University, St. Louis, 1965.

Hughes, Jean. *50 Ans d'Édition de D.H. Kahnweiler*. Paris: Galerie Louise Leiris, 1909–1959.

Hüter, Karl-Heinz. *Henry van de Velde*. Berlin: Akademie Verlag, 1967.

Janson, H.W. *History of Art*. New York: Prentice-Hall and Harry N. Abrams, 1965.

Johannes Itten—Der Unterricht. Catalog. Vereinigte Seidenwerke, Krefeld, February 17 to April 23, 1973; Museum Bellerive, Zurich, May 5 to July 29, 1973; Kunstverein, Ulm, September 9 to October 31, 1973; Kunsthalle, Nürnberg, November 30, 1973 to February 3, 1974; Bauhaus-Archiv, Berlin, March 8 to April 21, 1974.

Johannes Itten. Catalog. Gesellschaft der Freunde Junger Kunst, Baden-Baden, May 10–31, 1965.

Johannes Itten. Catalog. Kunsthalle, Bern, September 4 to October 10, 1971.

Johannes Itten: Die Jahreszeiten. Catalog. Kunsthalle, Nürnberg, February 12 to April 3, 1972 and Kunstmuseum Winterthur, April 16 to May 28, 1972.

Johnson, Philip C. *Mies van der Rohe*. New York: Museum of Modern Art, 1953.

Josef Albers, Painting, Prints, Projects. Catalog. Yale University Art Gallery, April 25 to June 18, 1956.

Jürgen-Fisher, Klaus. "Die II Documenta in Kassel—Fazit eines Unbehagens." *Das Kunstwerk* 3 (August–September 1959): 30–64.

Jugendstil. Sammlung K.A. Citroen, Amsterdam. Catalog. Hessische Landesmuseum, Darmstadt, August 31 to October 28, 1962.

Der Junge van de Velde und sein Kreis 1883–1893. Catalog. Karl-Ernst-Osthaus Museum, Hagen, October 18 to November 22, 1959.

Kahnweiler, Daniel-Henry. *Klee*. Paris: Braun & Cie.; New York: E.S. Herrmann, 1950.

Kállai, Ernst. "Das Bauen und die Kunst." *Der Kunstnarr* 1 (April 1929): 2–16.

Kandinsky, Wassily. *Concerning the Spiritual in Art*. New York: George Wittenborn, Inc., 1966.

———. "Die Kahle Wand." *Der Kunstnarr* 1 (April 1929): 20–22.

———. "Mes Gravures sur Bois." *XXe Siecle* 1 (July–September 1938): 19–31.

———. *On the Spiritual in Art*. New York: Solomon R. Guggenheim Foundation, 1946.

———. *Point and Line to Plane*. New York: Solomon R. Guggenheim Foundation, 1947. First published as *Punkt und Linie zu Fläche*. Munich: Verlag Albert Langen, 1926.

———. *Rückblick*. Baden-Baden: Woldemar Klein Verlag, 1955.

Kandinsky. Catalog. Solomon R. Guggenheim Foundation, Museum of Non-Objective Paintings, New York, March 15 to May 15, 1945.

Kandinsky 1901–1913. Catalog. Berlin: Verlag der Sturm, 1913.

Katherine S. Dreier. Catalog. Academy of Allied Arts, New York, 1933.

Klee, Paul. *Pedagogical Sketchbook*. New York: Nierendorf Gallery, 1944. First published as *Padagogisches Skizzenbuch*. Munich: Albert Langen Verlag, 1925. New edition published Mainz and Berlin: Florian Kupferberg, 1965.

————. *On Modern Art*. London: Faber and Faber, 1948. First published as *Über die Moderne Kunst*. Bern Bümplitz, Benteli Verlag, 1945.

Klumpp, Hermann. *Abstraktion in der Malerei: Kandinsky, Feininger, Klee*. Berlin: Deutscher Kunstverlag, 1932.

Kocher, A. Lawrence, and Dearstyne, Howard. *Colonial Williamsburg: Its Buildings and Gardens*. Revised edition. New York: Holt, Rinehart and Winston, 1961.

Kreis, Wilhelm. "Die neue Einigung." *Die Form* 1: 12–13.

Kurt Kranz bauhaus and today. Catalog. Organized by Stephen Reichard for circulation by the Smithsonian Institution, Washington, D.C. Exhibition shown in 1973, 1974, and 1975 in twelve American art galleries.

Lane, Barbara Miller. *Architecture and Politics in Germany, 1918–1945*. Cambridge: Harvard University Press, 1968.

Lauterbach, Prof. Heinrich, and Hoff, Claudia. *Für Berlin Geplant und nie Gebaut*. Catalog. Akademie der Künste, Berlin, August 1 to September 15, 1957.

Lauweriks, Jan. *Nieuwe Nederlandsche Ruimtekunst*. Blaricum: De Waelburgh, 1927.

Leo, Peter. *Werner Graeff—Essen*. Catalog. Städische Kunstgalerei, Bochum, March 3–31, 1963.

Leonhard, Kurt. "Die Malerin Ida Kerkovius." *Die Kunst* (October 1959): 10–13.

Lindner, Werner. "Architekt und Ingenieur." *Wasmuths Monatshefte für Baukunst* 12 (1928): 412–417.

Loos, Adolf. *Trotzdem 1900–1930*. Innsbruck: Brenner Verlag, 1931.

Luckhardt, Brüder. "Ein Einfamilienhaus." *Innen-Dekoration* 42 (July 1931): 264–266.

Luckhardt, Hans. "Vom Bauen." *Kunst der Zeit* 3 (1928): 84–87.

Ludwig Mies van der Rohe. Catalog. Akademie der Künste, Berlin, 1968.

Lyonel Feininger 1871–1956. Catalog. Hamburg, Kunstverein, January 21 to March 5, 1961; Essen, Folkwang Museum, March 15 to May 7, 1961; and Staatliche Kunsthalle, Baden-Baden, May 14 to June 26, 1961.

Lyonel Feininger—Marsden Hartley. Catalog. The Museum of Modern Art, New York, 1944. Contains essays about Feininger, by Alois J. Schardt and Alfred H. Barr, Jr.; and a foreword about Hartley, by Monroe Wheeler.

Mahlow, Dietrich and Zahn, Leopold. *Der frühe Klee*. Catalog. Staatliche Kunsthalle, Baden-Baden, April 18 to June 21, 1964.

Maillard, Robert, general editor. *Dictionary of Modern Sculpture*. New York: Tudor Publishing Co., 1960.

Malevich, Kasimir. *The Non-Objective World*. Chicago: Paul Theobald and Co., 1959.

Malewitsch, K. "Suprematistische Architektur." *Wasmuths Monatshefte für Baukunst* 11 (1927): 412–414.

Matare, Ewald. "Ein Wort uber Plastik." *Kunst der Zeit* 3 (1928): 25–26.

Meidner, Ludwig. "Besuch einer Kunstausstellung." *Das Kunstblatt* 12 (October 1928): 289–296.

In Memory of Wassily Kandinsky. Catalog. Solomon R. Guggenheim Foundation. Museum of Non-Objective Paintings, New York, March 15 to May 15, 1945.

Mendelsohn, Erich. "Erich Mendelsohn, Bauten und Skizzen." *Wasmuths Monatshefte für Baukunst* 8 (1924): 1–66.

Michel, M. "Wohnraum und Biologie." *Innen-Dekoration* 42 (July 1931): 259.

Mid-century Review of German Watercolors, Drawings and Prints, 1905–1955. Catalog. Circulated by Thomas M. Messer, Director of the American Federation of Arts.

Mies van der Rohe, L. "Die Wohnung unserer Zeit." *Innen-Dekoration* 42 (July 1931): 257.

Mies van der Rohe. Catalog by James Speyer and Frederick Koeper. Chicago: The Art Institute of Chicago, Chicago, 1968.

Mock, Elizabeth L. *Built in USA, 1932–1944*. New York: The Museum of Modern Art, 1944.

Moholy, Lucia. "Das Bauhaus Bild." *Werk* 55 (June 1968): 397–402.

Moholy-Nagy, Laszlo. *Ausschnitte aus einem Lebenswerk*. Bauhaus-Archiv, Berlin, February 18 to March 30, 1972.

——. *Malerei, Fotografie, Film*. Mainz and Berlin: Florian Kupferberg, 1967.

——. *vision in motion*. Chicago: Paul Theobald and Co.1947

Paul Citroen en het Bauhaus. Utrecht/Antwerp: A.W. Bruna & Zoon, 1974.

Muche, Georg. *Blickpunkt—Sturm, Dada, Bauhaus, Gegenwart*. Munich: Albert Langen-Georg Muller, 1961.

Müller-Wulchow, Walter. *Bauten der Arbeit und des Verkehrs aus Deutscher Gegenwart*. Königstein im Taunus & Leipzig: Karl Robert Langewiesche Verlag, 1928.

——. *Bauten der Gemeinschaft aus Deutscher Gegenwart*. Königstein im Taunus & Leipzig: Karl Robert Langewiesche Verlag, 1928.

München 1869–1958—Aufbruch zur Modernen Kunst. Catalog. Haus der Kunst, Munich, June 21 to October 5, 1958.

Muthesius, Hermann. "Kunst und Modeströmungen." *Wasmuths Monatshefte für Baukunst* 11 (1927): 496–498.

Neumann, Eckhard., ed. *bauhaus and bauhaus people*. New York: Van Nostrand-Reinhold, 1970.

——. *Functional Graphic Design in the 20s*. New York, Amsterdam, London: Reinhold Publishing Corp., 1967.

——. "Russia's 'Leftist Art' in Berlin, 1922." *Art Journal* 27 (1967): 20–23.

Nierendorf, Karl. *Paul Klee, paintings, watercolors, 1913–1939*. New York: Oxford University Press, 1941.

Offset—Buch- und Werbekunst. Special issue devoted to the Bauhaus. Offset-Verlag, Leipzig, 7 (1926).

Otto, Karl, and Reidemeister, Leopold. *Berlin, Ort der Freiheit für die Kunst*. Catalog. Arranged by the National Galerie der Ehemals Staatlichen Museen Berlin and the Hochschule für bildende Künste, Berlin, and shown in Rechlingshausen, June 2 to July 17, 1960; Vienna, August 2 to September 4, 1960; and Berlin, September 18 to November 6, 1960.

Oud, J.J.P. "Uber die Zukünftige Baukunst und ihre Architektonischen Möglichkeiten." *Baukunst* 1 (May 1925): 98–101.

Oskar Schlemmer und die abstrakte Bühne. Catalog. Kunstgewerbemuseum, Zurich, June 18 to August 23, 1961.

Painters of the Bauhaus. Catalog. Marlborough Fine Art, London, March–April 1962.

Paintings, Drawings and Prints by Paul Klee from the James Gilvarry Collection. Catalog. Krannert Art Museum, College of Fine and Applied Arts, University of Illinois, Champaign, September 25 to October 25, 1964.

Paul Klee. Catalog. Akademie der Künste, Berlin, December 18, 1960 to January 19, 1961.

Paul Klee—Works from Chicago Collections. Catalog. Arts Club of Chicago, January 16 to February 20, 1962.

Paul Wieghardt. Retrospective Exhibition. Catalog. Chicago: Art Institute of Chicago, September 12 to October 20, 1974.

Pehnt, Wolfgang, ed. *Encyclopedia of Modern Architecture*. New York: Harry N. Abrams, 1964.

Peters, Heinz. *Die Bauhaus Mappen—"Neue europäische Graphik" 1921–1923*. Cologne: Verlag Christoph Czwiklitzer, 1957.

Petitpierre, Petra. *Aus der Malklasse von Paul Klee*. Bern: Benteli-Verlag, 1957.

Pevsner, Nikolaus. *Pioneers of Modern Design. From William Morris to Walter Gropius*. New York: The Museum of Modern Art, 1949.

————. *An Outline of European Architecture*. Baltimore: Penguin Books, 1963.

Pinder, Wilhelm. *Deutsche Dome des Mittelalters*. Königstein im Taunus und Leipzig: Karl Robert Langewiesche, 1925.

————. *Deutscher Barock*. Königstein im Taunus und Leipzig: Karl Robert Langewiesche, 1924.

Platz, Gustav Adolf. "Poelzigs Entwürfe zum Salzburger Festspielhaus." *Wasmuths Monatshefte für Baukunst* 9 (1925): 27–32.

Poelzig, Hans. "Vom Bauen unserer Zeit." *Die Form* 1 (1922): 16–29.

Poelzig, Endell, Moll und die Breslauer Kunstakademie 1911–1932. Catalog. Akademie der Künste and the Städische Museum Müllheim-an-der Ruhr, 1965.

Rave, Rolf, and Knöfel, Hans Joachim. *Bauen seit 1900: Ein Führer durch Berlin*. Berlin, Frankfurt-am-Main, and Vienna: Verlag Ullstein, 1963.

Read, Helen Appleton. *German Art from the Fifteenth to the Twentieth Century*. Catalog. Pennsylvania Museum of Art, Philadelphia, October 3 to November 1, 1936; Cleveland Museum of Art, November 12 to December 13, 1936; Art Institute of Chicago, December 22, 1936 to January 24, 1937; Brooklyn Museum, February 5 to March 5, 1937; Boston Museum of Fine Arts, March 15 to April 15, 1937; Carnegie Institute, Pittsburgh, May 3–31, 1937.

Read, Herbert. *Education Through Art*. New York: Pantheon Books, 1945.

————. *Klee 1879–1940*. New York and London: Pitman Publishing, 1949.

Rebay, Hilla. *Kandinsky*. New York: Solomon R. Guggenheim Foundation, 1945.

———. *Wassily Kandinsky Memorial*. Catalog. Solomon R. Guggenheim Foundation, Museum of Non-Objective Paintings, New York, March 15 to May 15, 1945.

Redslob, Edwin. "Kirche und Handwerk." *Die Form* 1 (1922): 20–25.

Reverdin, Raymond and others. "Hommage à Pierre Jeanneret." *Werk* 55 (June 1968): 377–396.

Rewald, John. "Last Visit with Maillol." *Magazine of Art* 38 (May 1945): 164–167, 205.

Richards, J.M. *An Introduction to Modern Architecture*. Baltimore: Penguin Books, 1956.

Riemerschmidt, Richard. "Zur Frage des Zeitstiles." *Die Form* 1 (1922): 8–12.

Riezler, Walter. "Religion und Kunst der Gegenwart." *Die Form* 1 (1922): 1–10.

———. "Drei Bücher über Technik." *Die Form* 6 (November 15, 1931): 427–430.

Rischowski, Edith. "Die Wohnung unserer Zeit." *Innen-Dekoration* 42 (July 1931): 251–257.

Robb, David M. and Garrison, J.J. *Art in the Western World*. New York and London: Harper and Brothers, 1942.

Roethel, Hans Konrad. *Modern German Painting*. New York: Reynal & Co., n.d.

Rogers, Ernesto N. "Henry van de Velde o dell 'evoluzione.' " *casabella* 237 (March 1960): 1–9.

Roh, Franz. *L'art allemand au vingtième siècle. Documents*. Special number, edited by the Bureau International de Liasion et de Documentation, Offenbourg-en-Bade, 1951.

Rudolf Belling. Catalog. Akademie der Künste, Berlin, May 6 to June 17, 1962.

Sachs, Paul J. *Modern Prints and Drawings*. New York: Alfred A. Knopf, 1954.

Sartoris, A. and Terragni, G. "Rebbio, a satellite town for industrial workers." *Plus* 3 (May 1939): 42–43.

Schardt, Alois J. *Franz Marc*. Berlin: Rembrandt Verlag, 1936.

Scheffler, Karl. "Unser Programm: 25 Jahre 'Kunst und Künstler,' " *Kunst und Künstler* 26 (October 1927): 3–10.

Scheidig, Walther. *Bauhaus Weimar, 1919–1924—Werkstattarbeiten*. Munich: Süddeutscher Verlag, 1966.

Schlemmer, Oskar. *Briefe und Tagebücher*. Munich: Albert Langen-Georg Müller Verlag, 1958.

————. *The Theater of the Bauhaus*. Wesleyan University Press, 1961.

Schlemmer, Oskar, Moholy-Nagy, László, and Molnár, Farkas. *Die Bühne im Bauhaus*. Mainz and Berlin: Florian Kupferberg, 1965.

Schmidt, Diether. *bauhaus—weimar, dessau, berlin*. Dresden: VEB Verlag der Kunst, 1966.

Schmidt, Paul F. "Schlemmer, Fuhr und Kriegel." *Das Kunstblatt* 12 (December 1928): 361–372.

Schnaidt, Claude. *Hannes Meyer: Buildings, Projects and Writings*. New York: Architectural Book Publishing, Co., 1965.

Schreyer, Lothar. *Erinnerungen an Sturm und Bauhaus*. Munich: Albert Langen-Georg Müller, 1956.

Schuster, Franz. "Die klare Aufgabe." *Innen-Dekoration* 42 (July 1931): 277–278.

Segal, Artur. "Ich Selbst über Mich Selbst." *Kunst der Zeit* 3 (1928): 42–44.

Selz, Peter. *German Expressionist Painting*. Berkeley and Los Angeles: University of California Press, 1957.

Sevenhuijsen, Aug. M.J. *Nieuwe Bouwkunst in Nederland*. Blaricum: De Waelburgh, 1927.

Sörgel, Herman. "Historische Architektenbilder: Karl Friedrich Schinkel, 1781–1841." *Baukunst* 1 (March–April 1925): 66–67.

————. "Holländische Architekten—Charakterköpfe." *Baukunst* 1 (May 1925): 102–103.

————. "Neue Wege, neue Ziele." *Baukunst* 1 (March–April 1925): 35–48.

————. "Reisebericht über neue Holländische Baukunst." *Baukunst* 1 (May 1925): 83–97.

————, Spaeth, David. *Mies van der Rohe*. New York: Rizzoli, 1985.

Speyer, A. James and Koeper, Frederick. *Mies van der Rohe*. Catalog. Art Institute of Chicago, 1968.

Speyer, A. James et al. Ludwig Mies van der Rohe. Catalog. Berlin: Akademie der Künste, 1968.

Staatliches Bauhaus Weimar 1919–1923. Bauhaus Verlag Weimar-München. Issued in collaboration with the art dealer Karl Nierendorf in Köln.

Steneberg, B. "Die Ungeduldigen." *Das Kunstwerk* 13 (August–September 1959): 3–26.

Stuckenschmidt, H.H. "Musik und Musiker in der Novembergruppe." *Kunst der Zeit* 3 (1928): 94–101.

der Stuhl, seine funktion und konstruktion von der antike bis zur gegenwart. Catalog. Hochschule für bildende Künste, Berlin, February 17 to March 17, 1962.

Taft, Robert. *Photography and the American Scene*. New York: Macmillan, 1942.

Taut, Bruno. *Die Auflösung der Städte oder Die Erde eine gute Wohnung oder auch: Der Weg zur Alpinen Architektur*. Hagen-in-Westfalen: Folkwang Verlag, 1920.

Theo van Doesburg, 1883–1931. Catalog. Eindhoven, December 13, 1968 to January 26, 1969; Gemeentemuseum, the Hague, February 17 to March 23, 1969; Kunsthalle, Nürnberg, April 18 to June 1, 1969; and Kunsthalle, Basel, August 9 to September 7, 1969.

Triumph der Farbe: Die europäischen Fauves. Catalog. Schaffhausen: Museum zu Allerheiligen, July 5 to September 13, 1959; Berlin: Nationalgalerie der Ehemals Staatlichen Museen, Orangerie des Schlosses Charlottenburg, September 20 to November 15, 1959.

Van de Velde, Henry. *Geschichte meines Lebens*. Munich: R. Piper & Co. Verlag, 1962.

———. "Tre scritti di Henry van de Velde." *casabella* 237 (March 1960): 23–42.

———. *Zum neuen Stil*. Selections from his writings, chosen and introduced by Hans Curjel. Munich: R. Piper & Co., Verlag, 1955.

Veronesi, Giulia. "Van de Velde architetto realista." *Comunità* 12 (October 1958): 50–56.

Verzeichnis der Gemälde und Bildwerke der Nationalgalerie in der Orangerie des Schlosses Charlottenburg, 1961. Catalog. Nationalgalerie des Ehemals Staatlichen Museen, Berlin.

Vetter, W. "Der Entwurf von A. und G. Perret für das Völkerkundegebäude in Genf." *Wasmuths Monatshefte für Baukunst* 11 (1927): 416–419.

Von Alten, W. "Georg Kolbe." *Die Kunst* 23 (April 1922): 212–221.

Vorhoelzer, R., Wiederanders, M., and Hacker, Chr. "Wohnräume im Boarding-Haus." *Innen-Dekoration* 42 (July 1931): 273–276.

Wagenführ, Max. "Architektonische Entwürfe von L. Hilberseimer." *Deutsche Kunst und Dekoration* 22 (July 1919): 206–216.

Walden, Herwarth. *Einblick in Kunst: Expressionismus, Futurismus, Kubismus*. Berlin: Verlag der Sturm, 1924.

Waldmann, E. "Kunstausstellungen." *Kunst und Künstler* 23 (December 1924): 112–115.

Wattjes, J.G. *Nieuw-Nederlandsche Bouwkunst*. 2 Vols. Amsterdam: Uitgevers-Maatschappij "Kosmos," 1926.

Wedepohl, Edgar. "Die Weissenhofsiedlung der Werkbundausstellung 'Die Wohnung.' " *Wasmuths Monatshefte für Baukunst* 11 (1927): 391–402.

Weitemeier, Hannah. *Licht-visionen. Ein Experiment von Moholy-Nagy*. Berlin: Bauhaus-Archiv, 1972.

Wensel, Dr. Alfred. "Lebensgefühl und Wohnraum." *Innen-Dekoration* 42 (July 1931): 278–280.

Werbegrafik 1920–1930. Catalog. Göppinger galerie, Frankfurt-am-Main, June 27 to July 20, 1963.

"Werkbund Ausstellung 'Die Wohnung' Stuttgart 1927." *Stein, Holz, Eisen* 41: 531–532.

Werner Graeff. Catalog. Kunsthalle Grabbeplatz, Düsseldorf, November 9 to December 9, 1962.

Wetzel, Ines. "Die Linie." *Kunst der Zeit* 3 (1928): 59.

wilhelm wagenfeld, dreissig jahre künstlerische mitarbeit in der industrie. Catalog. Die neue sammlung, Munich, March 23 to April 30, 1961.

Willi Baumeister 1889–1955. Catalog. Akademie der Künste, Berlin: May 30 to July 1965.

Wingler, Hans M. *The Bauhaus*. Cambridge: MIT Press, 1969.

———. *Das Bauhaus*. Schauberg: Verlag Gebr. Rasch & Co. and M. Dumont, 1962. 2nd edition, enlarged, 1968.

———. *Bauhaus in America*. Berlin and Darmstadt: Bauhaus-Archiv, 1972.

———. *Herbert Bayer—die druckgrafische werk bis 1971*. Catalog. Hamburg, Münster and Wiesbaden, 1974; Berlin: the Bauhaus Archiv, 1975.

———. *Johannes Itten—Der Unterricht*. Catalog. Krefeld, 1973; Zurich, 1973; Ulm, 1973; Nürnberg, 1973–74; and Berlin: Bauhaus-Archiv, 1974.

———. *Kleine Bauhaus-Fibel*. Berlin: Bauhaus Archiv, 1974.

With, Karl. "Hoetger, Hoeger, Högg und der Ziegelbau in Deutschland und der Sahara." *Wasmuths Monatshefte für Baukunst* 11 (1927): 476–480.

Zehder, Hugo. *Wassily Kandinsky*. Dresden: Rudolf Kaemmerer Verlag, 1920.

Die Zwanziger Jahre in Hannover. Catalog. Kunstverein Hannover, August 12 to September 30, 1962.

index

photo credits

We are grateful to the following for permission to reproduce the pictures on the pages below. Unless otherwise stated all other photographs are from the estate of Howard Dearstyne.

Josef Albers 90. Klaus G Beyer 98, 106, 120, 128, 129, 190, 191, 194. Hermann Blomier 230. Busch-Reisinger Museum 108, 109, 110, 170. *Casabella* 36. *Cimaise* 66. Die Neue Sammlung 192. Walter R Drewes 158. Andreas Feininger 43. Estate of Julia Feininger 108. Fogg Art Museum 44, 68, 81, 133, 141, 163, 170, 173, 213, 214. Folkwang Museum 108. Werner Graeff 66, 111. Walter Gropius 40, 48, 58, 76, 80, 87, 89, 90, 103, 112, 115, 121, 124, 135, 146, 162, 166, 167, 171, 183, 184, 193. Walter Gropius and Hans M Wingler   Solomon R Guggenheim Foundation 144, 152, 157. Hamburger Kunsthalle 29. Ludwig Hilberseimer 217. Wilhelmina Hoffman 120. Mrs Hattula M Hug 116. Knoll International 99. Kunstgewerbe-museum, Zurich 34, 37. Dirk Lohan 221. Edward Ludwig 91, 231. Georg Muche 124, 201. Georg Muche and Walter Gropius 61. Georg Muche and the Museum of Modern Art 202. Museum of Modern Art 47, 92, 100, 104, 200, 203, 204, 246. Nationalgalerie, Berlin: Staatliche Museum Prussischer Kulturbesitz 57. Eckhard Neuman 255. New York Review of Books 61. Pius Pahl 159, 222, 229, 240, 241, 243, 252, 253. Mrs Oskar Schlemmer 41, 43, 78, 163, 165, 175, 176, 177, 178, 179, 181. Mrs Oskar Schlemmer and Walter Gropius 178. Mrs Oskar Schlemmer and Hans M Wingler 162. SPADEM 138, 139, 140, 169. Streendrukkerij de Jong & Co. 24. Paul Theobald & Co. 212. Mr and Mrs Burton Tremaine 63. Ullstein GMBH Bilderdienst 50. Verlag Ernst Wasmuth 29, 68, 198, 248. Verlag Florian Kupferberg 113. Verlag Julius Hoffman 25, 211. Verlag R Piper & Co. 34, 86. Hans M Wingler 28, 57, 75, 89, 90, 93, 98, 100, 103, 107, 116, 117, 126, 127, 128, 130, 136, 147, 153, 185, 186, 189, 190, 193, 194, 199, 206, 207. Würtembergischen Kunstverein 78, 129, 167.